African Traveller
Twenty years of adventures as a documentary filmmaker

Neil Shaw

D0924882

African Traveller
Twenty years of adventures as a documentary filmmaker

Copyright © 2022 Neil Shaw

All rights reserved. No parts of this book may be reproduced, scanned or transmitted in any forms, digital, audio, or printed, without the expressed written consent of the author.

Contents

CHAPTER ONE - Beginnings..1
CHAPTER TWO - Morocco with a backpack...................................7
CHAPTER THREE - Africa's east coast islands............................23
CHAPTER FOUR - Passport to travel...45
CHAPTER FIVE - South African ghosts....................................63
CHAPTER SIX - Zimbabwean farmers and other video journalism.......67
CHAPTER SEVEN - Wildflowers..89
CHAPTER EIGHT - The Mulanje Cedar....................................91
CHAPTER NINE - The rejuvenation of Gorongosa National Park........97
CHAPTER TEN - Back to Malawi...105
CHAPTER ELEVEN - Highway to Mauritania..............................115
CHAPTER TWELVE - Mozambique forest expeditions....................129
CHAPTER THIRTEEN - My year of living dangerously....................149
CHAPTER FOURTEEN - Road trip to East Africa.........................177
CHAPTER FIFTEEN - Elephant dictionary................................189
CHAPTER SIXTEEN - Saint Helena island...............................193
CHAPTER SEVENTEEN - The most expensive Primus beer.............. 199
CHAPTER EIGHTEEN - Angola..203
CHAPTER NINETEEN - Namibia...209
CHAPTER TWENTY - The youth and democracy across Africa...........215
CHAPTER TWENTY-ONE - "If It Works"...................................235
CHAPTER TWENTY-TWO - Smashing xenophobia through theatre.....237
CHAPTER TWENTY-THREE - Suzete -- a return...........................241
CHAPTER TWENTY-FOUR - Refugee camp musician.....................247
CHAPTER TWENTY-FIVE - The rock..253
CHAPTER TWENTY-SIX - What could possibly go wrong?...............255
CHAPTER TWENTY-SEVEN - The forgotten Western Sahara...........267
CHAPTER TWENTY-EIGHT - Ghana by Uber...............................269
CHAPTER TWENTY-NINE - Bumpy ride to a prison island...............279
CHAPTER THIRTY - Back to the childhood haunts.......................281
CHAPTER THIRTY-ONE - Cape to Cairo..................................289

CHAPTER ONE
Beginnings

As a child in Malawi, my friends and I would collect and swap African country flags. These small flag cards were sold in chewing gum packets. The flags are imprinted in my mind. A seed was sown: to visit all these places.

My family lived in Lilongwe, Malawi from 1982 to 1985. This was when I became an African boy. I attended Bishop Mackenzie School and my friends came from places like Iran, Trinidad and Tobago, the UK, Zimbabwe, Malawi and many other countries. My friends and I roamed far and wide in the suburbs and bushveld surrounding a small and safe capital city.

One day at home I sang at the top of my voice in the lowest pitch an eight-year-old can "Shosholoza," the Zulu mineworkers song from South Africa. My father, who had been out jogging rushed back worried there was a problem. Malawi was the only African country with full diplomatic relations with South Africa during apartheid, and my father was the South African Deputy Ambassador there. He came running up the driveway only to discover that there wasn't a Zulu mineworkers strike under way at our house.

That my friends were of every hue, and that race was never an issue or discussed at home is ironic. The irony is that my father's job which was representing the apartheid state, allowed me to have a childhood free of racism, well outside the white suburban bubble that was the norm in South Africa at that time.

At Lake Malawi's Monkey Bay our family would walk up the hill at sunset that looks down on the hippo pool, and we'd listen to them grunting down below. At the railway cottage right on the lake shore, the adults would drink Carlsberg "greens" (beer) and Malawi G and T's (gin and tonics), and the children would play in the lake. It's called the Calendar Lake because it is 52 miles wide by 365 miles long—the number of weeks and days in the year. It's like a sea without the salt.

When we left Malawi it was directly to Scotland for another three and a half years. My last Malawi childhood memory is my father turning around at the aeroplane door at Lilongwe airport, not for a last look at the country but to fill his lungs one last time with this air. And every time I have returned through the years that first lungful is so redolent for me—the wood fire, bushveld aroma so particular to Malawi.

***

Years later, wanting to make documentaries in Africa, and see all the places where the flags had ignited my imagination, I take the advice of a South African television producer, "Just do it."

In 1999 the digital revolution is under way and I get my hands on a small cheap Panasonic mini DV palmcorder. I then recruit a university friend, Andrew Schmidt to be my presenter. I invite him to my house, informing him we are going to be watching a TV travel series for inspiration.

"In that case, go and get us a six-pack of beers," he demands.

I comply and 20 minutes later start screening the entire Michael Palin's Pole to Pole BBC travel series.

"Be like Michael Palin," I tell Andrew.

We then set off, using only trains from Cape Town to Dar es Salaam in East Africa. I have no training or experience in filming or filmmaking.

Four weeks later after completing the 5100-kilometre journey to Dar es Salaam on five different trains, I find myself in the village of Nangurukuru. The ancient Leyland bus has brought us late in the evening, travel-weary, into this crossroads village on Tanzania's east coast. We're directed through a collection of ramshackle buildings to the Fourways Guesthouse. It is extremely basic and costs only US$2 per room per night. We each padlock our door with the lock provided and walk to the market where we eat a simple bowl of rice. Fifteen minutes later we return to the hotel. My room door is standing wide open. *That's strange*, I think. I enter and see that my backpack is gone. All five tapes that recorded our journey by trains from Cape Town to Dar es Salaam is missing. In other words, my first documentary is gone. Also stolen are my battery charger and clothes. The video camera, hidden under the bed is still there. I immediately say to my travelling companion Andrew, "Wait here, I am going to look for them." I rush out and ask the hotel manager, and people outside the hotel if they have seen anyone suspicious. I dash around the somnambulant village making enquiries. It is to no avail. It is so disappointing.

The next day I report the theft at the local police station in Kilwa Kivinje. It's a square concrete bungalow under a large palm tree. The Police Chief types out the list of stolen items on an ancient typewriter slowly, letter by letter, carefully tippexing mistakes as he goes along. Afterwards, Andrew and I head down to the nearby coast at Kilwa Masoko and settle into the New Mjaka Enterprises Hotel. Andrew plays checkers with locals. I, feeling sorry for myself drink too much beer. The Police Chief, a Mr Mangalla, is also staying at our hotel, which is handy for my daily questioning of progress in their investigations. Seeing him arrive I rise and before I can open my mouth he says:

"I am very sorry my dear."

The investigation, such that it is, is not delivering results.

In my diary, I write: "Note for future travelling: keep most important items apart and with me at all times." The footage is the most crucial of all. Everything else is replaceable. I feel crestfallen and disheartened.

In the town of Kilwa Masoko, I replace my stolen clothes. At the market, I buy a few *mitumba* items. *Mitumba* in Swahili means second hand. In other parts of Africa, these clothes have more interesting names. In Ghana, they are called "dead white man's clothes." *Mitumba* is used clothing that is donated to charities in the West. It's a strange business where donated clothes end up being sold in Africa. Items not sold in first-world thrift shops are resold in bulk and exported to parts of the developing world, including many African countries. Charities like Oxfam say they use the profits for their development work in developing countries. But the trade has been detrimental to local textile industries. I also buy some African cloth and have a couple of shirts made for me by the market tailor, something I keep doing in the years ahead.

I revisit Mr Mangalla, the policeman, a few more times ("I am very sorry my dear") and am feeling pretty down about the theft. My faith in the police investigation is driven more by persistence than realism. On the third afternoon of drinking some beers alone, Andrew approaches me and says, "Come on!" in his inimitable cynical manner. He's right—snap out of it and make a plan. This is the turning point. The documentary will experience a renaissance on our return journey: Dar es Salaam to Cape Town by public transport.

We travel back up the east coast to Dar es Salaam by bus. I search the city high and low for replacement tapes. I stick out my thumb and hitch rides on my elusive mini DV cassette quest. Shop after shop doesn't stock these tapes. In the evenings Andrew and I rendezvous for beers at the Milk Bar across the road from the Holiday Hotel, where we are staying. It's probably the cheapest hotel in Dar es Salaam, and square in the Indian district of Upanga. I get chatting with a Tanzanian at the bar and ask him about the Indian influence.

"They keep to themselves. They have been here for two, three generations but they have not integrated at all."

Any native population anywhere in the world expects outsiders who settle in their parts to make at least the minimum effort to fit in.

I ask what my fellow beer drinker at the Milk Bar does.

"I'm a lawyer. I was the first Tanzanian to get a master's degree in the 1960s. What have you studied?"
"I have an honours degree in African Politics," I say.
"What are you waiting for? Study for an MA. Strike while the iron is hot!"

All I have on my mind is finding tapes.

I finally track down a little Indian-run shop a stone's throw from our Upanga neighbourhood hotel, which has a good selection of electronics. He is genuinely friendly and asks where we are going.

"Kigoma, on the shores of Lake Tanganyika."
"Ah, that is where we are from." In this dusty little store, my luck turns. He stocks mini DV tapes. I buy all eight that he has available.
"I also have this battery for my camera but no charger. Do you have a universal charger?" I ask.

My battery charger was also stolen in Nangurukuru. He examines the battery, then finds a charger for a different battery and solders new wires to it. Attaching my battery and plugging it in shows it is charging. In Africa, it is always possible to make a plan. I am back in business! A new documentary of our return trip to Cape Town is born. Andrew and I travel west to Lake Tanganyika, south into Zambia, onwards through Zimbabwe and finally to South Africa, on trains, buses and ships.

Back in Cape Town, and following advice from Cape Town filmmaker Paul Morkel, I log my nine hours of footage. That is writing out a description of each shot. A shot is from when you press record until when you press stop. It's the basic element, the word, in the language of film. Then I write out a paper edit, which is the making of a selection of which shots will be used and in which order for the documentary. While reading a magazine I come across a biography of a South African filmmaker of Indian origin doing work for the United Nations, and I think to myself, "That's what I want to do," so I find her number and call her. She is friendly and suggests I speak to Cape Town filmmaker Glen Thomas to get my Dar es Salaam documentary edited. I phone Glen out of the blue and he says, "Come over." He proceeds to give me two weeks of his time (the use of his editing machine after some brief instructions) for free, and the documentary gets finished. It is an accomplishment and I love every moment of making it.

I sign a distribution deal with Ice Media. One of the criticisms from them is that I should use a tripod. Indeed, many of the handheld shots make the documentary look amateurish. Unfortunately, despite having to provide all kinds of publicity material, Ice media never make a sale. The documentary will sit on the shelf for a long time. But then finally nine years later I will sell it.

In the meantime, in the early hours of a Sunday morning in a Cape Town night club I meet the boyfriend of a friend and ask him:

"What line of business are you in?"
"I work in the film industry."
"Oh, I'd like to work in the film industry."

By the next Wednesday, I meet him in his office and begin working as a location scout the following day. I go out with my camera to find locations with literally no training. I arrive at Chapman's Peak Drive wondering to myself, *what do I do next*? I call Chris, one of the other location scouts, and he tells me how to photograph the location. "To start with, photograph all four directions..." A baptism of fire.

The work means travelling the Western Cape province by car, seeking out and photographing potential locations for TV commercials, features films and music videos. Being seasonal work, I have time off in winter. In 2002, I head north out of Cape Town, to make my second shoestring budget, a self-made travel documentary.

CHAPTER TWO
Morocco with a backpack

I am keen to get to West Africa via Europe. In the end, I don't make it as far as West Africa, but I still have a real adventure travelling and making a documentary in Morocco.

The South African Airways flight makes a Zurich stop-over en route to France. In that different plane of being one enters after a long journey I experience what alcoholics refer to as a moment of lucidity: the Alps jutting through clouds, the green valleys, the dense forests, and the occasional matchbox house village. Everything becomes clear: this trip, my next trip and everything else that dogs me as a 27-year-old.

Under a leaden sky, vast trees flash past the TGV high-speed train heading south in a blur. Passengers around me seem completely lost in their thoughts. In the distance a building: a farmhouse? A shed? We're travelling too fast to tell. Behind me lies Paris. Ahead lies Africa. And still, the train goes faster, and still, the countryside becomes more of a green-grey blur.

I walk the streets of Grenoble, the nearest town to where I am staying with my sister. The weather is beautiful and so are the women in their short summer dresses. Lovers don't hold back in expressing themselves. I buy a pizza. The French are polite.

"Hello."
"A pizza with ham please."
'Here you are, and thank you."
"Thank you," I say.
"It is for me to thank you!"
"Have a good day," he says as I leave.

It is true, it is him to thank me—I'm giving him money!

It's time to get to Africa. After taking a bus to Barcelona, I baulk at the 4.50 Euro locker fee and walk the streets with my backpack which is too big, too heavy, with too much stuff. The girls are very pretty.

On the next bus the driver gets on board:

"Let's go," he exclaims out loud.

We pass through more faceless Spanish coastal towns but the passengers make up for it. A Chinese guy shouting at his cell phone. A red-eyed mariachi-looking character with his guitar and sombrero. An Arabic lady. We stop at generic highway truck stops. Finally, we get to the port town of Algericas. 30 kilometres across the Straits of Gibraltar is Africa.

My five weeks in Morocco start when the ferry arrives in Tangier.

It's day one in a new country. I am slightly anxious and on the defensive after reading that there are many dodgy characters in Tangier. I need to get from the harbour to the bus station via a bank. I take a taxi.

At the first bank, I ask the taxi driver to wait, taking my bag with me inside. They don't change money. At the second bank, I again take my bag. Again they can't help me. When I return to the car, the driver mollifies me:

"Trust me," he says. "Relax, I'm an old man," he adds in the face of my apparent nervousness.

Nonetheless, I haul my bag with me into the bank. Again they don't change money. Finally, I manage to change cash at the fourth bank.

We had agreed on a 30 Dirhams fee but when he drops me off at the bus stop he demands 60 Dirhams because of the extra driving around. I say, "No way". To be fair he did some extra driving. But I am very much on the defensive having just arrived in a new country and having read about so many Tangier shake-down stories in the online forums.

Unwilling to accept the original fee the driver starts driving away from the bus station with me inside.

"Wait, where are you going?" I ask.

He is insistent on the new price. I concede:

"Ok make it 50 Dirhams."

He stops the taxi. But I only have a 100 Dirham note. He gives me back 30 Dirhams. But in his other hand is a 50 Dirham note. I grab it, drop his 30 Dirhams, take my bag and slam the door shut.

My nervousness here is why it may be better to not read the online forums and travel advisories.

It's a long bus ride south to Chefchaouen, but as I write in my diary when I arrive it is "…all, all, all, worth it." At my hotel:

"Hand me your passport, and we'll return it at 7 pm."

"No, I'll keep this."
"Ah, like all South Africans."
"Do you have a lock for the door?"
"Ah, like all South Africans."

Until a hundred years ago this village was off-limits to any outsiders, and just a handful of Westerners risked their lives to visit in disguise. There is still much character and authenticity in the photogenic mountain village of Chefchaouen with its labyrinthine alleys, and striking blue and white painted buildings, reminiscent of the Greek Cycladic islands.

A green-eyed Berber tailor repairs my backpack, and I film him at work. When I thank him he touches his heart with his hand. I start filming the town and its people and find what will become the theme of the travelogue: the craftsmen, artisans and artists of Morocco—a sights and sounds documentary of Morocco. Watching the travelogue 15 years later I am struck by how easy-going the Moroccans were—to allow me to hang out with them and film them going about their work.

After a flea-bitten night, I move out of my room and up to the open rooftop area of the hotel. There's a Norwegian hippy with a serious sound system who's been here for one and a half months. Leftfield's Leftism is playing at full volume—and full bass. He tells me about his India travels:

"In India, they separate business and friendship. Even if a good friend cheats on another friend in business it does not affect their friendship." I often think back to that philosophy.

I also meet three South African guys on holiday from London who say to me:

"Without alcohol, there's tranquillity and non-aggression here."

It says more about South Africa or the UK than Morocco. Nonetheless, this area is renowned for hashish too, so that probably plays a role in the tranquillity.

In the early evening, after a particularly lazy and very hot day, I have a refreshing shower, put on some decent clothes and walk down to the entrance of the Ibn Batuta Hotel to watch the world go by. First, a deformed dwarf comes by for a conversation with me in broken French and Arabic, then totters away. Since then I've been entertained by a cute girl of about five or six who chats away to me in Arabic, looking entirely happy in her community. It's now dusk and the weather is balmy. The place seems magical. Even the girls are smiling at me tonight. The little girl is still talking to me, giggling, breaking my reverie from time to time. I nod and smile. It's nighttime now and the *medina* comes alive with the folk of Chefchaouen—laughing families, hobbling old men wearing the fez, young boys carting steel wheelbarrows, old women in black, kids running about in the meleé. There goes the *muezzin*. Magic.

I greet a shopkeeper in French who I recognise from the night before. He seems surprised.

"Are you Canadian?" he asks.
"No, South African."
In other words, you're not French (who form the majority of tourists) are you?

Departing at the Chefchaoun bus stop I meet a Moroccan called Charlie. Though illegal, he is smoking hash in the open, and I don't say no to a puff. He tells me he smokes 20 to 25 grams of hash a day. As is often the case in Morocco he has a pitch. He has a house in a village in the mountains where foreigners and hash smugglers stay.

"There are three women from Germany there now," he says. "You should come."

"Next time," I tell him as the bus pulls away.

It's a nice way to leave Chefchaouen. But the heady relaxed state quickly changes just outside town. The bus is stopped at a police checkpoint. Like the character at the start of the film Midnight Express, I'm overcome with red-eyed paranoia. The cop slowly walks up the bus corridor carefully checking everyone and their bags. I have nothing to hide, yet I am overcome with paranoia. That is the flip side of smoking hash.

In the late afternoon, the bus pulls into Meknes, one of Morocco's four imperial cities. It's a 1000-year-old town with impressive gates along its walled circumference. Sitting at a street café as dusk turns to night I watch the passing parade of people. I am struck again by the magic in the air turning to surreal when Pavarotti plays on the café's speakers. I stroll through the open-air evening market. A seemingly drunk, high, or just very intense Moroccan man approaches me.

"Where are you from?" he asks.
"South Africa."

Without missing a beat or listening he tells me:

"I live in Boston. I'm a mechanic. Fix cars."

His approach is somewhat harassing and aggressive. I disappear from him into the crowd. Four young Moroccan guys in the main square invite me to join them. I spend the evening with them, and they give me lessons in Arabic which I jot down in my notebook.

I greet the owner when I return to my spartan Meknes hotel room. His initial friendliness is in contrast to his demeanour the next morning when I pass through the entrance. He is rinsing his face and looks up bleary-eyed without a smile. It makes me wonder about what a French traveller said to me about the private drinking phenomenon in Morocco.

I bus it to the Roman ruins of Volubilis. It is over 40 degrees centigrade as I meander through the vestiges of this far-flung corner of the old Roman Empire. It's amazing to think that a community of 5000 Romans lived here 2000 years ago, and to see their faces and the animals that once roamed here on the mosaics that are still in good condition after two millennia. The empty plains are also a vestige: this was a forest before the Romans got here. An early environmental disaster.

The next journey is a 475-kilometre air-conditioned modern train to Marrakech, the most well-known of Morocco's four major imperial cities. Arriving at the central plaza, or Djamâa el Fna, I see hundreds of pale faces, package tourists being whisked about in air-conditioned tour buses. Every time I pull out my camera someone approaches me for money. At dusk I spring into action, asking politely at the myriad food or fruit juice stalls permission (and often buying something first) and then filming.

It's time to move on and find a more authentic Morocco again. Stopping at Agadir, I get talking to a Moroccan guy at the bus station. I tell him I am heading south to Sidi Ifni.

"That is good," he says.
Talking about the package tourists he says, "I don't understand how someone would take the trouble to fly a long distance to Morocco (from Europe), go directly to a beach hotel, spend a week lying on the beach and then fly home."

I agree.

The next morning I continue south, in the hopes of a mellow beach place. Sitting in the bus waiting for our departure I watch a procession of beggars traipsing in and out, murmuring, almost in tears with their long-winded furtive stories in Arabic. Another visitor to the bus appears to be preaching. What an adventure.

After installing myself at the Hotel Suerta Loca in Sidi Ifni I walk along the coast to the modern harbour. A policeman stops me and questions me. He loses interest when it becomes apparent I am a young innocuous traveller. There is also a soldier walking around the port. But I go ahead and chat with the fishermen offloading their haul of fish. As usual, they don't mind me filming them. The fact that my video camera is a small unobtrusive palmcorder helps.

The sea breeze at Sidi Ifni is cooling, the Atlantic is chilly. I like this town. It's very laid back. It was a Spanish enclave until 1969 and there are many lovely Art Deco buildings. By chance, a festival celebrating the town's independence and reintegration into Morocco is in a few days. I'm going to stick around. I break my dry spell by drinking three beers at a bar that evening. There are a handful of Moroccan men drinking, each sitting quietly by himself. It's not a merry atmosphere.

If you need something when travelling find the right person, don't trust someone who approaches you. This I am learning the hard way. A guy furtively offers to organise hashish for me on the street. I agree and give him some money. I never see him or that money again.

But on the beach, I meet Lisham and Ackram, local lifeguards who share their joint with me and promise to organise some more of this strong Moroccan hash. They also share their tasty lentils with chicken which they warm up on a gas cooker on the beach.

Lisham and Ackram invite me to their house that evening and I am presented with a djellaba, the flowing dresses men wear in these parts. I also meet Hanain, an 18-year-old Moroccan woman. In a divided society like this, it is not easy to make contact with the opposite sex. Hanain and I converse in basic French. She is 18 and beautiful. I walk home thinking, *More Moroccan magic.*

At the Hotel Suerta Loca in the morning, I get talking to two American Peace Corps volunteers.

"We're based in the Atlas mountains."
"What are you doing there?"
"We're hoping to find jars to package the locally made honey."

This sounds a bit like being tasked to assist in the developmental sector, and then just making up some random and unsustainable project so that it seems like you are doing something worthwhile.

Sidi Ifni is practically as far south as you can get in Morocco and it's a quiet outpost kind of town. It has an end-of-the-world feel to it. In a way, it is the end of the world. Further south is occupied Western Sahara and beyond that is Mauritania and the Sahara.

In 1975 Spain withdrew from its Western Sahara colony, and instead of the territory getting its independence just as every other European colony in Africa did, Morocco duly and violently took control of the 266,000 square kilometre chunk of Sahara desert and coastline. Many of the inhabitants of Western Sahara fled to neighbouring Algeria where they have been languishing in camps ever since. I will visit these camps many years later.

Ironically, the former Spanish enclave of Sidi Ifni has an air of excitement about its upcoming independence celebrations when I visit. Ironic, considering Morocco is itself a coloniser.

I join Ackram and Hisham on the beach while they carry out their lifeguard duties. I write in my diary:

"At home in a foreign land, a foreigner in a homeland, I watch the winds change, currents turn, and I watch the horizons for a sign. I am, floating."

At sunset, Hanain arrives at the beach. We are alone and I spontaneously kiss her. Just a peck on the lips.

Together with my lifeguard friends, we all walk through town. I hold Hanain's hand.

The moussem, or week-long independence from Spain celebrations of Sidi Ifni, are about to begin, and I have met a local, Bachir Mardi. Bachir offers to show me around. First, he takes me home. On the way, he explains to me that he is a Berber. It's my first introduction to the indigenous Berber people as distinct from the Arabs who migrated across North Africa in about 700 AD. Bachir's house, on a hill away from the whitewashed town, is a simple structure made of cinder blocks. As we walk into the lounge his wife quickly gets up and without a word disappears out of the room. Bachir plays the guitar for a while before we go to the festivities.

The week-long event begins, literally, with a bang. Horsemen fire shots in the air as they gallop past spectators. Berber traders have travelled from around Southern Morocco to sell their wares ranging from blankets to spices, earthenware to clothing, and carpets to vegetables. Today lorries and transit vans have replaced camels as a means of transport for these traders. But other than that one has a sense of going back in time. There are games for adults and children, such as basina, a gambling game that entails throwing a coin onto a disc floating in water. I film the celebrations.

I speak to a taxi driver, Mohamed, about the market.

"This year the market is smaller than usual. I think it's because of 9/11, but in general, unemployment is high and money is short in Morocco."
We talk about the big divides in the world and he says, "If people, not politicians, were to talk openly, that would help."

I agree. Next year the USA invades Iraq for no good reason other than to show the world who's the boss.

Surreally "Rule Brittania" is playing on a radio at a sidewalk café. It's 2002 and "Rule Britannia" is no longer to be played officially by the UK. Perhaps the irony of singing the words, "Britons never, never, never shall be slaves" finally sunk in? It's fitting that a song that glorified colonialism should breathe its last gasp across the road from an independence celebration in an obscure corner of the world, in a country that oversees the so-called last colony in Africa.

I meet my lifeguard friends in the evening. Hanain is there, but she is cold. She is also angry.

"I didn't know you were just visiting. I thought you lived here."

She doesn't talk to me again. The lifeguards chuckle when they ask me about her.

One of my lifeguard friends, Hisham, invites me to join him that evening. I meet him at a house. Inside a bare room, about 15 men are sitting against all four walls. I join them. They are smoking a light brown hash. There seems to constantly be another joint coming around, which I duly smoke and pass on. This stuff is knocking my socks off. At first, I am high as a kite. But then intense paranoia follows. Who are these guys and what is their motivation? My anxiety is building up. Why have I been invited here? I jump up and get out of the room, get out of the house, and stride back to my hotel. Here, alone, my head settles down. I have read so many "shakedown stories" (especially on Lonely Planet Thorn Tree), and the hash was kick-ass too. Nonetheless, I still support this rather than alcohol.

In the morning I say goodbye to Bachir on a hilltop outside Sidi Ifni. He has been an unofficial guide during the festivities, and he features in my sights and sounds of Morocco documentary. He'd like something:

"Whatever you can spare—I don't know what is in your pocket."
I give him a relatively small amount because my budget is tight. As we part, he says with much compassion, "It's okay, I know you are American." He thought I had pretended to be South African in the fraught months after 9/11.
"No, I'm South African."

"It's okay," he says compassionately. He remains convinced.

Originally I had hoped to keep going south into West Africa but budget and time won't allow it, so getting into a "grand taxi" I start the slow and long journey back north. Bis'Millah says the passenger next to me.

"What does that mean?" I ask.
"In the name of God," he says. It's an incantation to bless the journey.

The "grand taxis" are old Mercedes Benzes carrying six passengers each: four in the back seat, and two in the front passenger seat. Their speedometers usually show the mileage stopped turning at around 500,000 miles! One of these solid old German cars takes me up into the Anti-Atlas mountains to the town of Tefroute. En route, a veiled lady sitting in the back row throws up. The driver doesn't flinch—he just keeps driving.

Tafroute is a pretty town whose shades of brown match the mountains in which it is dramatically set. But the heat in July is extreme. Enervated I enter a café and order a tea. Moroccan green tea is loaded with sugar, giving a welcome boost to flagging energy on a day like this. A minstrel walks in playing his guitar and singing to the patrons. I ask him if I can get some video of him playing and he agrees. I record it in my hotel. First outside but it's too noisy. Then in the reception but too many people walk in and out. Finally, with the minstrel starting to look a bit bewildered, upstairs on a landing. I give him 20 Dirhams. The minstrel doesn't appear in my travelogue. Thank you for your patience, minstrel of Tefroute.

I don't sleep much as I am getting bitten by fleas. At some point in the night, I move to the slightly better rooftop. I figure out that any hotel under 35 Dirhams a night, such as this one, is probably a flea hole. I can barely see out one eye that is bitten ("by mosquitoes," says the hotel manager) the following day. In the late afternoon, I hike in the ochre hills that surround Tefroute, enjoying the exercise and spectacular scenery. In the evening I walk to the five-star hotel on the hill, get transported to another world in the lounge area, watch BBC news and drink a beer, before returning to reality, and my 20 Dirham flea-hole.

The coast makes for a welcome break from the sweltering interior. The next town is surf spot Taghazout where I install myself at the Auberge de Taghazout on the beach. I meet two English girls, Leone and Elizabeth who smoke hash incessantly. I am invited to eat dinner in a room at the hotel with the girls and some Moroccan guys. We sit around a large tajine and eat with our hands. At one point I accidentally take a bite with my left hand. One of the Moroccan guys looks at me unable to hide his disgust. In Morocco one eats with one's right hand only—the left hand is for toilet matters. There is red wine and beer. At one stage one of the Moroccan guys turns to me, and just loud enough not to be heard by the two girls says, "English pussy tastes like chicken, smells like fish." I think that sums up the evening quite well. I leave the girls with their clutch of admirers and an everlasting supply of hash.

The owner of the Auberge is a 67-year-old Hungarian who according to Abdella who works here, subsists on cigarettes and coffee. I get talking to her.

"Although they are chauvinistic, men here are also very proud, take good care of their wives, and their wives live like queens because the men provide everything." She says that "In Morocco, the men rule the streets and the women rule the homes." And, "Gradually drink and drugs (stronger than hash) are becoming a problem."

Later Abdella tells me this auberge owner was a spy in the second world war. Of course, I ask her, and she shakes her head, "Nonsense." But Abdella is convinced and shows me a newspaper cutting. It looks like her.

In the evening I hear the Ella Fitzgerald song, "Summertime" emanating from upstairs. I walk up to find the source. A guy is sitting outside his hotel room smoking a cigarette.

"Good evening."
"Good evening."
"This music is great."
"Yes, it's peaceful."

As I walk past I catch a glimpse of a woman sprawled on the bed, and the smell of sex is in the air.

One of the best aspects of travelling alone and without a firm schedule is making spontaneous travel decisions. That is the definition of freedom. In the morning as I finish breakfast the Hungarian spy owner asks me how I am.

"Fine. I've just decided to go to the mountains."

Twenty minutes later I am on a bus heading inland again. I travel via Marrakesh where I am accosted at the bus station by a guy:

"Where you from?"
"South Africa."
"Oh very good," he says and gathers trust. "I have a friend in South Africa."
"You like to smoke?"

"Maybe."
"You come with me, we smoke at my house."
"No thanks."
"It is close by."
"No."

The final destination is a little town called Imlil in the High Atlas mountains. This is the end of the tarmac road and the starting point for ascents up Jebel Toubkal, at 4167 metres above sea level, the highest peak in North Africa. It is why I am here.

I spend the first three days doing day hikes up into the mountains around Imlil, getting some shots with my camera. Alone on a saddle between two peaks and in the middle of nowhere I meet another hiker. He is a teacher from Rabat.

"Every year I take two weeks' holiday by myself. I leave my wife and children in Rabat, and I walk in the mountains."

Then we shake hands and each goes off on our wanderings.

On another day I come across a small shop high up along the footpath, with a large Coca-Cola sign on it. Is it impossible to get away? In a village with stupendous views, I am invited for tea. I watch the elaborate tea-making ritual: mint tea is poured back and forth between the teapot and glass pots to ensure good mixing of the Chinese gunpowder tea, mint leaves and copious amounts of sugar. Thus energised, the journey continues.

I am filming general mountain shots and there are some impressive views across the High Atlas mountains. I write in my diary: "Film is a deceit. The filmmaker captures various images, narration and music, and arranges them to create a story—of his making. It is art, and because it draws from so many mediums it truly is the richest, most powerful and most deceptive of all the arts."

After my three days of acclimatisation, I finally set out for the peak of Jebel Toubkal. I am alone, without a guide, no muleteer and no map. And I am carrying about 12 kilograms on my back. There is a French group with a guide and muleteers ahead of me, so I keep them in my sights, stopping only for a quick orange juice sold by locals along the way. It's hard work keeping up with the group in front but they are my unwitting navigators, so I have no choice in the pace. Three hours and 45 minutes later I arrive at the Toubkal Refuge, 3200 metres above sea level. It is the base camp for the Jebel Toubkal peak. I am so tired I lie down and immediately sleep for a couple of hours on a dorm bed.

Guides discuss tomorrow's ascent and hikers rest for the final assault. Most of the hikers are French—they all seem to have the same Gallic mouth, quite sexy on a woman.

The following morning at 6.30 am I begin the walk up a steep scree slope. At a col, I turn left for the final walk to the summit. It is wild up here, feels like a different world. All of North Africa is spread out below. I feel exultant. The achievement is complete.

At the summit, I bump into a French guy I had met at the Marrakesh bus station.

"Are you smoking a cigarette?"
"No, it's a joint. Do you want some?"

I am already on both a natural high and an altitudinal high, but I join him to smoke a bit of his hash. Then I really am high: a triple high. I am smiling all the way back down to the refuge and onwards back down to Imlil village.

At the hotel in Imlil I get talking to a Spanish couple. I tell the beautiful wife that I read where the term "blue bloods" comes from: the Spanish aristocracy who hid out in mountain caves during the Moorish invasion, and whose veins showed blue against their pale skin. Her husband looks disbelievingly at me. They give me a lift to the next town, and when I greet him outside the car I get a hard look and a very firm handshake.

Feeling rather stiff after the mountain ascent, I continue the long journey back to the coast. Our Mercedes Benz "grand taxi," loaded with the usual six passengers is stopped by a traffic cop. He wants to see everyone's identification. I pull out my South African passport. He studies the front and looks inside at my picture. He frowns.

"But you're not Black."
"We have all the colours in South Africa."

He gently taps my knee for it to be inside the car, and closes the door for me.

I write in my diary: "the lone traveller, moving about at will, by chance, spontaneously, carrying only the bag on his back, attains an unsurpassed level of purity. Responsible only for himself, answerable to no one, a stranger who melds into his constantly changing environment, a master of disguise, a chameleon reaching heights of inner peace, control, content in oneself."

On my first morning in Essaouira, a laid-back and fairly authentic coastal town, I awake early, the first shops opening for business, the light still golden, the narrow *medina* streets still. Rounding a corner near my hotel, I come upon a restaurant whose every wall is entirely covered with bright paintings—floor to ceiling. I sit down trying to take in the vivid colours and shapes resembling abstract fires and other seemingly cataclysmic natural forms. A shy pretty waitress takes my order. Today I have coffee and a slice of cake.

This town used to be a hippy hangout. People like Cat Stevens and Jimi Hendrix spent time here. Music is heard from every nook and cranny, whether it's djembe drums at the waterfront, or Gnaoua music (with its West African roots) coming from rooms in houses. There are also many artists, painters, potters, jewellers, and craftsmen making chess sets through to boats. I enjoy the music and it seems that instead of drinking in a bar or watching television, these guys, who come from all walks of life, meet every evening to jam, to celebrate life together. I poke my head around a doorway and find a group of guys playing music. They usher me in. I sit quietly just soaking it all up. The West has lost something important in its continual spiral of technical efficiency. Perhaps the West has lost life itself, for its soul has retreated to some dark recess making space for material wealth instead.

It's good to spend time with my friends Stephan and Leah who I met in Sidi Ifni, once again. At the harbour I film Stephan selecting his squid and sardines, watch them being grilled, and enjoy a classic Essaouira lunch. Following the sounds of Gnaoua music leads me to make friends with some of the musicians, hanging out with them while they play music in their homes. They never hesitate to welcome me.

And I befriend Hassani Majid, an artist who paints Arabic script on parchments. While I am outside his studio I experience another benevolent beauty-and-the-beast moment as I did in Chefchaouen. An erratic guy dressed in rags approaches me from time to time. He's not menacing, just unbalanced, dirty, clasping a bottle of whisky. Then a little girl approaches me, giggling, chatting, and clasping my knee as she hides from the social outcast. Such innocence. Together we are unafraid. It's another magical moment in Morocco.

With the djembe drums beating and echoing along the castle walls at sunset I write a part two to my lone traveller musings: "The lone traveller is answerable to no one. The tide is coming in."

I bus it up to Casablanca and revel in exploring a new city, supposedly modelled on Marseille—just a bit grubbier. Just like Cairo is a grubby version of Paris they both just need a good scrub down.

My Morocco journey is coming to an end. I find a run-down colonial-era hotel with period-heavy furnishing. Then I buy a bus ticket. It'll be a 44-hour ride direct to Lyon, France. Being a Monday departure the ticket is half-price. I've heard an old French song playing a few times over the last few weeks, and it runs as a soundtrack as I walk these streets. *Ne me quitte pas*—don't leave me.

A charming fellow sidles up to me.
"Did you enjoy Morocco?"
"Yes."
"Where did you visit?"
I run through the places.
"And what was your favourite?"
"Chefchaouen."
"When are you leaving?"
"Tonight."
"Oh very sad. By plane?"
"Yes"
"Oh," he says gathering trust, "I work at the airport. I'll be working night shift."
I doubt that.
"So when you were in Chaoen you smoked?"
"Yes, good stuff."
"The best. Come with me, I'm stopping at my house to smoke a little. I've made couscous." An extra incentive.
"No thanks, I don't want to smoke today."
"You sure? Good stuff."
"No."

He has followed me into a dusty little shop selling alcohol. I buy a couple of small bottles to take back to South Africa as gifts. My new friend is eyeing it closely. I buy a third bottle and give it to him. His eyes widen, and he grabs it and dashes out before I change my mind.

Even on my last day in Morocco, I have dished out money. But I have to take my hat off to some of these guys for their persistence. And I'd rather hand over a bit of money to a talker than be killed for it in South Africa by a thug.

I eat my last meal in Morocco on a busy street at a worker's cafeteria. A brochette (kebab). Across the road is the once regal but now very dilapidated Hotel Lincoln. In front rush hour traffic: *petit taxis*, scooters, *grand taxis*, harassed pedestrians. *Au revoir* Morocco.

During the two-day bus ride to Lyon I enter the awake-dream state. We stop at a garage and I alight. Which country are we in now? I listen to the conversation inside the mini supermarket. Spain. The wheels turn, and the journey is hypnotic in washed-out mid-summer sunshine. A police checkpoint on a highway in France. A policeman with police dogs walks through the bus inspecting everyone's passport. Fortress Europe. I am inside.

In France, devoid of any funds I am limited to walks in the forest and reading at my sister's house in Sassenage, a village near Grenoble. I also watch my footage of Morocco and make notes on how a story can be made of the material.

Back in Cape Town, I upgrade my computer to be able to handle video editing and buy a basic video editing software called Pinnacle Studio. I edit the sights and sounds of Morocco documentary. I love every moment of the editing process. This is what I want to do for the rest of my life.

I arrange a screening at the Armchair Theatre in Observatory. And I make a sale to South African Airways as in-flight entertainment. The circle is complete and I can call myself a filmmaker. I wait and wait to get paid. Finally, I follow up. "Where did you send an invoice?" Oops. I hadn't sent an invoice. How did I think I think I was going to get paid? I have no idea. Lesson number one learnt!

The following year I become a full-time student once again at the age of 29, to study for a master's degree in Film and New Media at the University of Cape Town. I start working on a screenplay, but by the end of the year, I have decided to stay focused on factual TV content. What I learn in terms of filmmaking during that master's year is minimal. Almost everything I have learnt about filmmaking has been on the job, working alongside, reading about, watching and learning from industry professionals, and asking for tips from experienced professionals.

This is not to say a good teacher couldn't teach a lot about the ins and outs of filmmaking in a short time, and help students leapfrog many common technical and creative mistakes. But unfortunately, our teacher disappears after one month when he gets a TV series commission, and my class of five students is left to fend for ourselves. But I get to make a documentary on Cape Town's Long Street, with no input from anyone except from our cameraman teacher. I ask him to view my project near the end of post-production, in the university edit suite. As he sits down he says: "Get me a bottle of red wine." I cross the road, return with the wine, and he proceeds to drink it out of the bottle after popping in the cork, and then gives me his feedback.

The only time I cross the line from observer to activist is in that student year of 2003. George Bush's USA is about to invade Iraq with the fake reason that Iraq has weapons of mass destruction. Together with my class, I picket outside the old US Embassy in Cape Town's City Centre. Down with imperialism.

CHAPTER THREE
Africa's east coast islands

At the start of 2004, with a master's degree completed, I sell my car and use the proceeds to fund my next adventure, and documentary: the Swahili islands off East Africa. In the gradual genesis and evolution as a documentary filmmaker, this journey is to be part backpacking adventure, part filmmaking project.

Leaving behind the enormous valleys with their picturesque vineyards and Cape Dutch buildings, the train rises to the vast plateau of the South African interior. Here the Karoo begins. It consists of dry wide open spaces, and the air is sparkling and clear. With the setting sun leaving a red pall over the horizon, I make my way to the restaurant car for a sundowner.

I sit down next to an old gentleman, who turns out to be a retired ex-policeman. "Man, in the old days there was still respect, people didn't talk back to policemen," he grumbles. "If they didn't listen to you, you just klapped (hit) them. There was law and order then."

He excuses himself, and I wander off, past the second-class compartments. Darkness has fallen, and the train's hypnotic and repetitive rumbling lulls passengers into preparing their beds.

Later, back in the restaurant car, I meet Janice. She is a Coloured widower from Cape Town.

She launches right into things. "I see you as a human being. Not as a blonde-haired person. White people have always treated me well, spiritually and emotionally. I've always gotten on so well with them."

"I look forward to the day South Africans don't see people according to their colour," I reply.

It turns out that Janice has visited Gabon, but hates it. It's one of the places I love.

I excuse myself and head back to my compartment, beer under my arm. I settle into my top bunk.

The Cape under the Dutch East India Company rule was pretty brutal, but it was the British who created race classifications. In other words, you have to fit into a White, Brown or Black category. Many White Afrikaners have a drop of Brown blood in them, myself included I would guess. If only we had all embraced the mixed heritage so many of us have from the get-go. How much further along we would be as a nation. We are all creole in South Africa.

An old Zimbabwean gentleman passes me a cup of Fanta and a banana. Two young boys pass by the cabin and give me a packet of chips. It always amazes me how much generosity there is in people with little.

As I set up my sleeping bag, Charles, the garrulous train conductor, walks in, and takes a seat, asking me where I come from. When I tell him I live in Tamboerskloof, Cape Town, he launches into the English White South African versus Afrikaans White South African debate: the Afrikaner is a racist; the *soutie* (English-speaker) a liberal. The defining moment for him was when he saw English Whites at an ANC rally in the apartheid days.

If only it were that simple, for in reality racism is found across the board.

Breaking away from politics, Charles lets me into a few secrets about womanising. Good manners and communication are his credos, and he goes on to tell me about the women he sleeps with on the train.

"White, Brown, Black, any colour, so long as the train driver is okay with it, then I bring them back to my compartment." For the record, Charles, is Coloured guy.

He doesn't stay long—something about a girl who works in the kitchen.

And so, as the Trans Karoo Mainliner cleaves through the thin desert air, I make myself comfortable for the night ahead. The moon's reflection briefly skirts a Karoo farm dam but otherwise has little effect on the inky black night. The new engine that has been added to the train in Beaufort West adds impetus to the journey. I think about Charles, the train's rocking motion, all his women, the racial divides, the humanity, the fucked up but oh-so-beautiful country.

In Johannesburg, I take a walk around the city centre. It's now entirely African compared to my first forays circa 1988 - 1992 when my family lived in nearby Pretoria. Since then many white businesses moved out to the suburbs. In the centre sooty, dusty buildings tower over shouting hawkers and jostling pedestrians. I walk purposefully without a destination. Wandering about cities, including getting lost, is one of my favourite pastimes when travelling. I don't find anywhere to stop off and have a coffee, as I would in Cape Town. Finally, I need to find my way back to the train station. I ask a passing pedestrian. Viktor, a young man, berates me for walking around alone in the dangerous CBD. He grabs my arm and leads me back inside the station, with a firm warning not to leave again.

"It's not safe!"

A day later, leaving Pretoria my sister asks me, "Won't you be lonely going to Mozambique by yourself?" I just smile. How could I be lonely when I am in the company of *the people*?

The train conductor comes to my compartment to let me know we'll be a bit behind schedule because "The signals were out." Oh, the joy of travel. To be on the move again!

In the morning the acrid smell of burning brakes fills the compartment. At the South African side of the Mozambique border, I climb off the train and walk across. There's a Portuguese-South African guy on the South African side running a small shop.

"Where are you going?" he asks.
"Maputo."
"Why would you want to go *there*," he asks with obvious distaste.

I guess he was one of the many Portuguese who fled Mozambique soon after independence in 1975 having lost everything. When we cross to the other side we'll get on a third-class-only train. The shopkeeper says, "It's because when the South African train went all the way to Maputo it would return stripped of its seats and tables... and anything else of value."

Over the border at the Ressano Garcia station, a deranged man rants and raves up and down the platform. Passengers settle down into the tatty, overcrowded interior of the third-class-only compartments. They are Mozambicans with extra baggage ranging from queen-size beds to bags of potatoes, boxes of sunflower oil, and other goods in zipped-up checkered made-in-China bags. The train passes the occasional village, each hut surrounded by a patch of maize. Here and there lies a crumbling Portuguese-era building. A passenger buys a *vondo*, the Shangaan name for a giant rat. This meal he tells me lives in the sugar cane fields, where this one was caught.

Then we crawl into Maputo, Mozambique's capital city.

The last and brightest stars are being washed out by a faint glow silhouetting the massive concrete apartment blocks that characterise Maputo's skyline. Dawn is breaking and already the air is an intoxicating tropical punch that is breathed in with large gulps.

A chocolate croissant which melts in the mouth is chased by an espresso to kick the metabolism back into shape. I'm sitting at the Pastelaria Nautilus, a pavement café where Maputo's well-heeled are watching the city wake up. Traders touting batiks or cigarettes walk the pavements in search of customers while regulars to the café stop to shake hands and greet each other.

Mozambique has been at peace since 1992 following a 17-year war, and the last decade has seen Maputo repaint, resurface and rebuild. Amongst the towering concrete edifices lie some 1960s glam style and Art Deco panache that is gradually being revived.

Art Deco's geometry and simplicity set in vibrant colours characterise Maputo's architecture. Look beyond the cracked black-and-white mosaic pavements and grimy shop fronts and find a city that is both retro-cool and elegant.

Stepping back into the muggy summer morning, I head downtown, stopping to photograph vendors sitting next to their wares—bottles and cans of cold drinks and beers piled high on top of each other. Dazzling red flame trees line the wide boulevards, contrasting sharply against the pale blue sky and grey buildings. A traffic policewoman, in a pristine white uniform, directs rusty trucks belching black diesel smoke and sparkling new four-wheel drives on a busy intersection.

Walking the streets at night with other backpackers from Fatima's Lodge, we are accosted by police. The stamped and notarised photocopies of our passports are not sufficient evidence of identity. Armed with AK47s this police, time and again in my personal experience, target foreigners to create a problem which has to be bribed out of. The first time this happened to me in the 1990s it was unnerving. They're intimidating. This time, we are eventually set free. But it takes some negotiating.

I catch a very early *machimbombo* (bus) north to Tete, a two-day trip through lush summertime Mozambique. There are some interesting shirts worn on the bus. There is an Osama Bin Laden T-shirt, a very colourful Saddam Hussein t-shirt, and finally "Save Ferris," referring to one of my all-time favourite movies, "Ferris Bueller's Day Off"—"one man's struggle to take it easy."

My fellow passenger, Sam, from Zimbabwe, epitomises the flux of Southern African politics. He has been looking for work in Maputo. Just ten years ago, Mozambicans would have been looking for work in Zimbabwe. But following the commercial farm invasions in Zimbabwe the economy there is tanking. Sam has had no luck and is heading back home. In a small village north of the Save river, the bus stops for a few hours for the driver to rest. As usual in these rural parts of Southern Africa, the night sky is a spectacle of a trillion ultra-bright stars.

After Tete, I press on to Malawi, the country of my childhood. My destination is east of Malawi, back into Northern Mozambique, and on the Indian ocean, my first East African island, Ilha de Mozambique, where I can start filming my documentary. The plan is to make a sights and sounds travelogue of seven East African islands, using the dhow (an Arab-origin boat used in the Indian Ocean) as the central thread of the story.

I enjoy moving about with just my bag and me, taking things as they come, able to go as and when I please. From Malawi's commercial capital city, Blantyre, I take two hopelessly overloaded minibus taxis to Chipoka, on Lake Malawi. At one stage I count 27 passengers inside a Toyota minibus. It makes me wonder what the purpose of all the police roadblocks is—to illicit bribes, one assumes. Finally, I hop onto the back of a bicycle taxi to the waiting Ilala ferry, another piece of the jigsaw of my childhood memories. It's a characterful ship that was built in Scotland in the 1950s, disassembled, transported to Lake Malawi, reassembled and has been in regular service ever since. This ship must have so many stories to tell, and I will return to seek them out.

But by now I am starting to feel not quite right. When we arrive at Metangula, on the underdeveloped Mozambique side of Lake Malawi I am decidedly ill. Of the six times I have had malaria, almost every time was after a night of a few beers. It's like the parasite lies await in your liver and at a moment of weakness, it kicks into action.

Here at the age of 30, I think about my mortality for the first time. There is no medical help, and I am isolated. No medical help is an exaggeration. There is a hospital, but they have no medicine at all. Not even headache tablets. Malaria can be fatal and if it's cerebral malaria you could go to sleep and never wake up. I don't want to die. If I were to die, then it's my family I think about. This signals a shift away from the arrogant invincibility of youth.

Fortunately, I am travelling with a course of coartem, the best treatment for malaria. And, James, a local who speaks English (in a Lusophone country) takes it upon himself to keep an eye out for me, bringing me a meal and water every day. Thank God for the kindness of strangers.

A few days later, after leaving a note of thanks for James stuffed with a few metical notes, I catch public transport—the back of an overloaded Toyota pickup—up the rift valley on some truly atrocious roads.

I spend a few more days recovering at Lichinga, the regional capital of Niassa province. At an internet cafe I do some reading about malaria: According to the World Health Organisation, 90% of global malaria cases are in sub-Saharan Africa, with an estimated 435,000 annual deaths as of

2017. And looking at the bigger picture, malaria is but one of many tropical illnesses that have impaired Africa's development through the ages. It's why the progeny of those who left Africa and spread around the world 100,000 years ago were able to fare better, in healthier climates.

I camp at Quinta Capricornio. It's a pleasantly cool high-altitude campsite surrounded by forests. There is a coterie of expats who hang out here in the evening. They have various theories about malaria. I'm told to take one and a half fansidar tablets in addition to the course of coartem, to ensure there are no parasites left in my liver. Later I am told that in this area mosquitoes are immune to fansidar.

Hanging out with these Western aid workers, at first I listen. Then I ask a Danish lady working in HIV AIDS:
"So tell me, is the development, developing?"
My premise is that Africa needs to stand on its own feet. She replies after a bit of thought:
"Hmmm, yes, that's the first time I've thought of that."
Another expat called Jackesh chimes in:
"On the micro level, yes: roads, pumps, you can see some improvements, but the country has so little industry, how can it develop without outside help?"

The aid workers seem to spend a lot of their time talking about which exotic destination they'd like to work in next. A part of me doesn't blame them for that. I wouldn't mind having to choose between Brazil, Sri Lanka or Haiti but it does make me wonder about the perceived altruism of the aid sector. Perhaps there is no such thing as altruism anyway—don't we all act in our interests? But is there a link from the slave trade to missionary work to colonialism, culminating in a continent still under foreign control by the development sector?

Zambian Economist Dambisa Moyo in her book Dead Aid says that in the five decades until 2010 US$1 trillion was been spent on aid in Africa, yet the continent is poorer. The outcome has been aid dependency, which diminishes the incentive to build a sustainable economy. And, a great deal of this aid has been lost to corruption or administration.

Moyo says the solution to the aid question is for each African country to be informed that in five years the taps will be switched off. Free of aid "corruption would fall, entrepreneurs would rise, and Africa's growth engine would start chugging…" For Moyo aid doesn't create jobs, trade and foreign direct investment do. Her solution seems harsh. But maybe it's time for radical change, for which there are precedents.

It has been rare for a post-colonial African state to eschew foreign aid. In the mid-1980s, Burkina Faso was run by the modernising, progressive, social revolutionary Thomas Sankara, who said, "Our country produces enough to feed us all. We can even produce more than we need. Unfortunately, for lack of organisation, we have to beg for food aid. This type of assistance is counter-productive, and has kept us thinking that we can only be beggars who need aid... The one who feeds you usually imposes his will on you."

In the four years he was in power Sankara stood up to the French (who generally like to retain some control of their ex-colonies), carried out mass vaccination and mass literacy programmes, built roads, a railway, schools and health centres, improved women's rights, planted ten million trees to halt desertification, achieved food self-sufficiency and eradicated hunger, and much more. This was achieved with very limited foreign aid. Unfortunately, Sankara was assassinated in 1987. Why was such a seemingly progressive state so short-lived? On the one hand, the revolution entailed a lack of human rights (shades of the Cuban and Russian revolutions), and on the other hand, many vested interests wanted their privileges back. Those vested interests are the ones who knocked him off.

Self-reliance is a sovereign and therefore political issue. Yet aid is more complex than saying simply Africa must go its own way. Humanitarian crises require assistance from the global community. There's no justification for anyone going without a meal or shelter, and dying from diseases that have cures, and the global community simply must help those fleeing wars and dictatorships, or climate crises. These are not political issues but humanitarian ones.

A week later I am well enough to hit the road. I climb aboard a bus that will depart once it is full. And then it will add a few more passengers. The engine overheats several times on the red earth road to Cuambo. It's quite pleasant to have these roadside breaks in the northern Mozambique bush, the landscapes of my Malawi childhood.

I love the unpredictability of this form of independent travel. The week before I was stricken with malaria on a lakeshore village, this week I am in transit in Cuambo, and I have no idea where I'll be the following week.

The next day I take a train trip due east from Cuambo to Nampula and then finally by bus to Ilha de Mozambique. Enjoying my first post-malaria beer at the hole-in-the-wall Copacabana bar on Ilha I watch the passing parade while having a broken conversation in Portuguese with some local guys. It's balmy, and I don't think I ever want to return to Cape Town. A few things have changed around here since my previous 1996 trip. The run-down main hotel, the *Pensado Mozambique*, where I stayed eight years ago is now the renovated, expensive and generic-looking Hotel Omuhipiti. So I camp.

Ilha is the first of the seven islands that will comprise my one-hour travel documentary, "Swahili Islands." When I had shown my previous sights and sounds of Morocco documentary to Cape Town filmmaker Paul Morkel he suggested that I start the story with a theme or a "hook" and that I then stick with it.

The Swahili people are those of Africa's East Coast (predominantly the Kenyan and Tanzanian coast) and their language is the *lingua franca* for the East African region. The dhow, an Arab-origin boat that Swahili traders used historically in their trade between East Africa, Arabia and India is the theme of my documentary. I need to find what aspect of the dhow I'll film on Ilha.

As it was the capital of Portuguese East Africa for four centuries, Ilha certainly has a lot of character. It is only about three kilometres by 500 metres in size, with a rather precarious single-lane 3.3-kilometre bridge linking the island to the mainland.

Northern Mozambique is very far east in its time zone, so sunrise is at 4.30 am here. I watch the sun appear over the palace and chapel of Sao Paulo, a grand faded rose-coloured colonial building that used to be the residence of the Portuguese governor when this was the capital city of the entire Mozambique colony. The capital city moved down to what is now Maputo in 1898 because of the pre-eminence of trade with South Africa. After that, the island went into decline, but the Portuguese had been there since 1507, so that is a long colonial period. Stepping inside the dank interior of the chapel blocked off the muezzin calling the faithful to prayers, and ancient wooden stairs led up to a bell tower for a view of the island, all faded pastel colours and palm trees.

Indeed the island is photogenic, in a charming faded Portuguese way. I set about filming. Cape Town filmmaker Paul Morkel, upon viewing my Morocco sights and sounds documentary, had said I should try to make stories within the story. To explore and explain each story within the greater story. This is a good tip especially if you are taking on a long-form documentary: break it down into mini-stories. This I do with segments on the fishermen and the historic fort.

The stones that were used to build the impressive fort on the northern part of the island 500 years ago were brought from Portugal as ship ballast. And the fort played a key role in fighting off other European colonial powers vying for their slices of the world.

I write in my diary: as filmmakers we take control over space and time, re-jigging it to create our illusion of a space and time. These are such elementary parts of life that we as filmmakers are almost like deities, altering, shifting about, creating our vision, our stories out of the reality that is all around us.

A few days later the excitement of being on Ilha is wearing off. There have been too many nights of too little sleep. I'm camping in a noisy neighbourhood at Casa de Luis and the humidity is extreme. "*Epa*" exclaims Luis when he sees the rash across my chest from the non-stop sweating. On the streets, the kids,' "Amigo, give me money" is starting to grate. It's time to move on, although I will be back to investigate the island's unique architecture, or whatever other excuse I can find to return.

After a fast lift with an Italian hotel owner from Ilha I find myself drinking a beer at Russell's—a landmark in the region for backpackers. Pemba is also changing, becoming a busy little town. Russel is an Australian who landed up in Northern Mozambique as a trader in African curios. His piece of land outside Pemba evolved into a campsite, bar and chalets. One of the travellers started off in South Africa and is heading north, "Looking for my piece of paradise."

"What about South Africa?"
"Too many walls up."
He means between people as well as literally. Indeed.

That night disaster strikes. When I go back to my tent, it is unzipped, and open. Inside several items are missing: my tripod, some books, sunglasses, and backpack. I learnt my lesson the hard way back in 1999 with the theft at Nangurukuru, and I had placed my most important items such as the video camera and tapes in the campsite safe. But this is frustrating. I go to the police. All they can do is provide a letter for my insurance. I then go to the on-site carpenter at Russel's and ask him to make me a replacement tripod made out of wood. When Russell finds out he is furious. This seems strange to me considering I experienced a theft at his place with nary a word from him. The camp security guard who helps me go to the police and also try and ask around about the theft tells me an anecdote. When 100 US dollars went missing from Russel's house, Russel blamed locals in the neighbourhood without for a moment considering the possible culpability of the Westerners staying in his house. And this guard was once an interrogation soldier for Frelimo (the ruling party) during the war. Later Russell approaches me, calm now, and asks if I'd like to share the costs to hire a vehicle to head north.
"No."

I've got my replacement tripod made of wood, and at this stage, I am done with backpackers, foreigners, and towns. I want a wilderness experience. In my wisdom, I decide I am going to hike through the bush to Quissanga, which is the stepping-off town to my next island, Ibo.

Someone at Russell's bar draws me a map. Take the road north by bus, and get off at the village called 19th October. From there head due east 47 kilometres to Mahate. Then it's 15 kilometres north to get to Quissanga.

In principle that all sounds fine. And the makings of an adventure. However, my replacement backpack is the cheapest Chinese quality and is already falling apart. And the region is a wilderness zone. It is inhabited by lions, elephants, buffaloes and much more.

Smithy, a South African guy who landed up living here following a divorce, gives me a lift into Pemba where I spend the night in a cheap hotel. My wilderness adventure begins at 5 am with a taxi ride to the bus stop. We arrive to find the bus has left, but as we drive off we see the bus coming from the other direction. "Catch that bus," I shout to the taxi driver, and we chase after it, flashing our lights. The bus finally stops at a police checkpoint and I can get on.

Not too long later I get off the bus at the village of 19th October. Finally, it's me and nature. 60 kilometres to Quissanga. I think to myself, this should take two or three days. I start walking. The cheap backpack is very uncomfortable, digging into my back. It is also of such poor quality it is breaking in multiple places. It is weighed down with too much stuff. All I have to eat and drink is a packet of biscuits and a bottle of water.

After two kilometres I hear a truck coming from behind me. It pulls up next to me. The driver looks down at me.

"*Epa*," he says, looking at me like I am crazy.
He berates me for walking in an area known to have dangerous wildlife. Then he says, "Get in."
"Okay." It is probably the right thing to do. En route along this Northern Mozambique back road I spot baboons and monkeys but no larger wildlife. However, I do get a glimpse back into time: a man out hunting with a bow and arrow and aiming at a quarry I cannot see, oblivious to our truck.

I stay the night in Mahate. It is not a hotel, but a bedroom in someone's house. As I negotiate my way to the hole-in-the-ground toilet outside the house, a black cat approaches me, meowing, screeching and staring at me. I stare back, holding my ground, and then I step slightly forward. The cat runs away still screeching. It's as if I've chased away the bad spirits there. After that, I feel secure, despite shall we say not being the most hygienic of quarters.

The following day I bus it to Quissanga where I meet a local called Dino, who leads me five kilometres away to a village called Tsangangi from where boats depart for Ibo. First, we have a lunch of rice at a friend's house. Finally, at 4 pm I am on a dhow under sail, crossing the channel to Ibo island. The wind stops entirely halfway across, and we start rowing. However, I can think of worse places to get stuck than on a dhow under a million stars next to an ocean as flat as a billiard table.

Ibo island is stuck in a time warp. The Portuguese were here for 500 years but in the last century, the island gradually sunk into decay and stagnation. I stay at Bella Vista Lodge where an Englishman, James, who was also staying at Russel's the week before says to me:

"I didn't want to say anything while we were at Russell's, but theft out of the campsite is regular. Weekly!"
It's a goldmine in the context of poverty.

Ibo's dark history is, as with Ilha de Mozambique, as a slave entrepot. Today, at first glance, it appears to be a ghost town, long derelict. Yet people are living here, in and amongst the ruins of a Portuguese colonial-era town. Serving the trickle of tourism is the small and historic silver jewellery industry. I enter one of the silversmith's houses and he lets me film while he works. Using rudimentary melting equipment coins are turned into intricate jewellery. I'm told these are ancient Arab techniques and tools, yet the designs are unique. One of the shots I utilise is a "reveal"—I start on a close-up of a piece of jewellery being made and pan up to reveal the jewellery maker. It's a useful shot but it is also a useful concept in filmmaking. To only reveal the truth or the full story after having teased or pulled in the audience.

"Ghost town" is the name I give Ibo for my storyline. And the peace, quiet, and unique atmosphere ultimately make this my favourite of all the islands I visit.

With my work done on Ibo, I take a dhow ride across to the mainland. Being so far away from things I know and am accustomed to is what I enjoy most about travelling. It allows one to get perspective. But I also like the anonymity of it. I'm just another foreigner passing through. And not understanding the language makes everything seem a bit more removed. And in time one becomes a bit more attuned to body language and tone of voice. There are dusty, hot, long bus rides, but there are also dhow trips on the placid Indian Ocean.

Heading north, I take a detour up to Mueda for a side project on Makonde art. Mueda is located on a plateau in the far north of Mozambique.

Mirroring South Africa's Sharpeville massacre of 1960, Mozambique's war of independence was sparked off in the same year when the Portuguese colonial forces mowed down about 600 protesters.

In the following decade and a half, Mozambicans fought for independence. Mozambique became a sovereign nation in 1975 after 500 years of Portuguese rule. But soon thereafter war started again. This is often referred to as the civil war, but it was not. It was a war of destabilisation created by outside forces. Minority White-run Rhodesia created and trained a force known as Renamo whose aim was to destroy infrastructure and terrorise civilians in Mozambique. When Rhodesia became independent (and thereafter known as Zimbabwe in 1980) minority White-run South Africa took over the training and support of Renamo, which continued to create havoc, death and destruction until a Mozambican peace treaty was signed 1992.

Why would White-run Rhodesia and White-run South Africa put so much effort and money into so much destruction? Ostensibly their fear was communism, as the ruling Mozambican party Frelimo while not communist, was aligned with the communist block during the cold war. So Mozambique was a cold war proxy? Yes, but beneath the "*rooi gevaar*" (red peril), lay the "*swart gevaar*" (black peril)—the fear that White-run Rhodesia and later White-run South Africa had of black majority-run politics. And at their doorstep was just too close for comfort. During Mozambique's "civil war" one million people died. In South Africa, apartheid was a criminal act of colonial subjugation, but next door in Mozambique, South Africa's National Party can also claim responsibility for all these innocent deaths.

In Mueda, at the only hotel in this little town, I am greeted by the South African, "Howzit?" The fellow resident is Joao who works for a South African company involved in mining gemstones. There is also a Senegalese in flowing robes, and a Tanzanian that he is talking to, involved in the gem trade in this region. I say to them, "Africa Unite!" as we represent different parts of the continent.

Joao invites me to join him for lunch, where we eat *nsima* and antelope. It's delicious but then I haven't eaten much aside from bananas and bread for two days. *Nsima* is the staple food in Southern Africa, a kind of maize porridge. They had shot the antelope recently while out on a gemstone trading bush trip. This was a fantastic meal for me, but Joao couldn't stop talking about Nando's, the chain of chicken restaurants in South Africa: "You order a chicken, and then fifteen minutes later it's ready!" Considering I have waited up to half a day for a chicken to be prepared in Mozambique's more out-of-the-way restaurants I get what he is saying.

Makonde art is what brought me to Mueda. I fell in love with these sculptures during my solo backpacking trip up the Mozambique coast in 1996. I was on such a tight budget I couldn't afford a US$ 5 Makonde art piece. Later I read that traditional Makonde Art can be viewed in prestigious anthropological museums around the world and has been put on show in art galleries globally since the 1960s. And the Mueda area is where this art form originated.

The starting point of Makonde Art is usually a piece of the African blackwood tree, known locally as mpingo. This hard, heavy, dense wood is fashioned into the three broad types of modern Makonde art: *Binadamu*—naturalistic portrayals of Makonde people pursuing their traditional activities; *Ujamaa*—also known as people poles, they often depict village life, and frequently incorporate ancestral spirits watching over the village; and *Shetani*—representing the complex and rich spirit world. These tend to be more abstract, often with exaggerated features or combinations of figures in a piece.

After a chilly bucket shower at 5 am, I set off on the back of a bicycle to a village 15 kilometres away where I meet some of the artists making these sculptures. A couple of years later I'll incorporate this footage with a Makonde artist in Maputo who I'll interview, for a TV news feature.

After a few days of shooting different aspects of Makonde art, I head for the Tanzanian border. It's a long day on the back of an overloaded and open lorry from Mocimboa da Praia to Palma. To say I am travel-weary after this 13-hour trip is to make an understatement. But after a wash up in a basic hotel, I take a stroll through the village, passing the beached boats under a blanket of stars, and palm trees silhouetted by the moon, and I think to myself—considering I'll leave at dawn the following day—that some of the most fleeting of experiences can leave the most lasting impression.

At five am the next day I am led three kilometres to the main junction by a hotel employee, where an Isuzu 4X4 pulls up.

"Border?"
"Yes, let's go."
"Hello, Mr *Mzungu*," (White man) says one of the passengers to me. To be called *mzungu* is an all-too-often refrain in these parts.
"Hello, Mr *MwaAfrica*," (Black man) I reply. He did not expect that! We all laugh.

It is a quick trip through the wild bush and sandy tracks. The border post has been upgraded since my last trip. Instead of a reed table under a tree, there are two buildings now. We get stamped out, and the vehicle takes us right up to the river's edge where a dhow takes us over the Ruvuma river into Tanzania.

As with my trip eight years earlier, the first town in coastal Tanzania, Mtwara, seems like civilisation after the isolated and underdeveloped Northern Mozambique region. At the Blue Bay Resort I enjoy a decent room with a hot shower, a swim at sunset in the billiard table smooth ocean, followed by dinner with two beers every evening. I also catch up on the world of news and emails at an internet cafe. Yet, looking back at the trying times, the dives I slept in, and the long days on rough transport, in a strange way, those are the highlights, because they were the tests. Aside from the fleas, the Blue Bay Resort is a luxury.

Getting up to the city of Dar es Salaam is a fourteen-hour marathon bus ride, passing en route the village of Nanguruku, where my first documentary's tapes lie moulding in a field. From Dar es Salaam I take a *matatu* (minibus) down to Kisiju. Aside from losing a wheel—it just popped off, fortunately at a low speed—an uneventful trip.

Kisiju is a dirty and smelly little coastal village with its hyperbolic "Pentagon Shop," "Las Vegas Pub," and large dhows with hopeful names like "Titanic," "One Way," and "Mercedes Benz." I'm here to arrange passage on one of these boats over to Mafia island, my third "Swahili island."

I start making enquiries about a boat. While walking around this bedraggled village I am approached several times and given the third degree. At first, I am quite defensive, sure that they just want something from me. Then I decide that my cynicism is unwarranted and that these have been efforts at genuine hospitality. I wish I could have a camera filming me during some of these conversations. I meet Mpiri who asks me what religion I follow.

"I am not religious but I do believe in God and I do respect all religions," which is uncharacteristically diplomatic of me.
"That is fine. Though I will pray for you, it is not my place to judge you," he says.

At the Golden Harvest Office, I buy a ticket for a 9 pm motorised boat to Mafia island. 9 pm comes and goes, and we wait. A "pastor" strikes up a conversation with me. He is friendly. Then he pops the question.

"I and my two pastor colleagues are short for the ticket to Mafia. Can you assist with two thousand shillings?" I do help them.

The boat doesn't depart that evening as "it is broken." We all spend the night on the floor in a reed structure. In the morning I have many itchy bites and welts. It's going to be another day spent in grubby Kisiju with its somnambulant locals. I'm told the boat will leave that evening.

Just then I'm saved by Pastor Elisha Mkeu from the Korea Church Mission. He finds me wandering around the village, takes me to his nearby church and gives me a decent room to sleep in. After a wash up I feel like a new man. Pastor Elisha invites me to join the service. On the way there he turns to me and says:

"You have come here for a reason."

In the small concrete-walled tin-roofed room, Elisha reads from Mark Chapter 10 verses 1 to 14. It's about not getting a divorce and that marriage is forever—two become one. So, choose carefully. And if there's a problem, pray.

There's a medical doctor at the Korea Church Mission who gives me antibiotics for my welts (the standard medical treatment for pretty much everything in my experience in Africa).

Pastor Elisha fills me in on Kisiju's problems: over 70% AIDS rate, prostitution, illiteracy (and as I've mentioned it is really dirty). He puts many of the problems down to Islam, which, purportedly, promotes reading the Koran only, and no other education. Elisha also blames the villager's indifference to the slave trade.

"But that ended a century and a half ago!"
"It's still in their collective conscience. The rationale is, we don't like to work."

But he, a Tanzanian, and two or three other Tanzanians at the mission are trying their best to uplift the village—they've begun a primary school, and a clinic, and have other plans: Tanzanians helping themselves. Charity begins at home.

Pastor Elisha prompts me a few times about my opinions about Kisiju. I am reluctant to judge the state of the village. But I am struck by the lack of pride to let rubbish pile up like that, and the air of lethargy.

At one am Elisha drives me back to the Golden Harvest "office" but it turns out that that night's boat has already left for Mafia island. So we return to the Korea Church Mission.

Four days of attempts to get a boat ensue and finally I succeed. Elisha drops me off in the middle of the night for my transport across to Mafia, and it is in the driving rain that I disembark and wade waist-deep to reach the island that afternoon.

After eating a packet of chocolate biscuits for a sugar buzz after a sleepless night, I take a walk through the town of Kilindoni's main drag. It consists of a row of low, square concrete buildings with rusted corrugated iron roofs, under towering palm trees. I start filming in a shop selling a variety of beans and rice, the staple in these parts. A short, thin, unfriendly, officious-looking fellow arrives.

"Where is your authorisation to film?"
I smile and give a stupid tourist, "Yes."
"You come with me to the district office."
Again I smile and give a stupid, "Yes," and keep filming.

A guy like me wearing shorts and filming in a one-horse village with a palmcorder attracts the ire of officialdom? Wow.

This particular official looks increasingly irritated but I just keep filming the trader. Eventually, he leaves but not without threatening me.

"I will report you."

Chill out man.

It's a lush green island, and the dense tropical vegetation and trees spill over onto the beaches. Here I spot large boxes full of freshly caught fish packed with ice being loaded onto dhows that will take them under sail to the capital city Dar es Salaam. The traders allow me to film them loading their dhows, and I have a theme for my third Swahili Island: the traders. And although the long-distance Indian Ocean dhow trade to Arabia and India is no more, it's great to see dhows still being used for the age-old purpose, ocean sea trade.

The owner of the hotel I stay at, Colonel Kimbau, is the former Member of Parliament for Mafia island and was part of the Tanzanian delegation to South Africa when the country became a democracy in 1994. South Africa is the only country in Africa to not achieve "independence" but instead to have achieved "democracy." That is because it wasn't colonised by an outside power that could exit, but was run by a minority who don't have a "mother country" to return to. My roots in South Africa reach back to the French Huguenots on both sides of my family, who arrived in the Cape in the 1680s, meaning ties to Europe were cut a long time ago. Nonetheless, White South Africans, in a minority, and with our 350 years of subjugation behind us, are strange bedfellows of the "New South Africa."

Colonel Kimbau was impressed with South Africa, with its level of development. But like everyone who visits, or reads anything about the country, the security situation concerned him. Tanzania is so much poorer than South Africa, but crime, particularly violent crime is lower. Like my experience in Morocco, you are more likely to be "asked" for money (for example the 2000 shillings I handed over to the "pastor" at the Golden Harvest office in Kisiju). The approach is blunter in South Africa. Some might say that is because South Africa was built on violence, and so violence becomes the means of interchange. Violence begets violence.

I'm not about to hang about for several days waiting for a boat back to the mainland, so I splurge on a flight in a tiny plane over to Dar es Salaam. Here I meet up with Andrew Schmidt who had I roped into being the presenter of my first travelogue documentary. Andrew is carrying out PhD research into Zanzibar politics, and we cross together to my fourth Swahili island.

Evocatively names Zanzibar, with its winding labyrinthine historic Arabic Stone Town, its wonderful Indian restaurants, and its sundowners overlooking the ocean at Africa House, has a lot of charm. It shares the same dark history as a slave entrepôt with many of these islands I am visiting. Slaves captured deep into mainland Africa were sold here and exported to the Middle East, Indian Ocean islands and the Caribbean.

After my Kisiju village experience, I am intrigued by the story of The Al-Sultanah, which I read about at the island's museum. The Al-Sultanah was a 305-ton Zanzibari barque that docked at New York harbour on 30 April 1840 after an 87-day journey from Zanzibar, purportedly the first African ship to visit the USA. There is a painting of their disembarkation at New York harbour at the museum. The New York locals were very welcoming, handing out drinks at every corner bar to the exotic visitors with their turbans and daggers. These wayfarers' usually teetotalling Muslim ways were temporarily tarnished. And the returning inebriated sailors were told by the grave old Muslim mariner waiting for them at their ship, "Wretched, if you go on at this rate you will soon be as low and degraded as the Christians."

Andrew and I head up to Nungwi on the northern tip of the island. Since I'd been here nine years before the village has been changed beyond recognition: tourism on turbo charge: restaurants, hotels, dive centres where there had been practically nothing before. Walking down the coast away from the development, I come across a dhow builder who agrees to let me film while he works.

One of the tips I picked up from Roy Macgregor, a cameraman who taught us during our master's degree year, is to track your shot from start to finish. Find your endpoint, then go back to the start and shoot the shot. I start on the dhow and twist the camera 90 degrees to work my way up to the top of the palm tree. It's a good lesson for life, working out your endpoint first, and then slowly making your way there.

Back in Stone Town, the woodworkers and carvers allow me to film them while they work. I have a theme for my fourth island: the craftsmen.

While working the wood, Ahmada Yussuf tells me the story of Zanzibar. "Arabs from Oman colonised the island from 1845 until they were ejected in a bloody revolution in 1964." That explains the narrow winding streets with tall buildings, more Middle Eastern than African. Yussuf makes the elaborately carved doors that Zanzibar's Stone Town is renowned for.

Writing in my diary I remind myself that filmmaking is, "Your vision, your voice, your style." Generally, filmmaking is the most collaborative art form. The way I am doing it is not: self-shooting and editing. Yet my plan to make a pure "sights and sounds" later evolves into a slightly more personal approach based on advice given to me afterwards.

From Zanzibar we take a short hop by plane to Pemba island: the step, unloved and forgotten sister of the two islands that make up the Zanzibar archipelago. The island looks more Asian than African with its rice paddies and dense forests. I get some "establishing" shots from the little plane as we descend onto verdant Pemba island.

At our basic hotel in Chake Chake Andrew spots a female traveller, and says, "She looks like she doesn't know what she is doing here." As touristy as Zanzibar has become is as off-the-map as Pemba is. That suits me fine.

At a beach, near Chake Chake I come across fishermen selling their catch in a kind of auction and set about filming. Adding the town's fruit and produce market gives me this Swahili island's theme: the markets.

Three days later, early in the morning, after a delicious spicy tea with black pepper, cloves and ginger I depart on a motorised boat over to the mainland at Tanga.

A side-project of mine is taking photos of any historic cinemas I see en route. In Tanga, I spot one such relic, a lovely old crumbling Art Deco cinema. No sooner have I taken a photo, and turned to walk to the bus station than I am accosted by an angry man.

"You cannot photograph a building without permission."
"Oh," I say, giving the confused dumb tourist look.
"You have to come with me to the police station."

"*Oh*," I say, thinking to myself, *what is this guy on about*? I have just taken a photo of a cinema and he wants to arrest me. I just keep walking to the bus station. This guy is now getting hot under the collar, trying to keep up with my fast pace.

"You cannot do that. You must come with me."
"Oh," I keep acting dumb. And I keep walking.
He persists for a while, but eventually trails off. These people need to chill about the photos.

From Tanga, I take a *matatu* up the coast into neighbouring Kenya. Although speaking the same language, and the people are part of the same region, crossing from Tanzania to Kenya is a significant shift. In Kenya English is much more widely spoken, and crime is more of an issue. Kenyan journalist Catherine Awuor observes that, "It's always been accepted that a major difference between Kenyans and Tanzanians is that Tanzanians are friendlier. Kenyans grow up knowing you must never accept any food or drink from someone in a bus because it is probably laced with some drug that will make you sleep as they rob you blind."

The border is at Lunga Lunga. On the Kenyan side the immigration official says to me:

"A visa costs US$50."
I am sure it is free, so as politely as I possibly can muster I say: "Oh, I see. I had spoken with the Kenyan Embassy in South Africa and was told there is no charge for South Africans."
"No."

Oh bugger, I think to myself. *I am pretty sure there is no fee, but what can I do?* I am about to start extricating my money bag, hidden under my trousers, when the immigration official's colleague pipes up from the back. The official I had been interacting with then stamps my passport, passes it to me:

"It's okay Sir, here you go."

Approaching the outskirts of Mombasa, our *matatu* is stopped once again. At this stop, there is a large contingent of both plain-clothed and uniformed police, all heavily armed with large machine guns. They ask all the passengers to get out of the vehicle and stand in a group. They search our bags. Then they body search us, and then we are on our way. After the US Embassy bombings of Dar es Salaam and Nairobi in 1998, and ongoing terror attacks in the region, security continues to get stepped up.

Mombasa is a slightly dilapidated yet historic small tropical coastal city. I

take long walks around the town, as I like to do, and catch up on emails. My friend Richard Goldstein says, "It must be great to be on a long backpacking trip."
"Yeah, it is."

In the taxi to Mombasa airport, the taxi driver, John, tells me his story.

"I am a lubricants engineer by training. I worked with AGIP Oil but I was made redundant when they pulled out of Kenya. They left because there wasn't enough business. Driving a taxi earns me very little. It's my wife's small government salary that keeps our family going. Many mouths to feed."
"How many children?"
"Eight. We were looking into emigrating to the USA but after 9/11, that became harder. Now we're considering Botswana".
"Botswana is good. It has a strong economy and is safe."
"Yes. My friend is a tour guide—speaks many languages. He went to South Africa. But he left soon afterwards. He said the xenophobia was so bad that he left in such a hurry that his belongings are still there."
"That's terrible," I say.
"Yes, and you'd think Africans would help Africans... I suppose it's survival of the fittest." I think now he is being diplomatic.

South Africa experiences outbreaks of xenophobic violence from time to time—targeting African and Asian foreigners. Human Rights Watch says, "Foreigners are scapegoated and blamed for economic insecurity, crime, and government failures to deliver services, and have been targets of nationwide protests and shutdowns characterized by mob violence, looting, and torching of their businesses."

My flight from Mombasa takes me to my sixth island, Lamu. It is possible to travel by bus but I have read that there is a risk of terrorist attacks. Al Shabaab has attacked buses on this route, and passengers have been killed.

Lamu, like Zanzibar, has a lot of character, with its winding alleyways and mosques. I am told that in a few days the annual Maulidi festival will be taking place. This event celebrates the birth of the prophet Mohammed and is attended by pilgrims and visitors. It seems like a good opportunity for my documentary, with a "festivities" theme for this island.

At an internet cafe, I notice a few stout marine-looking Americans. There is a military base here used by Kenyan and US troops. The purpose of their presence is to counter the threat of terrorism in the region. I am not an activist but if the US ever tries setting up a military base in South Africa, I'll protest on the streets. Fortunately, that hasn't happened.

Next to me in the Lamu town internet cafe is also an American, a peace corps volunteer, Rachel. I strike up a conversation and she invites me to join her friends at a Lamu home that evening. We meet at a house where a local is giving a short talk on Lamu culture. It's a badly lit bare room in which we sit on the floor.

First, I ask the other American peace corps volunteers, all about 19 years old, what activities they are busy with. "We're looking at finding new markets for the wooden furniture that is made here." I wonder how Americans would take to have a group of 19-year-old Kenyans arrive in their cities or towns and give advice on how Americans should do things better. Especially if said advice is as nebulous as the above.

The Kenyan begins telling some folk stories from Lamu, and the group of Americans keep giggling and laughing. I am mortified at how disrespectful they are.

Finally, it is time for Maulidi. Tom Olali from the University of Nairobi describes the Maulidi festival as, "A hybrid festival that is a part pilgrimage, part carnival and part mystical Islamic ceremony." Although the birth of the prophet Mohamed is celebrated across the Sunni Muslim world, the annual Lamu event is a unique Swahili version. The donkey races and dhow races are nice visuals for my documentary. There are also poetry readings, mock sword fights, and long meditative-like dances by men in white robes set to hypnotic drumming.

I hang out with some travellers during my three weeks on Lamu. The highlight is a paganistic-feeling fireside party during a lunar eclipse at Shela beach. There is drumming and dancing. As the sun disappears behind the earth, the shadow of the earth covers the moon. It becomes three-dimensional, and it's as if you can reach out and grab it with your hand, and put it away in your top pocket. Keep it for another occasion.

The foreign girls are approached by the so-called "beach boys," who are local guys found up and down the Kenyan coast. These young men get romantically involved with Western female tourists, with the expectation of financial rewards in return. When asked where I come from and I reply South Africa, one beach boy tells me disdainfully: "You're not African." I don't say anything, although if not African, then what? Returning to Lamu town, the foreign guys are approached by Ethiopian prostitutes. We shrug them off and the whole group goes for the last beer at one of the local joints.

CHAPTER FOUR
Passport to travel

It's useful to have a mentor. I didn't have one, but I approached any filmmaker I could for advice in the early years. About becoming a filmmaker, Paul Morkel said it's the final destination that counts. The journey there can take any form. I would say I have taken an organic approach to that journey.

2006 is a watershed year for my career. For seven years I've made shoestring documentaries that have made little money. Hence working in the film industry in the rather mindless role of finding locations. Soon I'll find a way to be a filmmaker, or at least a video journalist, full-time. And journalism is something one can never get bored with. It's a constant education, every project is different. Most of all it's an opportunity to meet people from all walks of life.

Always on the lookout for new opportunities, I come across the website of a Dutch videographer. This is the kind of work I'd like to be doing: documentaries or video news features. Scrolling through the list of clients he has worked for I don't recognise any of the broadcasters except for the Associated Press. At that stage I don't know anything about the Associated Press, I just recognise the familiar AP acronym. So I write to AP with two story ideas in Mozambique and Tanzania. One Saturday morning, still in bed, my phone rings, and it's the AP bureau chief in Johannesburg. "We're interested in these ideas…"

I'd assumed I would focus on arts and culture stories, yet from the start, as a video journalist, I veer towards nature and the environment. And the more I do so, the more I see how destructive humankind is towards our planet, and the more important these stories are to tell. And how over time, it starts to feel like one is on repeat, again and again highlighting examples of trashing the planet and its wildlife.

The first of the two news features that I get commissioned to produce is on the Unity Bridge. This will be the first road connection between Tanzania and Mozambique, thus connecting Southern and East Africa. The second story is on the Selous-Niassa Wildlife Corridor, a zone linking two of Africa's largest game reserves and thereby allowing animals like elephants space to follow their old migratory routes with some safety. It's a great opportunity but with one catch. What AP pays is less than what I will spend to get there and produce these two stories. But I see it as a kick-start. So I draw money from my home loan account. Basically, I mortgage my house! I borrow my father's Suzuki jeep and head over to Maputo, capital city of Mozambique.

Another piece of advice I received was from Carte Blanche producer Hein Ungerer, who said about travelling in Africa, "Whatever you do, just make sure you have the right documents allowing you to film, with all the right stamps on them." Upon arrival in Maputo, I head over to the Information Office on Avenida Francisco Orlando Magumbwe. Getting the general national film permit is easy and it's free. The next stop is the national parks offices to meet and interview Baldeu Chande. Baldeu is the director of the Niassa Game Reserve. This is Mozambique's northernmost reserve covering 42,000 square kilometres. It is the southern of the two massive game reserves linked, at least on paper, by a wildlife corridor which is the focus of one of my two stories. The northern game reserve is the even bigger Selous, at 50,000 square kilometres. It's like connecting Slovakia and Switzerland with a travel corridor.

African borders are mostly arbitrary, invented by Europeans without any consideration for the local situation. This took place with the European powers sitting around a table in Berlin in 1884 and 1885, deciding among themselves who gets what in Africa. They drew random lines, many straight, on a map of Africa. The result is people of the same ethnic group, speaking the same language, and sharing the same culture became split up by what amounts to artificial frontiers. Academics say around 177 ethnic groups are split up by colonial-era borders. The same goes for the natural environment. As Baldeu puts it:

"The Rovuma river was used as a colonial border between Tanzania and Mozambique, and this split the catchment area," the region where rainfall feeds into the river. Elephants, antelope, buffalo and other animals migrate over the river between the two countries. The idea of the wildlife corridor is to improve the conservation status of the zone between the two game reserves, allowing these animals to move and migrate in more safety from the threat of poaching, as well as better protect the biodiversity of the miombo forest. Although the corridor links the two parks it falls on Tanzanian territory, so when I go north of Mozambique, I'll find out how they are trying to balance the development needs of the people within the corridor with these conservation goals.

As they cover the same geographic area, the two AP stories I am working on are intertwined, so I shoot them concurrently. I also interview Baldeu about the Unity Bridge. The point of my story is to explore the two sides to the development coin: it's great that the first bridge and land connection between Mozambique and Tanzania is finally being built, which should surely boost development in these two isolated and underdeveloped regions. But at what cost does that development come, both in terms of people and the environment? That is what I will investigate.

"Promoting development means we face more challenges to keep the environment in good shape. With such a good infrastructure—a good road running between the two countries—we might face an impact on the forests. Logging will take place where it isn't currently taking place due to lack of infrastructure," says Baldeu. Although not against the bridge, Baldeu prefers that it would have been built elsewhere.

I pack up my gear, thank Baldeu and am on my way out of his office when he adds seemingly as an afterthought, "You should say hello to Dr Rodrigues, head of all Mozambique National Parks. She's in the next office."

I say "Okay" to Baldeu, but I don't stop in at Dr Rodrigues. Why? I guess it seemed less like a request than a suggestion. But it was a request. And it's an error I'll pay for later.

For these first days, my friend Tessa joins me and is assisting me on my shoots. Together we take on the marathon 2500 kilometre six-day journey north on Mozambique's EN1 highway—a blur of dust, tar, radar gun-toting traffic cops, and road works. It is good to see the country's infrastructure on the mend, but road works in progress make for slow driving.

Like wounds, fissures in the ground, potholes scar the tarmac, the trucks, the cars pounding them, driving open the gaping wounds until one day the roadworks company arrives to patch up the hole with new tar, and then over time the cars and trucks pound this patchwork quilt of scar-mending, and eventually some of them reopen, exposing the red earth underneath to the elements, like pink flesh breathing again, making the vehicles bounce and damage their suspension... until one day another road crew arrives and this time they resurface the whole road, and it is rejuvenated, good as new again, billiard table-smooth.

The hours merge into days of pot-hole dodging and subsisting on bananas and peanuts. Eventually, we make it to the holy grail of Pemba, Mozambique's northernmost town, as late afternoon turns to dusk, baobab trees resplendent in the last pink red purple dusty light, the ocean beckoning for a swim.

A few days of dashing around Pemba ensue, getting interviews, and learning a little about HIV AIDS in Mozambique along the way. This is the potential impact on humans of a new bridge. It is a fairly safe assumption to make that a corollary of the Unity Bridge will be an increase in the HIV AIDS rate in the region—which is to date pretty wild and isolated. As with other highway corridors, like the Maputo corridor or the Mbeya-Zambia/Malawi corridor, it is the truck drivers who spread the disease along these routes, through their brothel visitations. In extreme cases, whole villages have been wiped out along these corridors. In Mozambique, the rate of infection along these roads is around double the national average, one in seven versus one in fifteen. I will also look into this issue on the Tanzanian side of the bridge.

It is time for Tessa to leave, as she has to get back to work in Cape Town. I head north towards the Niassa Game Reserve. Driving past Montepuez and into the hinterland I suddenly feel quite alone. And I am. This dirt road passes through some fairly isolated wilderness areas. Virgin land all around.

My reverie gets broken by a test from above. As I approach another river crossing, instead of stopping and checking the best route as I usually do, I drive slowly towards the water and mud area. Then, the car just slips into the mud. I engage low-range, four-wheel drive, but it is too late. The car is good and properly stuck in a rather smelly patch of sludge. *Hmmm, now what?* I think as I look up to see the sun is getting low. I am by myself in the middle of nowhere with a stuck little car!

I smoke a cigarette and take some pictures with my cellphone camera. The silence is pleasant after the bumpy roads. Driving on bad roads requires concentration, and these stops are rare moments to appreciate the surroundings. And I know that sooner or later I'll get out, somehow.

Soon, two old men arrive, and without saying anything set to work by digging out the mud with their hands and placing branches under the wheels. It's not the first time this sludge has trapped a vehicle. Despite their effort, no joy. The car is sitting on its chassis, wheels spinning freely. More and more villagers arrive, and everyone, including a mother with a baby wrapped around her, gets to work digging out the mud with their hands.

I assist and now and then I try again to drive out but to it is to no avail. Eventually, I get everyone to lift the car. The Suzuki Vitara only weighs a ton, and there are twenty people by now. And that's how the car gets out. I hand over a high denomination note. There are some arguments amongst the group about how this money will be split. I hand out some cigarettes, shake hands all around, and hit the road again, feeling elated. There's nothing like a challenge overcome to raise the spirits.

I spend the night in Marrupa, where I spot some South African registered trucks. I amble up to one of the drivers, to say a friendly hello. He is wary and sceptical about why I am greeting him. Ah, the joys of South African racial barriers. It's what I love about being in other parts of Africa—that generally speaking there are no automatic walls up between the races. It's not that there aren't issues, but fewer than in South Africa. This truck driver is highly suspicious of the White guy greeting him just because we are both South African. Ugh!

The following day I head up through the wonderful miombo forests and bush to get to the Niassa Game Reserve.

While the war of destabilisation of the 1980s led to the decimation of most animals in the country's other reserves, the Niassa Reserve, located up in the isolated far north was left relatively unscathed. The 42,000 square kilometre reserve consists largely of virgin miombo forest interspersed by dramatic inselbergs—the enormous dramatic rocky outcrops that characterise the region. Roaming the protected area are approximately 12,000 elephants, as well as sable antelope, lion, leopard, wild dogs, buffalo, Lichtenstein's, hartebeest, reedbuck, kudu, wildebeest, zebra, hippo and much more. Remarkably, I am the only visitor during the three days I spend in the reserve, which is one of the last wilderness zones in Africa.

When I met Baldeu back in Maputo, he mentioned that as well as deforestation, poaching is a second concern of the bridge development near the reserve. With better roads and increased traffic, Baldeu is concerned about the potential for increased illegal hunting. In the ensuing years following my visit, elephant poaching for their valuable ivory will reach catastrophic proportions. According to the Wildlife Conservation Society, the elephant population drops from 12,000 to 3675 by 2016. I'm not blaming that on the bridge, but development is a double-edged sword.

The only person at the campsite I am staying is Greg, from Kenya. He is building new offices for the reserve management. When I mention the Unity Bridge opening up the area to business, he tells me about the local traders who follow some of the ancient trade routes of this region. At the Lugenda river, they load up their bicycles with fish, then cycle through the reserve up to the Ruvuma river where they trade with Tanzanians returning with items like plastic buckets. The catch is they can only go up safely after August at the end of the dry season when they have burnt down the bush lining the road, thus improving visibility. Without doing this, the risk of being eaten by wild animals is too great. A new road and bridge are likely to benefit these traders as well of course as larger-scale trade.

While at the reserve I get some general park shots, an anti-poaching unit, and some wildlife. The highlight is when as I walk back to my tent one afternoon, I see three elephants some ten metres away. *Elephants!*' I grab my camera, and make my way as close as possible, shooting as I go. Now I'm within about five metres and can make out intricate details of the pachyderm: creases and frown lines, wrinkles covering every inch of its skin. The elephant has such a regal bearing. It is the only animal that fears none in the animal kingdom. Certainly, man with his guns is his only threat.

Suddenly, the wind changes direction. It's a mother with her infant, and she turns to me, trumpets, flaps her ears and, all in the space of less than a second, or so it seems, charges me. I turn, and can honestly say I have never run so fast in my life. The camera is still recording, so it's quite amusing to watch the footage and see the world suddenly swing topsy-turvy, and to hear my ragged breath. I climb up an ant hill in time to get out of her way and wait until she leaves. The first thought that comes to mind is how when I interviewed Baldeu, he said when people see elephants, their first instinct is to run, and he said it kind of mockingly, a smile playing on his lips. Indeed most elephant charges are mock charges. Let me assure you I am not sticking around under these circumstances. I run for my life. This is not the first nor the last time I am chased by elephants, so it is one of those things I seem to do. Most importantly I have some great general shots of the elephants, including walking through a patch of vegetables. This will be useful to later illustrate the issue of elephant-human conflict with the Selous-Niassa Wildlife Corridor.

Then disaster strikes. Baldeu's polite request that I pop into Dr Rodrigues' office when I was in Maputo comes back to haunt me in a very real way. Greg, the Kenyan at the Niassa Reserve, in his wisdom, sends an email to Dr Rodrigues, "Just to keep her informed," that a journalist is visiting. Dr Rodrigues writes back an urgent email saying she does not know about me and I must leave the reserve immediately. I write to Dr Rodrigues using the local "bush mail" email that works on radio frequency rather than the internet, explaining that I have met Baldeu, the reserve director, and he had given me permission. Rodrigues is adamant I must leave the reserve immediately.

The good news is I have sufficient footage. But I am not allowed to try and head due north through the park to see if the back roads are passable up to the pontoon Ruvuma river crossing. I have to retrace my steps back to Pemba town first. This I do, avoiding the slimy mud patch where I recently got stuck.

I then drive due north, towards the Ruvuma river, and the pontoon that takes vehicles across. The last stretch is on a sandy track which leads to the Mozambican border post. I'm told that this is the last pontoon for a week, as it works according to tides. Three other South African-registered vehicles arrive. So much for intrepid travelling.

While waiting for the pontoon, the minutes turn to hours, as they do. The Barnards, a South African family in two Toyota Hiluxes are getting fidgety, as they are on a rather intensive tour of Southern and East Africa. Their very busy schedule entails being on the road practically every day for four weeks. In fact although well planned and prepared in many ways (not to speak of being self-sufficient) they had thought there was a bridge here and not a pontoon. They are lucky to make this pontoon. Nonetheless, Mrs Barnard at one point throws her hands in the air and says simply, "Africa." The rest of the brigade look on in understanding. What is Africa anyway? It is many things. The Barnards themselves are Africans. The Afrikaans speakers of South Africa are called "Afrikaners," which means "Africans." So, the Ruvuma river is a different Africa to the White Pretoria suburbs.

Speaking about their drive here on the last days Mrs Barnard says to me, "The locals seem so happy." What she is implying is that despite their poverty they are happy. But how on earth would she know how they feel from her car window speeding past? This smacks of romanticising poverty. According to UNICEF, 43% of under-five year old children in Mozambique suffer from chronic malnutrition. Is that a recipe for happiness?

I am feeling relaxed in this beautiful wilderness corner of Africa, and lie on a tree trunk to wait. The Barnards, with their hectic schedule, are getting pretty stressed. Mr Barnard asks me to ask the immigration official about the pontoon. As if that will bring the pontoon to us quicker.

We finally cross the river at night time following the tricky entry and exit onto and off the pontoon which requires the use of four-wheel drive.

Over in Tanzania, we get stuck in no man's land until immigration opens up the next morning. As with most South Africans—except me—the Barnard family travel fully self-sufficient and invite me for dinner. I pitch my tent near their camp.

The somewhat intoxicated customs official comes to visit us a couple of times in the evening. Mrs Barnard invites him for coffee, saying to him:

"We are all children of Africa."

The official gives one of those quick nose exhalations. Ah, the complications of identity!

I then enjoy a couple of Tusker beers from a little shop which I buy with some leftover local currency from a previous trip to Tanzania. The customs official notices, and does a double take, making that very African surprise exclamation sound. I can see he is wondering how I could buy anything if I haven't been able to exchange money but he doesn't say anything.

The next morning, we all present ourselves to the customs official—officially. He is swaying gently. He asks me:

"Do you have any explosives?"
"No."
"Can I assist you any other way?"
"No, thank you."

Then, together with the Barnards and the other South African group, we head over to get our passports stamped. These officials have an interesting theory, which they propose to us. Because we have paid less for our visa in South Africa, US$50, than the price at the border, US$60, we have to pay them the difference! This is a little scam, but it's hilarious in its way, and I settle down to wait a bit. Patience and politeness are the watchwords on these occasions.

Aggression and shouting are not. Even though one knows this is an act of corruption, one has to be cool and calm and as I said, patient. Something like, "As I understood it from Mr X at the Tanzanian embassy in Pretoria, this visa would be sufficient for my entry into your country." "Oh? There is an additional fee?" "If only Mr X had informed me of this fee then I would have been prepared for it..." et cetera... Or better yet, act dumb.

Unfortunately, the South African group immediately start hurling all sorts of moralistic invectives at these guys—"We refuse," "You guys are just going to keep the money," (Really?! You think?!) and generally taking a very aggressive tone with them. It drags on like this for a while. How disappointing that I am unofficially part of this South Africa group. The officials keep our passports and get on with some other things. Eventually, we are allowed to leave with our passports, but unpleasantly so.

Be patient, and act a bit naive. I'm not saying I always get it right at all, but if one can, then one will be amazed at what one can achieve.

Ian Barnard has been unwell for a few days and gets tested for malaria. Positive.

As I leave to make my way north Ian's parting words are, "I hope you don't get malaria too."

That very night in the first town of Mtwara I begin feeling slightly odd, and by the next day, I test positive for malaria. There is nothing to do but take a course of coartem treatment, and lay low for several days. I send off an email to an ex-girlfriend so that there is someone in the world to say a kind word while one feels pretty rough.

I then head west to the small town of Masasi, where I meet up with my local NGO contact here, Nurudini Nhuva. He drives us around on his *piki*

piki, the wonderfully onomatopoeic Swahili name for a motorbike. Still weak from malaria, I visit the local immigration officer with Nurudini, a decidedly unfriendly official. We also visit a local HIV AIDS NGO lady, and finally the District Executive Officer. I explain who I am and that I would like permission to visit the Unity Bridge construction site.

"You need to go to Dar es Salaam to get permission from the national level."

What started as an unprofitable three-week expedition to make my first television inserts is growing into a protracted and expensive adventure.

I continue west to Songea then north and east in a big loop towards Tanzania's de facto capital city, Dar es Salaam. It's a two-day journey. En route, the highway goes through the Mikumi Game Reserve. Always on the lookout for opportunities, especially if they entail free shots of wildlife, I stop on the side of the highway when I spot some giraffes. I pull out my camera and shoot. I hear a bus coming towards me. I look behind. It is not coming towards me, it is hurtling towards me. These Tanzanian buses travel at very high velocities and this driver has a bit of difficulty getting past me without rear-ending me. That was close. That's one of my nine lives gone.

In Dar es Salaam I go to the National Information Services and am told a national permit is US$1000.

"Is there any alternative?"
"You can speak to the Masasi District Commissioner and request an exemption."

Masasi is where I just spent two days driving from. I phone the Masasi DC, and he says, "Come here and we'll discuss it."

In the meantime, I learn that my Swahili Islands travel documentary has been chosen to screen at the Zanzibar International Film Festival. At this stage, it seems like a good time to take a break and go over to Zanzibar island.

I spend nine days on the island, watching movies and documentaries all day long, and drinking beers with the ever-growing crew at the festival. I have the good fortune to experience the music of Bi Kidude, an icon of the Taraab music style, singing live in a packed smoky bar. The Taraab style draws from Indian, Arab and African styles, much like Zanzibar. Although her exact age is not known, Bi Kibude is said to be nearly 100 years old, is still an engaging performer, and has a few years left in her. I'm told she is still a smoker.

I meet Susie, a Brit who'll join me on a short part of my next travels. When my Swahili Islands documentary screens, and I am in a room full largely of Swahili people, Susie asks me:

"How does it feel making a documentary about these people and screening it for them?"
"Uncomfortable."
"I thought it might be."

But all good things come to an end. I cross over the channel back to the cacophony of Dar es Salaam. It's a city of a handful of German and British colonial buildings, Indian architecture, and some modern buildings. It's where power outages are so frequent, diesel generators run in unison outside shops, the noise making it hard to think.

My new plan is to go back south to Masasi to meet the Distict Commissioner to request a film permit exemption, in person. But first I meet up with Benson Kibonde, Chief Warden of the Selous Game Reserve in his Dar es Salaam office. The Selous is one of the two-game reserves linked by the Selous-Niassa corridor. The Selous is one of the largest protected areas in Africa, yet infrequently visited. After an hour or two in Chief Warden Kibonde's wood-panelled waiting room, we meet in his office.

Kibonde, who is friendly and engaging, says the highlight of a wildlife corridor is that the free movement of animals ensures a healthy gene pool. In other words the opposite of inbreeding. In a world of many people, and fewer and smaller wilderness areas, this is a very real issue.

Kibonde tells me an anecdote about African development while he walks me out to my car. Africans underwent a fairly quick switch from being hunter-gatherers to being agriculturalists. As various exotic foods such as bananas, sweet potatoes, potatoes, and maize arrived on the continent over the last two millennia, so Africans started settling down to be farmers. However, the way wildlife was perceived did not change. Africans did not lose their hunting instinct. That means that even as agriculturalists, Africans looked at wildlife positively, as food, even if not actively hunting. Proper agricultural protection from wildlife, such as fences, was not instituted. Hence animal theft and the destruction of agriculture curtailed Africa's development. Larger more prosperous farming couldn't evolve.

John Reader in *Africa: A Biography Of A Continent*, writes about how Africans struggled to prevent wildlife from raiding their crops, which hampered African development. "Oral histories recount how farmers succeeded in raising crops to maturity only when their fields were close together and the local community was large enough to supply the people needed to repel raiding elephants. Lone farmers stood little chance, and if conflict or disease reduced a community's manpower, elephants rapidly completed its collapse."

In the Selous-Niassa Wildlife Corridor, I hope to learn about the ways that animals and people can coexist. I'm surprised by Kibonde's parting words at my car. "Please, we need more funds." I'm a bit taken aback because it just seems a bit like a begging bowl statement. Is this the only way for the world's poorest continent to develop? To ask outsiders for money?

It's a long two-day drive back to Masasi. Here I meet the District Commissioner. There is no instant rapport.

"It's not possible to offer you any kind of letter or exemption. The bridge area is a border area and thus a sensitive zone."

So, now for the long two-day drive back to Dar es Salaam. For the third time.

En route, I meet Aloyse Temu in Mtwara. I ask him about what changes one can anticipate with the construction of the Unity Bridge over the Ruvuma river. He says the sooner HIV education is rolled out the better. In 2006 the official AIDS rate in Tanzania, as with Mozambique, is 7%.

Temu is doing some interesting HIV AIDS education work in the region. He says that in Tanzania, by law, every company has to have an AIDS education programme. He gets contracted by bigger companies to carry out AIDS awareness programmes. He does so in a grassroots style. Local drummers call surrounding villagers using a specific drum call. Once everyone from the area is there, a drama troupe perform mime acts that illustrate the dangers, the spread of, and the prevention of HIV AIDS. As Temu says, "The spread of AIDS has no language."

It seems a far cry from the little information I got in Pemba, Northern Mozambique, where I was told videos get made down in Maputo, and then distributed around the country. A video will get dropped off in your village, and even if you decide to watch it, it's in a different language, by a different ethnic group and lacking the immediacy of real drama.

Eventually, I am back in Dar es Salaam and at the National Information Office for the umpteenth time. I have come so far, and there is no giving up. So, I draw the necessary US$1000 from my diminishing overdraft! And I present myself to an official there.

"*Habari gani*?" he asks me.

At first, I start telling him how I am, and then I realise that he isn't asking how I am, but literally, "What's news?" I explain that I was not able to get an exemption letter from the DC down in Masasi and I'd like to go ahead and pay for a permit. Unfortunately, acquiescence to the system doesn't necessarily result in progress.

"There is a problem."
"Oh?"
"You must wait for the Director to return on Friday." That is five days away.

After some prodding, the story comes out. An Austrian filmmaker, Hubert Sauper, made a documentary the previous year, entitled "Darwin's Nightmare." It is about the alleged trade taking place out of Mwanza entailing Russian Antanovs flying Nile Perch fish from Lake Victoria to Europe and returning loaded with weapons destined for the unstable Great Lakes Region. Sauper also accentuates Tanzania's poverty to make his point clear about all the best fish being exported. This includes visuals of locals eating some pretty disgusting-looking fish offal—all that is purportedly left for Tanzanians.

So Tanzania's President Kikwete has just made a speech decrying this "scandal," and this is splashed all over the front pages of all the Tanzanian newspapers today. One article alleges that the president had just been to Paris to meet the filmmaker Sauper, asking for evidence of this arms trade. Sauper promised to produce this, then apparently, "Disappeared into thin air."

Whatever the facts are, the government is skittish about foreign journalists. This is bad timing for me.

I pour over the local newspapers at the Chef's Pride restaurant in the cheap hotel district of Dar es Salaam, Kisutu.

Hundreds of Mwanza residents march through the streets in support of the President's speech, "Denouncing the film 'Darwin's Nightmare' as a lie by some Westerners to derail Tanzania's development efforts... it was not immediately clear who organised the demonstrations," says the Sunday Citizen newspaper.

Local journalist Adam Lusekelo says in This Day newspaper, "What makes me go against the prez's speech is the style. Jack should not have graced such trivia with a comment. He has played into the hands of the producers. That is exactly what they wanted—free publicity from the president of Tanzania." He goes on to say it is the job of diplomats to sell a country abroad or "fix its image" if deemed necessary (at cocktail parties).

Regarding fish offal Lusekelo says, "And if you take a couple of fish heads, add some garlic in them, add a pinch of salt and some "pili pili," boil them for an hour, serve and wash down the soup with a cold drink. It's yummy!"

On Friday my Kafkaesque mission takes its next twist back at the National Information Services.

"The director is still at a conference. Please return on Monday."

And even if I get permission to go down to the Unity Bridge, it'll probably be with a minder.

These days I am staying at a Catholic Mission just outside of the city, and some evenings I see some of the crowd from the Zanzibar Film Festival who are based in Dar es Salaam. One evening heading back to the mission at about 8 pm I pull up to a set of traffic lights in the city centre. A character sidles up to my passenger window. I always keep my doors locked. But that doesn't mean opportunities don't abound. This character who has stopped next to my passenger window, looks at me, tilts his head, and appearing a bit like Gollum in the Lord of The Rings wrests the whole side mirror ("My precious") off the car, and then casually turns and saunters off. Well in the words of George Bush Senior, "This won't stand." I do a U-turn and drive onto the opposite pavement, up and over driveway entrances, squeezing between walls and trees. Gollum has spotted me and is now sprinting. I open my window while careening down the pavement and shout, "Stop. Thief." I know what they do to thieves in these parts. Golum jumps over a wall, into a graveyard. A night watchman chases after him. I stop the car. I don't want to leave the car unattended here. While waiting for the watchman, I meet some people who have gathered. A young man gives me his business card. "Chief of Prisons." It turns out that is his father's business card. The watchman returns. Gollum has gotten away with his "precious."

The next day I meet up with my friend, the Prison Chief's son, and he takes me to Kariakoo market. Here I find the identical mirror—could I be buying back my mirror? It's possible. I pay and get it fitted for US$ 15. I am also taken to my new friend's house where I meet the whole family in a run-down colonial-era bungalow.

Finally, I return to the National Information Services and miracles do happen. I have a permit and a letter of introduction.

So I set off on the long two-day journey south… again.

At Songea I present myself with my letter from the National Information

Services. A very pleasant lady helps me. She'll write the next referral letter.

Then I stop off at the small town of Namtumbo to get my next referral letter. The Namtumbo District Commissioner (DC) is a bit more friendly than some of the other officials I have interacted with previously in Masasi. He invites me to dinner.

"Can you see I have lighter skin than the people from around here?"
"Um, yes."
"It is because I don't come from here. I come from the north."

It seems that both the DC and I are both foreigners here in the deep south of Tanzania. Both Northern Mozambique and Southern Tanzania are the least developed regions of these countries—the Siberias if you will. How much the new bridge will change that time will tell.

The DC is proud of the conference facilities that he has recently built for US$500, and has already made US$2500 from renting them out. A businessman on the side. One of the unfriendly Masasi officials writes me numerous emails after my visit asking me to find an investor to develop some land of his. It seems everyone has a side angle.

With the referral letter from the Namtumbo DC, I can travel the final stretch down to the Unity Bridge. That is once I have presented myself at immigration. He is not a friendly official. And I make a mistake I won't repeat when he asks to see my passport. He pages through it slowly, and I reach over to take it and show him where the Tanzanian visa is. I don't recommend that you try that. Let the immigration officer leaf through your passport at his or her leisure!

I am finally at the Unity Bridge construction site. The holy grail! I am warmly welcomed by Mr Qin Li Hua, Site Agent of the China Geo-Engineering Corporation. Mr Qin reads my final referral letter written in Swahili. I am offered a room to stay in. It's basic, but it's fine, not to mention free.

At this stage, there is just a temporary bridge, as construction has yet to begin. Mr Qin and I walk over to the Mozambican side. Here I interview him on some of the engineering details of the bridge.

"That little camera!?" says Mr Qin.
"Yes!"

With the interview complete, we walk to the nearest village, Negomane. It's so good to hear Portuguese again. When I tell this to the village leader

Mario Mwankuto, he says:

"Stay, and I'll teach you!"

Mwankuto says the bridge should bring development to the rural area, and he's pleased that visa requirements will be dropped. People from the same ethnic groups remain split thanks to the river as a national frontier, dating from colonial times. There are strong cross-border family and community ties, spiritual pilgrimages take place, and of course, there is a cross-border local barter economy.

But he agrees about the possibility of HIV AIDS increasing, and that there could be a detrimental impact on the environment.

We retrace our steps back to the river and over the temporary bridge back into Tanzania, all without getting stamped in and out. I have a soft spot for Northern Mozambique. Sadly, later instability will be coming to the region following the start of large-scale gas exploitation.

I eat like a king in the Chinese construction camp. They have their vegetable garden, and every meal is fantastic if heavily laced with chilli. The one morning I have some free time I stay on after breakfast and incongruously watch models strutting up and down a catwalk on Fashion TV Channel in a Chinese cafeteria in the Tanzanian bush. It's the only sign of women in the place.

The Tanzanian surveyor is Andrew Egidius. He tells me how back in the mid-1990s he was working at the first post-democratic South African construction project in Tanzania, near Mbeya. A dispute arose about wages, and the Tanzanian labourers arranged a meeting with the management, sat around a table and negotiated a better deal. Meanwhile, the Zulu workers, from South Africa, laughed at the Tanzanians, and said, "You'll never get anywhere like that!" Armed with machetes, they moved en masse to the (White South African) management buildings that evening, toyi-toying (political protest dance), and threatening to burn down the buildings if the management didn't accede to their demands! For Andrew, this protest-action culture was pretty shocking. "Just sit down and discuss and then you can make progress," he said.

My work at Unity Bridge is complete. I've looked at the issue by providing different perspectives, without being editorial, and getting nice visuals including nice sequences (the stories within the story). This is journalism I like.

From here I drive a short way north to finish off the other story on the Selous-Niassa Wildlife Corridor. After all the wonderful, delicious Chinese food the usual local African fare seems even more dull and stodgy. Finally, I arrive at the Namtumbo district area where German Rudolf Hahn is a technical advisor for the Selous-Niassa Wildlife Corridor.

"Mr Shaw?"
"Yes it is I. Good to meet you."

Only later did I realise that was my moment to say, "Call me by my first name." South Africans are much more informal than Europeans so we usually start on a first-name basis, and I am not accustomed to going through this kind of rigmarole.

There may only be four people per square kilometre within the wildlife corridor, but that impact on the environment and wildlife movement and migration has to be mitigated somehow. Wildlife Management Areas have been established to empower local communities to control their land and resources. So instead of poaching wildlife, for example, training in alternative livelihoods is given. I am shown the genesis of a bee-keeping project, the idea being honey offers a good income. I also meet the anti-poaching team whose tasks include warding off wildlife that damage crops, using flares or pepper spray, or even culling a rogue troublesome elephant in extreme cases. Crop damage is a classic reason for local communities to attack and kill wildlife, aside from hunting for food.

Regarding two communities that recently moved into the wildlife corridor, the District Commissioner told me he is looking into finding them an alternative place to live outside the corridor.

The total area of the Selous, the Niassa, and the corridor is 154,000 square kilometres, roughly the size of Tunisia. If this giant conservation zone were a success it would be a fantastic refuge for wildlife and to preserve wilderness. But the challenges are immense: a fast-growing human population, the Tanzanian government de-gazetting parts of the Selous for resource extraction, and large-scale commercial poaching.

As we finish up our *bundu bashing* (off-road driving) through the miombo woodlands, Rudolf Hahn clears his throat:

"Uh, Mr Shaw?"
"Yes?"
"Could you contribute to our costs: petrol and so forth?"

Why not? I think. I am so wildly over budget what difference does another expense make? I hand over 40,000 shillings and hit the road back to South Africa. At a junction outside the town of Njombe, I stop at the side of the road to check my map, as there may be a shorter way. A traffic cop standing nearby saunters over, and we have the most convivial conversation about South Africa.

"I want to visit for the 2010 Soccer World Cup final... this is a globalised world we live in, we should all stay in communication."

And with that, we swap phone numbers.

I return to South Africa via Malawi and Zimbabwe, driving from dawn to dusk for four days.

In Cape Town, I update Associated Press on the status of my projects. I am told, "Thanks, when you have sent the stories in, we'll review them and let you know if we are satisfied." And I thought the stories were commissioned! I edit the two pieces, courier the tape to London, and get a positive response. The only criticism is that the Unity Bridge story would have worked better if there was actually a bridge, as opposed to a temporary structure! It's a good point! Anyway, I sold my first news inserts, but it was not financially viable. The way to make it work is to produce in South Africa where my overheads are lower, and then plan longer trips with multiple stories in other African countries. In other words, AP is my passport to travel Africa.

CHAPTER FIVE
South African ghosts

Although the focus of this book is my African adventures outside of South Africa as a documentary filmmaker and video journalist, it is worth mentioning some South African stories. This includes the first Associated Press story in my home country.

When South African President Jacob Zuma (2009-2018) said South Africa's problems started when Jan van Riebeek, the first European settler, arrived in 1652, he had a point. On the other hand, it is not exactly a unifying thing for a president to say in a fractured country.

Van Riebeek's Dutch East India Company built the Castle of Good Hope between 1666 and 1679. Today this is said to be one of the most haunted structures in South Africa. One might say Cape Town's Castle is a metaphor for the trauma the country experienced from 1652 until the advent of democracy in 1994.

Historically, escaped slaves, outlaws, and convicts were tortured and executed within the castle. There are frequent sightings of ghosts.

Arthur Goldstruck, writing in his book *The Ghost That Closed Down The Town* asks, "Could it be that the atmosphere of the castle, so steeped in history, and sometimes in horror, inspires belief in supernatural experiences even when they did not really take place?"

Not so says spiritual medium, Alida Riddell, who has agreed to participate in a TV insert on hauntings at the castle.

Alida and I take a walk through the castle together. She says the gardens are peaceful. But as time goes by she explains that there are pockets of negative energy.

At the clocktower, Alida describes a man who hung himself.

"He's not still here to harm you, he's looking for something he left behind."

I leave Alida for a while to meet Lolly Raa, the retired manageress of the castle restaurant.

"I've had many, many experiences of ghosts at the castle. Several times I saw a lady walking across the grass area... wearing a Dutch frock. She sort of floats rather than walks. At first, I was frightened, but then you get used to it."

Much other current staff have had experiences with ghosts, as have some of the tourists who visit the castle. I speak to other staff members, like Lydia Hassiem who has worked at the castle for 24 years.

"I didn't believe in ghosts until I started working here," she tells me. "The first time I was afraid for two months afterwards. It was a bride in a wedding dress, with a veil... moving across the grass area... she had no legs."

Lydia also describes hearing furniture being moved—when there is no furniture.

Ashley Frantz used to be a guard at the castle, which is still a working military fort, and he is now a tour guide.

"One night at about 2 am while I was on guard duty, I walked past Sally's Point. I had an eerie feeling. That's when I saw him. An old man with a white beard. He was waving and calling out to me.... Then I noticed he had no legs. I turned and ran! Most of the guards at the castle walk around Strand Street to avoid Sally's Port."

I catch up with Alida the spiritual medium, and together we step into the *Donkergat*. This is where tortures took place.

She describes an awful scene.

"I smell urine and faeces. The floor is disgusting. A man is tied up against the wall. These spirits can't rest because of the torture. They didn't have a chance to say goodbye to loved ones."

I don't see or feel anything. I am standing just outside the *Donkergat*. Alida describes a large Black man bleeding from the mouth, asking her why is he being punished just for acting out his culture.

"He is walking towards you. He asks you to help," Alida says to me. I don't know what to say.

When we walk away Alida says, "I can return and clear out the spirits. This whole castle is full of tragedy."

These ghosts are looking for peace, just as South Africa is.

But I don't think as a journalist I should be getting involved in changing events.

"I'm just here to document events," I say to Alida. I'm an observer.

This, my first AP story in South Africa is a pleasure to make after the run around I experienced in Mozambique and Tanzania. No issues with permissions, everyone speaks English, and it's my "home country" and "home city" so I get the cultural mores. But the adventures are to be had north of the Limpopo river. After more AP work in South Africa, I head up once again in early 2007, this time better armed for Mozambique having taken a beginner's course in Portuguese. And this time I have several stories commissioned.

CHAPTER SIX
Zimbabwean farmers and other video journalism

Thanks to my Dad I once again have the use of his Suzuki Vitara 4 X 4, and I arrive back in Maputo during a summer tropical downpour. I get myself a room at Fatima's, Maputo's original backpacker's lodge where I've been staying on and off since my first solo travels in Mozambique in 1996.

After picking up a national film permit, I head over to the Nucleo de Arte, an artist cooperative. I am working on several stories on this trip in a shorter time frame, i.e. this will be a profitable journalistic trip! I make a start on a story related to the previous wars and contemporary artists.

As well as artists at work, there are frequent exhibitions and music events at Nucleo de Arte. I'm here to meet Goncalo Mabunda, who has been turning Mozambique's weapons of war into pieces of art for the last ten years.

"We can destroy the guns used during the war, and then they will disappear. But if we transform it into a work of art, it's a way of showing what yesterday was used to kill people can today be used to promote peace," says Goncalo.

Goncalo welds together pieces of weapons ranging from AK47s and grenade launchers to mortars and handguns, to create metal sculptures. Goncalo is one of five artists making art from arms, and they've exhibited around the world, including at the George Pompidou Centre in Paris.

These artists' work is an offshoot of a project run by the Christian Council of Mozambique (CCM) and the Mozambican government. Following the war of liberation from Portuguese control from 1964 to 1974, and then the post-independence war of 1976 to 1992 in which the former South African government trained and armed Renamo to destabilise the country, Mozambique was awash with weapons. Although private ownership of weapons became illegal when peace came, the CCM created an opportunity for the legal handing in of weapons and gave in exchange various goods such as bicycles as an incentive. To date, 600,000 pieces of armaments have been handed in. That's where this weapons-to-art off-shoot project comes into the picture—recycling those weapons of war into something beautiful.

For artist Goncalo, the project is personal. "I lost many family members during the war, including my uncle. I remember as a child that he would visit us carrying a big heavy AK47."

Goncalo, who says he likes to subvert obvious meanings, shows me some of his pieces and I also film him at work. One of his biggest pieces is a helicopter made out of armaments. Goncalo explains that during the war there were many helicopters in the country used by the military forces. But then when peace came, and there was large-scale flooding, there were no helicopters available to help civilians. Neighbouring South Africa sent in their military helicopters to assist civilians. He wants to comment on this using his art.

The next step, which takes a few days of phone calls to organise, is an interview with the Christian Council of Mozambique. I meet Boaventura Zita who is the national coordinator of the Transforming Arms into Ploughshares project. It is so-called because it draws inspiration from a passage in the bible from the book of Micah: "They will pound their swords and their spears into rakes and shovels. They will never again make war or attack one nation." All I am missing for this story are visuals of the weapons being loaded up to be taken to the artists. Mr Zita assures me that can be arranged.

I'm sitting at my favourite place to eat or go for a coffee, at the corner of Avenida 24 Julho and Avenida Julius Nyerere. It's a good place to watch the world go by. I hear loud sirens. Everyone stops what they're doing and watches the road. A traffic cop on a motorbike flies past. This is the unwritten code for: all cars pull off the road! Another traffic cop on a motorbike flies past, and then another. The street is now deserted, all vehicles having stopped on the side. Then the cavalcade begins in earnest. A couple of black Volvos drive past, followed by a few black Mercedes Benz with tinted windows. More black Volvos pass and then more traffic cops on motorbikes. Then a military Toyota Landcruiser with soldiers sitting in the back drives past. The Big Man has left the scene. The president's cavalcade now gone, the vehicles that had edged to the roadside can slowly crawl back into the street. Normal traffic and life can resume. I think of the scene in the movie *The Queen*, where British Prime Minister Tony Blair is sitting in the back of a Daimler, and the car is working its way through normal London traffic.

Back at Fatima's Backpackers, although I have my own room, I am keen to stay somewhere quieter. Fatima is away in Brazil, but her sister, Mimi, has a room in her apartment available for rent, and I stay there for the next two weeks. Mimi is fairly scathing about the politicians in Mozambique and the lack of accountability. Or as the political scientist, R W Johnson describes them, "the crooks who run Mozambique."

I ask Mimi about the then-new Mozambican president Armando Guebuza. Mimi tells me the story of *Operacao Producao*. This was a project instigated by Guebuza back in the 1980s to move people to what was considered to be the country's richest province in terms of natural bounty and the lowest population density, Niassa, in the far north. This the government did by rounding up anyone on the streets of Maputo without an ID and sending them to Niassa in transport planes, without even an opportunity to say goodbye to their families. Upon arrival in Lichinga, they were told, "Find a wife, have children, take a hoe and work the soil." The tactics were quite similar to when the Portuguese colonial government forcefully rounded up young Mozambican men to work, or to fight during World War One.

My landlady, Mimi, worked with the United Nations to repatriate some of the people forcibly moved during *Operacao Producao* after the war in 1993. This included the town of Cuambo which she visited. Many didn't want to be repatriated as they thought they wouldn't be able to find their way home, or that anyone at "home" would even remember them. "It had been so long that wives and husbands would have remarried. There was one old man who was looking forward to returning home, and I visited him every day. He was quite ill though. Unfortunately, he died before the arrangements could be made to fly him home."

Staying at Mimi's is pleasant. It's quiet and I have the air conditioning on all the time to combat the oppressive humidity of summer in Maputo. From here I plan my other work projects which include another art story. Together with some of my existing Makonde Art footage from the visit to that region in the north three years earlier, I am also shooting and interviewing artists and experts in Maputo to make a TV feature on this form of art.

As I already discovered during my visit to the Makonde plateau in 2004, the Makonde make probably the most famous of East African art. Their shetani, or "spirit world" pieces are possibly the most interesting, being quite fantastical and grotesque.

My first contact is Giancarlo Gandolfini, an Italian who has been living in Mozambique since 1984. He is an architect by profession and an expert on Makonde Art. We meet for a coffee. I can't help but look up at the passing people from time to time. Giancarlo notices and says:

"Ah, the girls? They are beautiful!"

Looking at my business card, which includes the slogan "*A Luta Continua*" (the struggle continues) Gianfranco asks:

"Who's struggle is this? Your struggle?!"

A Luta Continua is a classic slogan for post-independence Africa, but one or two other people have raised their eyebrows at my use of this slogan. So as a White South African I can't say that the struggle for a better Africa must go on? Fine. I won't. But if I have to censor myself, and tiptoe around race and identity issues I don't know how I can call myself an African.

"What do you know about the spirit world?" Gianfranco asks me.
"I'm embarrassed to call myself an African and say I know very little!"
"Okay, you'll meet the artists and talk to them!"

Gianfranco explains that Makonde art has its roots in ceremonial masks and everyday objects, but that they branched into more market-oriented art in the 1930s, which is when the Portuguese colonialists made contact with them. Over time their art represented the colonial experience both directly and ironically, as well as later representing the war period. When I was up in Mueda three years before, I not only shot the artists at work in their villages, but had the good fortune to step out of my hotel one day, walk up to a small crowd, and watch an impromptu dance by Makonde wearing their masks. This is nice footage to add to my Makonde Art story.

Gianfranco's chief concern, and what will turn out to be possibly the most important lesson I learn as a journalist, is to not stereotype the Makonde Art when I tell this story. The European gaze on Africa is loaded. Firstly, most news is about war, disaster, and starvation. And, when the European gaze falls on African culture it is often in the most simplistic way: the primitive, backward peoples. Or the noble savage. Some of this is probably subconscious. Anthropology or ethnography is a tricky field. Who has the right to come in from the outside and talk about another culture? If you do, leave your prejudices behind, dig deep, do your research, and don't stereotype! It's a valuable lesson for life.

Gianfranco gives me some contacts for Makonde Artists in Maputo, and I duly meet up with Pascoal Mbundi. As rock-n-roll that Goncalo the gun artist is, is as down-to-earth that Pascoal the Makonde artist is.

Pascoal left the Makonde plateau during the war in 1984, studied art in Maputo, and now works at an artist's association. Although he has worked in the naturalistic style, and the "people pole" style (poles made up of people intricately carved into the wood), his preference is *shetani* (spirit world).

"We are the products of the additions of many ancestors. And what my ancestors were before me, influences the way I am. I believe in the reincarnation of somebody's soul. I don't know whether that soul has reincarnated in me was of somebody who was an artist, but I try to show the product of those who lived before me."
"And how do you do that?"

"It's something that comes from within me, that I identify with. Sometimes it's based on something that I dream about. When I wake up I try to create the image from my dream... It's an unknown or hidden science. Maybe the witch doctors understand."

I ask Pascoal about some of his pieces which tend to be abstract, often with exaggerated features.

One of them is a water goddess. Coming from the Makonde plateau which is a water-stressed area, Pascoal grew up with these concerns. The water goddess represents rain and the relief that brings to these communities.

Have I steered clear of stereotyping? I hope that by simply telling the story based on facts, and the artist's perspectives, I have. One thing is for sure as a journalist: telling art stories, which are interpretive, is a lot more complicated than science stories, which have clear hard facts as a basis.

I am phoning and texting Nicelau from the Transforming Arms into Ploughshares project to get my last shots, but so far I am not making any progress.

I have another story idea I am looking into, which is the Cahora Bassa dam, Southern Africa's largest hydroelectric scheme. I have just stopped the car to try and get directions to their Maputo office when a man with a big smile approaches me.

"Hello. What are you looking for?"
"The Cahora Bassa Maputo office."
"I'm a Customs Officer and it's my day off. I'll help you to find it. And next time you'll help me."
Naively, I say, "Get in, let's go." But it doesn't take long for his scam to fall apart.
"I saw you yesterday at the border," he says, trying to build confidence but taking it too far.
"I've been here for 30 days," I reply.
"Yes, yes I remember," he says.

Here we go—it's the remember me from the airport/train station/border scam.

He asks me to stop, and he asks someone a question. Then, getting out of the car and standing at the door he says, "Okay, I know. I'll call them," indicating for me to give him my cell phone. I reach for my pocket and then stop and say as politely as I can in my broken Portuguese, "It's alright, I am going to make another arrangement. Goodbye."

I make it to the Cahora Bassa office but filming up there is strictly forbidden, so that story is not possible.

Driving the Maputo streets and thinking about the artists I have spent time with, I revel in the textures of this city. The Portuguese architecture is stylish, and in a tropical, run-down way, Maputo oozes character. I see realist or street sculptures all around me.

Sidewalk car exhaust shops advertise their wares by sticking the exhaust systems onto tree-like metal structures. I call these *objets d'art,* "Clearing the air." A derelict unfinished 25-storey building allegedly sabotaged by the Portuguese at independence, I call, "The Portuguese Project."

These "realist sculptures" are more interesting to me than the "constructed artworks" of the "artists." Is art not simply that which is around us waiting to be noticed? The art of life, if you will. Samora Machel, Mozambique's first president, said, "Art is created by the people, and not by artists."

While in Maputo I pop into Nucleo de Arte a couple of evenings, and from time to time I go to nearby Fatima's. One such evening the manager Matheus tells me all his woes: he is working seven days a week, lives on the property, gets woken at all hours by the comings and goings of travellers, and is nearing total exhaustion.

I'm relaxing in Fatima's lounge later on when two French ladies walk in, the one in tears. I walk over and ask what the matter is. They've just been robbed 100 metres from the backpackers on the busy street. They had their backpacks grabbed off their backs, with their passports, cash, cards and absolutely everything of value taken. One lady is calm, while the other one is an emotional wreck. I know no one at Fatima's is going to help them, so I find the phone number for the French Embassy and call. It's the Ambassador who answers. Quite soon thereafter a lower-echelon Embassy official arrives to take them to a police station and assist them. It must be nice to be a first-world country nationality knowing if you have an emergency your government will be there to help you so efficiently. Aside from that, the experience makes me wonder if my real purpose is to help people.

On a more practical level, don't walk with any valuables in any African city. In many countries, including Mozambique, get your passport photocopied and stamped by a notary. Unfortunately, that is only the theory. As I know from my previous visits to Maputo, criminals are not the only menace on these streets. Walking with some backpackers near Fatima's we are, again, accosted by police armed with AK47s, who say "there is a problem" with our passport photocopies. My tolerance for these guys has gone, and I simply say "there is no problem," snatch my passport photocopy out policeman's hand, and walk away—fast!

I keep trying to phone and text message Niceleu to get my missing "loading the weapons to give to the artists" shots. He is evasive.

In the meantime, I start working on my next story. Land mines are designed to wound soldiers thus slowing down the opposing force during war. The problem is the land mines don't disappear when a war ends. They remain in the ground and injure or kill innocent civilians. This is especially the case if there is no record of where the land mines were planted, as in Mozambique. Fifteen years after the war ended in 1991, people are still losing their legs or getting killed. There are between 20,000 and 30,000 land mine victims in Mozambique.

NGO people tend to be nice folk to interview: earnest and engaging and open to discussing the issues at hand. And so it is when I visit Megan Lattimer, Land Mine Monitor 2007 Report Mozambique researcher.

Megan explains to me that the Mine Ban Treaty which outlaws land mines was signed in 1997 with an initial 122 members states. Since then land mine production has dropped considerably and trade has almost come to a halt.

Megan says that although the goal was to have Mozambique cleared of mines by 2009 that seems unlikely, especially considering that the extent of the problem is still unknown.

NGOs play a significant role in encouraging compliance with the land mine ban treaty. One of the key NGOs in this sector is Halo Trust. I meet Dan Bridges from this organisation at Maputo's iconic Costa da Sol restaurant.

"Halo Trust was started in 1988 and we were the first humanitarian mine clearance organisation. So in fact Halo started an industry. Before 1988 only military forces were involved in mine clearance."

To raise awareness of the issue, Lady Diana famously walked through an active minefield where Halo Trust was clearing mines in Angola, just a few months before her untimely death in 1997.

"Aside from the fact that records were not kept of where land mines were placed during the wars, the other challenge is during floods, land mines get shifted."

I make arrangements for a field visit to an active de-mining operation in Inhambane province, where I'll also meet a land mine victim.

I have now almost run out of time before heading north, and I simply must get the weapons shots to complete my arms-to-art story. I text Niceleu again and get a reply: "Access is not possible." So I get in my car and drive to his office determined to get these shots one way or another. It turns out Niceleu is there. He agrees to show me the warehouse where the weapons are stored. I bring my camera, and immediately start getting shots. Why wouldn't he help me? I have no idea. But persistence is the name of the game. And in this case, it paid off. And that feels good.

After a month in Maputo, I am pleased to finally leave the city. For the next while it will be rural areas and towns. My first stop is a Halo Trust active de-mining operation in Inhambane province. Actually, it's not the first time I walk through a minefield. When I backpacked up Mozambique using public transport in 1996, I went for a walk into the bush during one of the many roadside breakdowns. I was already about 50 metres into the miombo forest when all my fellow travellers from the old Toyota truck shouted out "*Perigo! Minas!*" It took me a while to get what they meant. Aaaah! "Watch out! Mines!" Being young and, foolhardy, I didn't immediately carefully retrace my steps. I walked another 10 metres to take a photo of the railway line that had initially caught my attention, then walked back to the road. If I think back to that now, all I can say is that was most definitely one more of my nine lives gone.

The minefield I visit in Inhambane province holds no risk. Halo Trust are busy professionally clearing the area using their metal detectors. They also use dogs that are trained to smell TNT. So it's painstakingly slow work, not least of all because the de-miners have to sift through whatever other scrap bits of metal they also find.

From here I am taken to meet a lady called Sara Julio Mavila. Today for the first time in over two decades Sara can till her field, which has been cleared of mines, safely. For the first time in over two decades, she can grow her food. I also meet her son who lost his leg just two years earlier when he walked through this field. Sara has suffered much. She tells me about the war of destabilisation—that is the South Africa-backed Renamo insurgency of the 1980s where one million people died. "It wasn't safe here. We were constantly on the run. Living in fear." I see in her and understand a little better, the sadness that one so often sees in the eyes of Mozambicans, and the extent to which the war period sits heavily in the psyche of Mozambicans.

I have visited Mozambique many times and read about its history, but here for the first time, its recent tragic history comes alive. For the first time, those abstract facts have meaning. That is the job of a journalist, to uncover the human meaning behind the cold facts.

A few years later, in 2015, after over two decades of hard work, Mozambique will be declared land mine-free. According to Halo Trust, they cleared 171,000 land mines in that time, having carried out 80% of the clearing work in the country.

I continue driving north, passing rapacious traffic cops en route, and finally arriving in the central Mozambican town of Chimoio. Back in December 1993, I was here with ten university friends travelling in a decrepit Land Rover and a Range Rover. The war had only just ended, so there was no tourism to speak of in Mozambique, almost no traffic, and diabolically bad roads. Arriving in the evening on the outskirts of Chimoio, slowly navigating the heavily potholed road, two *bandidos* walked up to the Land Rover driver's door, one of them firing off a shot into the air from a handgun. The driver handed over a small amount of cash and that seemed to satisfy the robbers. Traumatised, we headed for a United Nations encampment, knocked on the door and awaited the chief to arrive. I discussed with him, in French, our situation. He couldn't let us inside, but we could spend the night outside his camp. Thanks!

In 2007 I am back in Chimoio to produce a story on the Zimbabwean farmers of Manica province. Let's take a step back in time again. In 1980 Zimbabwe achieved its independence following a long liberation war. By that time Mozambique had been independent for five years, and nearly all of its approximately 250,000 Portuguese settlers had departed. Mozambique's president, Samora Machel, advised Zimbabwe's new president, Robert Mugabe, to take a conciliatory approach to Zimbabwe's White settlers, who love it or hate it, were the backbone of the economy. This was to be the policy in Zimbabwe for two decades until the land grabs began.

It's the combination of a weak economy and the growing strength of the opposition that sees the ever-wily President Robert Mugabe opportunistically appropriate the land invasion movement that has been growing for a few years. Instead of removing people who have moved onto White commercial farmers' land as he has in the past, Mugabe will allow them to stay and then simply make land reform an official policy.

The roots of the issue are colonial settlers who took the best land for themselves and their descendants still farming this land, a growing (indigenous) population in a post-independent Zimbabwe with the need for more land, in the context of a newly independent country.

The White commercial farmers are crucial to the country's economy, and over the next few years, in a chaotic and violent "fast track land reform" process, the vast majority of these over 6000 farmers will be violently pushed off their farms. A few will be killed, the rest leaving with the clothes on their backs. All are citizens including second or third-generation Zimbabweans. The effect on the economy will be devastating.

But Zimbabwe's commercial farmland invasions are a flashpoint that most African countries face in their decolonisation process, particularly those that had European settlers, i.e. more entrenched colonial systems. These flashpoints come in the guise of a form of nationalisation that however messy, serve as restitution, as a means of getting back dignity following repressive colonial rule.

Uganda's flashpoint was the expulsion of Asians, who dominated business, in the early 1970s. Academic Mahmood Mamdani, a Ugandan Asian himself, compares this incident with Zimbabwe: "[In Uganda]...people experienced the Asian expulsion of 1972—and not the formal handover [from the British] in 1962—as the dawn of true independence. The people of Zimbabwe are likely to remember 2000-3 as the end of the settler colonial era [as opposed to independence in 1980]. Any assessment of contemporary Zimbabwe needs to begin with this sobering fact."

And if this decolonisation flashpoint is more dramatic in former settler colonies (colonies where a large-scale settlement of Europeans took place), given their bigger colonial footprint, then should Whites in South Africa and Namibia be worried for their day of reckoning? South Africa had (and still has) the largest population of colonial settlers of any African country, so logically as the largest and longest-running settler colony in Africa, it will experience the largest decolonisation flashpoint.

Some of the Zimbabwean farmers expelled from their farms moved to the cities, and many emigrated to first-world countries, but some tried out commercial farming in other African countries. Zambia, just north of Zimbabwe, has the most similar farming conditions, so the Zimbabwean farmers fare best here, particularly Southern Zambia—not that it has been easy for them, starting all over again. Some of the farmers go to Nigeria, Angola, Tanzania, Malawi and Mozambique. The Chimoio area of Mozambique is a short hop from the eastern border of Zimbabwe. Since the farm invasions in Zimbabwe, 42 of these commercial farmers came over the border to farm in Mozambique's underdeveloped Manica province.

Of the ten Zimbabwean farmers still operating in Manica province five years later, one is Kevin Gifford. At his farm about 80 kilometres south of Chimoio, I asked Kevin why so many of his fellow farmers failed in the Mozambique endeavour.

"The Mozambican government saw us as refugees, invited us here, and gave us land." The hope was their expertise would help develop the region.

Kevin and his family were ejected from his Zimbabwe farm in 2000 and came to Mozambique, "With the clothes on our back." The Zimbabwean farmers may have been given land to use, but that was virgin bush, loans for development were not available, and the Zimbabwean agricultural support sector does not exist in Mozambique.

Also, although just across the border from Zimbabwe, Manica province is significantly lower altitude—it's sub-tropical. Fruit like avocados, litchis and mangoes would be ideal, but with no capital, the farmers had to go with what was offered them which was loans under strict conditions from tobacco companies, even though this is not an ideal tobacco growing zone. Gifford, who was fortunate to get land with an existing house, is growing 80 hectares of tobacco. The tobacco drying sheds that he has built, are enormous and impressive. "I'm also dabbling in soya beans and blue gums."

Sitting outside the old Portuguese colonial-era farmhouse, which lacks a coat of paint, Kevin says, "When you lose everything as we did in Zimbabwe, you lose your sentimentality. The value of things changes."

Aside from starting up a new commercial farming venture in a foreign country with no start-up capital, Kevin faces many other challenges here in Manica. As he says, "Malaria is a bitch." This is barely a problem in higher-altitude Zimbabwe. There is no frost here on this lower altitude land, meaning all the bugs and insects that can plague crops don't get killed off as they do in Zimbabwe's colder winters. And having to be extremely resourceful means not having time for anything else. He got hold of a cheap broken car and through phone calls to his father back in Zimbabwe, Kevin became a panel beater and mechanic, rebuilding the vehicle. "This is DIY commercial farming." It's not always been easy to adjust and Kevin says, "If you're a White man in Africa, unless you're with an aid agency, you're considered an exploiter."

Kevin has a British passport so he could go abroad. "It's financially stupid to be here. But in the UK society is in moral decline. Australia and the UK are nanny states with too many rules. Here in Mozambique, there are no gangs and no drugs. The children have space and apart from malaria, a healthy life."

Kevin's two kids are being home-schooled by his wife. "I don't expect to make money here. I expect to lay a foundation for my son to succeed."

Kevin says the perception of Zimbabwean farmers in the area is of being successful but also as drinkers and brawlers. I will meet some more of the remaining Zimbabwean farmers over beers in town that evening. When Kevin walks me to my car he says:

"I have a question for you. What is the purpose of interviewing me?"

I try to think of a good answer but only come up with a lame, "In order to document what happened to the Zimbabwean farmers who got kicked out of Zimbabwe."

Kevin throws his hands in the air, as if to say, and so? He then lets me know that he's had 27 TV crews visit and interview him already! So his question is a good one. Is it a case of the Western media giving excessive air time to the White commercial farmers of Zimbabwe, because they are White?

As a contextual aside, I think it is interesting that former Zimbabwean President Robert Mugabe was knighted by the Queen in 1994 despite the Gukurahundu massacres of the 1980s where an estimated 20,000 Ndebele civilians were murdered by Mugabe's North Korea-trained troops. That knighthood was revoked in 2008 following the death of a handful of White Zimbabwean farmers during the land invasions.

If you'll indulge a further aside, President Mugabe the Anglophile with his Savile Row suits must have been so pleased to receive a knighthood. In later years though, he became one of the harshest critics of the UK and the West. On the surface, this had to do with the UK reneging on its promise of funds to assist with land reform in Zimbabwe. But at a deeper level, there lies a contradiction of early post-colonial Africa, of mixed identity, of unchaining the mind. Decolonisation is a messy business.

That evening I meet some of the other remaining Zimbabwean farmers in Chimoio town. One of the more colourful characters is the grizzled Murray Dawson. "Nobody's making money here—it's a huge success if you're just holding on." The Zimbabwean farmers who didn't make it here were squeezed by the paprika and tobacco companies. "The farmers didn't read the fine print. The tobacco and paprika companies set the final prices."

Murray concurs with Kevin about moving to the UK: "I will do anything not to live in England. It is cold, wet and miserable." Nevertheless, you've got to be pretty tough, independent-minded, and resourceful to try and make it here in Manica province as a commercial farmer. When it comes to the development sector, Murray is scathing. "We had Scandinavians in Zimbabwe in the 1980s, and as soon as they left, their projects were ransacked and pillaged. All the delinquent kids in Scandinavia, for who there is no place in their prisons, were sent to Africa. And actually, it's just an excuse for them to taste some chocolate and leave behind a fatherless Coloured child."

As far as Kevin and all the other ex-Zimbabwean farmers here are concerned, the writing's on the wall for South Africa with a looming economic disaster, and bloodshed will be the result, "Because when the dutchman gets pissed off, he will lash out and fight for his land." Dutchman is a pejorative term for the Afrikaners of South Africa. When I am invited to a maize processing facility by another Zimbabwean ex-farmer, he does a double take and first checks, "You're not an Afrikaner are you?" These Anglo Zimbabweans are not a fan of Afrikaners, it seems.

With this story edited and the script written, I drive northwards, via Tete to Malawi. I arrive in Blantyre in the evening and start a hotel quest. The prices are too high for my tiny budget, and so, dog-tired I eventually settle for a campsite. I awaken the following morning at the crack of dawn. I have a hot shower that is worth the US$ 5 price of camping alone. Then I look around to realise it is the start of a beautiful day. There can be fewer more satisfying feelings than waking up in a new place, especially if said place is somewhere in Southern Africa. I think to myself I'd like to cover the back of the jeep with the flags of every Southern African country. I suppose that's a piece of nostalgia for the African flag cards we'd collect and trade as children in Malawi. But my reverie is quickly broken for it is breakfast time. I leave the campsite and stop at the first place—the five-star Mount Soche hotel where I splurge on a Full English Breakfast.

My mission in Malawi is a story on The Ilala, Lake Malawi's venerable passenger ferry. This somewhat sentimental journey is retracing steps taken as a child. I'm back, and I'm going to do the full loop—five days on board the old girl as she circumnavigates the entire lake. First I enjoy a week relaxing at the lake at Cape Maclear waiting for the next ferry departure.

There she was sitting by herself, and looking quite content to do so. In the bar that evening we speak for a little while, culminating in arranging to go on a boat ride the next day. Boatmen Benson and Patrick take us the following morning to a little island but she is not impressed by how rocky it is. She wants a beach. We are duly dropped off at a secluded beach. "So here I am on a secluded beach with some giant lizards," she says. *Here I am on a deserted beach with a blonde young lady*, I think to myself. Soon she has flung off her bikini top, and the sun and the boulders and the green vegetation meld into one.

Just before I catch the ferry a week later I check my emails one last time at Monkey Bay in a tiny internet cafe with the world's slowest dial-up connection. There is feedback from AP for my Makonde Art story. And unfortunately, it is critical feedback. The artist interview could have, "Benefited from better lighting," and the story would have, "Benefited from more interviews" to give more perspectives. This is what one might call "learning on the job." I can kick myself for not interviewing Giancarlo the

Italian Makonde expert in Maputo. Now I know: news features like these need about four or five different interviews.

I have many notes on interviewing and shooting. They include being well prepared by carrying out the necessary research, listening actively while interviewing, starting with the easy questions and moving to the harder ones, making sure there is good light, good sound and shooting nice sequences—the stories within the story. Despite this, I have made a couple of elementary mistakes and I am determined not to repeat them. Just as well I checked my emails before departing on the ferry.

Built in 1949 in the Yarrow shipyard in Scotland, the 640-ton Ilala was transported in pieces, assembled at Lake Malawi, and put to service in 1955 at a period when Malawi was a British colony. The ship's captain is Lameck Mponde. His father was a cook on the ship and Captain Mponde used to spend his school holidays on board. Mponde went on to study at Malawi Marine College and has been captain of the ship for twenty-two years. At the helm, Mponde looks across to the Malawi shoreline and tells me how he has watched the hills become denuded over the years. Later, when we cross the lake to the Mozambican side he will look at the land there wistfully and remark to me, "Just look at those forests." It is Malawi's human population pressure that is causing its forests to disappear. It has one of the densest populations in Africa.

Mponde refers to the Ilala as a "Lifeline vessel." In the early years of the Ilala, when there was no lakeshore road, the ship was a crucial means of transporting passengers. Today while the road network is better, there are still many villages that the Ilala connects to the outside world. Mponde says, "It's not just the passengers. We can carry about 100 tons of cargo." Maize, sugar, livestock, fish, building materials, reed mats, and diesel are some of the trade goods.

For local communities, the Ilala is the only transport option beyond the small local dugouts—the canoe-like boats that are hollowed-out tree trunks. I'd like to chat with some of the passengers, and with an interpreter, I make my way down to third class. We find a Mozambican woman, Maria Manuel, who is willing to be interviewed. But as we set up the camera her husband, Pedro Bernado Isufu arrives.

"What is this? Who are you to talk to my wife?"

Pedro is furious that we are talking to his wife without his permission. After some apologies and negotiations, we can interview them both. This we're able to do because although my interpreter is an anglophone Malawian, and the Mozambicans are lusophone, the indigenous languages of Chinyanja and Chichewa on either side of the lake (Malawi and

Mozambique) are practically the same. So much for colonial boundaries. Pedro tells me: "We used to walk long distances. The Ilala makes a big difference for us and allows us to visit family much easier."

Up on the top deck, the Ilala is a royal way of seeing the lake and many of the lakeside towns, villages and islands where the Ilala stops off. In the evening I meet Dudley, a South African wearing a t-shirt that says, "Tell your girlfriend I said thanks." Dudley is working on a construction project in Malawi and is now looking at getting a work permit to stay permanently.

"Crime in South Africa is just out of control. It's gotten too bad. My brothers have both left. One went to the UK, and one to Australia. This is home. All my friends in Lilongwe, [Malawi's capital city], are African."

"But aren't you African?" I ask Dudley.
"Yes I am, but I just call them that because I don't like to talk about Black and White."
"What about Mozambique?"
"Oh no, they've got a bad attitude!"

Later on, I'm in the small basic restaurant. At one table, three Kenyans on a stag safari (holiday) sit around a table, as usual, nursing a beer, no matter what time of day it is. Dudley walks in.

"What's available?" Dudley asks the staff loudly from across the room.
"*Kuku*" (chicken) comes the reply.
"*Kuku*! *kuku*! I've had it up to here with *kuku*!" he says drawing his hand up to the top of his head. "*Kuku* for lunch, *kuku* for dinner, *kuku* is all you eat!"

Dudley leaves, and the kitchen staff mutter amongst themselves, and I just catch "*mzungu*" (White person).

One of the 13 stops the ferry makes is at the colonial quirk of Likoma island. It's a colonial quirk because although it is 66 kilometres across the lake from Malawi, and just a stone's throw from a remote and underdeveloped region of Mozambique, it is Malawi territory. The Anglican Cathedral on Likoma island, with its British missionaries, is the reason the island was made Malawian (British) territory during the colonial period. The cathedral is the centrepiece of the island, and the standards of education here are high. In Malawi, there is a disproportionately high amount of intelligentsia that come from the island.

South African Craig Barlow runs Kaya Mawa guesthouse on Likoma, "Probably the best hotel in Malawi, and certainly the most expensive," he tells me. Craig has been on Likoma island for ten years. He tells me the ferry is critical to the survival of the 10,000 residents as not enough food is grown on Likoma.

"When the Ilala broke down a while ago, there was practically a famine on Likoma."

Compared to the overfished Malawi side of the lake, fish is more abundant here. People from Likoma transport dried fish over to mainland Malawi on the Ilala, and return with bananas, cassava, vegetables, firewood, sugar and other products.

Likoma island is a bit like one of the Greek Dodacanese islands where you can almost reach out and touch Turkey. But, "There's not much to trade with Mozambique, because it is an undeveloped region," says Craig.

I ask Craig how he sees Malawians as compared to Mozambicans.

"The Malawians are a nation of butlers."

On a future trip to Malawi I will find out that Craig, probably in his thirties, has died as a result of a tropical illness.

On the Ilala, people come and people go, but I remain on board for a full five days. I start feeling like the Tom Hanks character in the movie *The Terminal,* about a man who gets stuck in an airport for nine months (but based on a true story of a passenger who lived in Charles de Gaulle airport for 18 years). People come and people go.

Once in a while, there is a flurry of activity when the ship gets to its next port of call. Passengers load their bicycles, goats, and flour onto little dug-out canoes along the ship's side, and then join their cargo to make the trip to an inaccessible village. New passengers make the return trip to the ship, loading their chickens, fish and maize, and settling down on the third-class benches.

From dramatic mountains in the north, and dense miombo forests on the Mozambican side, to baobab tree shorelines and idyllic castaway islands, the journey is a slow cinema of striking landscapes.

Sadly, the round trip comes to an end, and I find myself editing the video and writing a script in a cheap hotel room on the beach at Monkey Bay, an upside-down chair serving as a table in an otherwise bare cement room, a raucous party outside.

From here I head due east, and the border crossing back into Mozambique highlights the difference between the two countries. On the Malawi side, the Immigration officer looks me up and down with distaste. I am unshaven, wearing an old shirt and shorts. When I hand over my vehicle papers he exclaims in surprise, "You have a vehicle?!" Why would someone, like most backpackers who come from wealthy countries, dress down? But more to the point, Malawi is conservative, and Mozambique is more easygoing. At Mozambique immigration, the officers are having a loud conversation among themselves. I greet them in Portuguese, and they do the same and stamp me through without blinking. It may be more easy-going but the people can feel downbeat after the friendly Malawians. I have a long chat with a waiter at a hotel in Cuamba but objectively he is a bit dour. It could be the impact of thirty years of war but I find people reserved—it's an adjustment after Malawi.

In the town of Nampula I meet one or two more Zimbabwean commercial farmers who lost their land back home. I ask one of them, Andrew Cunningham, what he sees as the main difference between running a business in Zimbabwe versus in Mozambique. He tells me that here in Mozambique you don't just go to the bank, fill out a form, and hand it in. You need to know the bank manager for things to happen.

"In Mozambique, it's all about relationships. Whether it includes bribery or is genuine, that is what it is all about."

I manage to arrange a government interview for my Zimbabwe farmers' story, to give another perspective on the issue. He confirms that there are no banks specifically designated to fund commercial agriculture—one of the main challenges to making it here as a commercial farmer. The story, together with my Ilala ferry story, can now be couriered on tape to London.

My car needs a repair and through my Nampula contacts I am sent to a South African mechanic called Ari who sets about telling me his woes:

"I've just come back from court."
"Oh, what happened?"
"I was driving up from the south, and as I slowed to go through a village, a person stepped in front of me. There was no way to avoid hitting her.... But, it's done on purpose. They target a foreigner's vehicle, someone who has money and then purposefully get injured. The law is completely on their side, so for sure, they will get paid out. That's what I've been fighting in court."

Then, taking extra care, I drive the final haul over to Ilha de Mozambique, the historic island town that was once the Portuguese capital city of their Mozambique colony. The story I am working on here is the unique architecture and its restoration. After the critical email I received about the Makonde Art story, I am determined to stay as long as possible, get enough different interviews, beautiful shots and sequences, and use the tripod as much as possible. I end up staying for a month, somewhat disproportionate to a six-minute video news feature. I could have made an hour-long documentary!

Before the Suez canal was built in 1869 all ships from Europe to the Far East went around Southern Africa. Like Cape Town, that was Ilha's strategic value historically—it lay on that route. The Portuguese annexed the Mozambique territory and successfully fought off the Omanis, Dutch, Turks and other powers all keen to have a base on the Europe to Asia route. The Suez canal shortened the journey from Europe to the East dramatically, rendering places like Ilha much less important, and finally the Portuguese moved their capital city down to Lourenco Marques (now Maputo) in 1898, as trade with nearby mineral-rich South Africa took pre-eminence.

Ilha was a Portuguese settlement for nearly 500 years and its architecture, while Portuguese design utilises elements from Arabia and India. The courtyards and narrow alleys draw from Arabia and the finishes from India. That makes this a unique island architecturally. Unfortunately, many of the buildings in the "stone town" (as opposed to the "reed town") are in various stages of dilapidation.

The good news is there are various efforts at reconstruction underway on the island. Casa Girassol is a mid-seventeenth-century building that through the years has been a slave market, a merchant's house and a police station. When I visit, restoration is nearing completion. The work is being undertaken with Norwegian government aid. Norwegian ethnologist Dunckard Monrad-Krohn explains that they are restoring these stately colonial buildings not only to look as they once did but by using the same building methods. French architect Yorick Houdayer has lived on Ilha since the 1990s, has been involved in other island restoration projects, and is the co-lead on this project.

Meeting Yorick outside the building I greet him with, "Dr Livingstone, I presume?"

Yorrick explains that they use lime in construction not only because it was used historically but because it is the superior building method. Lime allows for the permeation of water within these thick walls, which cement does not.

But standing outside the Casa Girassol, in the hot midday sun, Yorrick turns philosophical. "For what purpose are we renovating these buildings? European buildings made centuries ago are now squatted in by locals in an independent Mozambique. But how relevant is this eurocentric thing? They brought this European architecture to Africa despite Africa having its own building techniques—which are now rejected by modern Mozambicans as backward."

True to his beliefs, Yorrick has moved off the island to the mainland, where he lives in a house he designed using local materials. This double-story mud house is open to the sea breeze which blows through trees thus cooling the air, obviating the need for air conditioning.

At his house, he tells me how he ended up in this corner of Africa. "In the 1980s my girlfriend and I drove south into Africa from France in a Peugeot 504. As we made our way through West Africa, every night it was like we made a love nest. She wanted to get pregnant, but it didn't happen. We kept going until Zaire. Terrible roads. I sold the car and made a good profit. He was a missionary, but he didn't look trustworthy. Anyway, we continued to Kenya. I had tests done and it turns out I am sterile. My girlfriend left me. I had to see a psychologist because actually I love children. Within a few months of arriving on Ilha de Moçambique, I met a local girl, and since then I have worked on restoration projects on the island. I go back to France every year when all my friends get together. It's almost like I haven't left for them."

I say to Yorrick "I've been to France many times. And I thought on my last trip, this place must have been interesting 500 years ago." I don't get the sense that my comment is appreciated. Of course, France is wonderful! I guess I am just in "wilderness mode."

I make my way over the 3.8-kilometre single-lane bridge back to the island.

Tourism is growing, but it's not easy to get flights to Nampula, and from there it's a further three-hour drive to the island. So access limits tourism's further growth, and it's unlikely at this stage that Ilha will become another mass tourism destination such as Zanzibar, and thank God for that.

From time to time I chat with the owner of my little hotel, and one day on my way out he asks me, "But why alone?" Many people, especially in traditional societies, just don't get how someone could travel alone. But what difference does it make to him?

In stone town, I meet a few of the other home-owning foreigners. These expats live here, or holiday here. I'm invited into one of these restored homes. I ask one of the Western ladies here, who refers to her group of expats as, "The A Team," about the purpose of the architectural renovation on the island, which encompasses personal renovations such as her house.

"Well, I don't know how you thought the Mozambicans would pay for the building restoration?"
"Oh no, I didn't think they'd pay for it, I just wondered where Mozambicans fit into this all..."

But why would the "A Team" care? Later I interview the Mozambique Municipal Chief about restoration projects on the island. I mention funding issues with one of the donors. Referring to the small group of expats he replies, "Well then maybe all these people would just leave us alone."

As time goes by naturally one sees that the island is not just a charming historic relic—that there are many layers and complexities. That the beaches are used by the locals as a toilet is a downside. One of the more cynical of the approximately twenty Europeans who live on the island says to me: "Ilha is a rural village on top of a rubbish dump, surrounded by a latrine, with a world heritage site status."

Ilha de Mozambique was declared a UNESCO world heritage site in 1991. There are a little over 1000 of these "sites of outstanding universal value" globally.

When I visit, UNESCO is restoring the sixteenth-century fort of Saint Sebastian, which is claimed to be the oldest European structure in the southern hemisphere.

Portuguese architect Francisco Monteiro leads the UNESCO project. "There's a proliferation of trees growing out of the fort. That's because of a lack of drainage caused by no maintenance. So what is needed is good maintenance so that water can run out."

The Mozambican Minister of Culture is visiting the project and Francisco invites me to join them for a coffee at the Hotel Omuhipiti. We are discussing the fort restoration work. I am introduced as a journalist, and I find that mildly amusing. I didn't study journalism, and I am still new as a freelance journalist. But Franciso's saying that sort of cements it, and I feel like I'm in a scene from Michelangelo Antonioni's film about identity, *Profession: Reporter*. In talking about the fort's rehabilitation, I ask the minister, "But whose culture is it that is being taken care of, restored? Isn't it colonial Portuguese culture?" Franciso, the UNESCO emissary, is looking on fairly horrified and starts trying to downplay my question to the minister.

But the minister graciously answers that "All these layers of culture are what make us. We are a mosaic of influences. Take me. My surname is Portuguese, but I am Mozambican!" This is truly a profound statement, because when we can acknowledge all the different influences and experiences that have shaped ourselves and others, then we can reach acceptance. It makes sense to simply embrace all these layers.

The next day, Sunday, I attend a church service at the Misericordia church. It is a Catholic service, yet there is the most wonderful singing and drumming by a group of youth, a nod towards syncretism, which is what makes a place like Ilha unique.

Francisco and I have been discussing my making a documentary for UNESCO on the fort's rehabilitation. As time goes on, and despite follow-up emails, this, unfortunately, comes to nothing. It's time to start the long drive back to South Africa. At Nampula, I am pulled over by the traffic police. Just the day before Yorrick on Ilha had been telling me about these cops and the extent to which they are a law unto themselves. Apparently, to start with, they pay to have the job! Then they extract money from drivers by creating problems where there are none. This requires a bribe to be extricated. These bent cops will use the money to open bars, restaurants, night clubs but registered in family members' names! So here I am in Nampula and a traffic cop has just pulled me over. For a change, I don't give my usual friendly greeting. He asks to see my documents.

"*Hepa*! *Problema*! You can't have photocopied papers in Mozambique," the cop says to me.

I sit stoically looking forward. Then I switch to English:

"These are all the papers I got in Nampula."
The cop is groaning and moaning, and "*hepa*-ing" and I am simply ignoring him, looking forward grimly.
After a while, he passes my papers to me. Giving up he says, "Go."

The further south I get, the more I want the drive to just go on forever. The idea of permanently living as a gypsy journalist has been percolating, and now it reaches its fruition with a phone call to an estate agent in Cape Town. "Sell my house!"

Two days later, and further south, the last soft rays of sun pop in and out of the trees on the approach to Massinga. I see a Masaai warrior walking towards me. It can only be Muyire, the Kenyan who previously walked from Kenya to Cape Town, and is now returning. I reverse my car, and have a post-modern, "Dr Livingstone I presume" moment with Muyire the Masaai. I met Muyire in Cape Town. He has a filmmaker in tow, documenting his walk back up to Kenya. They have run out of mini-DV tapes. "No problem," I say, and give him a tape.

Muyire says, "I've been so surprised by Mozambique, by the hospitality, and the feeling of unity and shared values that are so universal... maybe that is why we met so that you could give me a tape!" Go forth Muyire and spread the message of unity and peace! As Yorrick, the French architect on Ilha said, "the 21st century is Africa's time to reclaim its dignity."

Turning back onto the road, I think to myself that when I met Muyire in Cape Town, I'd been mulling doing exactly that—making a documentary about Muyire's long walk home. Now I realise why I didn't. I am on my journey. It would make no sense to be traipsing along on someone else's journey.

A bit south of Massinga I find a local place to camp on the beach. Signing in the registration book I write "citizen of the world" for my country of origin.

CHAPTER SEVEN
Wildflowers

Back in Cape Town, I produce fifteen features for Associated Press during the rest of 2007. One of these is on the annual wildflower spectacle north of Cape Town. To give an idea of the Cape Floral Kingdom's biodiversity, despite occupying less than 0.5% of Africa, it holds 20% of the continent's flora, according to UNESCO. Or here's another comparison: Table Mountain National Park is just 221 square kilometres in size but has 8200 plant species. The British Isles have less than 1500 plant species, according to the University of Cape Town.

Every spring fields come alive in a profusion of colour in the Western and Northern Cape provinces. Setting off early one morning from Cape Town I drive fast on the deserted long straight roads. The first light of the day catches wisps of mist—ghostly in appearance—like apparitions hovering above the meadows. I am in Clanwilliam at 8.30 am to get some visuals and an interview at the annual wildflower show. Here I am told that this district has the world's highest concentration of wildflowers.

Looking at all the, mostly old, couples admiring the flowers inside the old church that houses the Clanwilliam Wildflower Show, I can't help but see the yin and yang that Joseph Campbell writes about—that that is why couples come together—they balance out the yin and the yang of each other. And why is it that mostly only old people admire flowers? As one gets to the winter of one's life does one start appreciating the wonders of nature, these miracles that many take for granted?

From the flower show, I head to the Remsbok Gardens where some of the wildflowers are now in bloom. It's a sea of yellow, orange, pink, and blue.

I interview a couple aged around 70. "We left Hout Bay when the squatters moved in. First, they were living on the beach, then they set up shacks on land in the neighbourhood. It's prime land!" Every time his wife started to answer or talk, he'd interrupt her and speak for her. "Now we live in Peddington, in Kwazulu-Natal." Cape Town's Hout Bay suburb is a microcosm for South Africa: wealthy and middle-class Whites, a Black township, and a Coloured township, all living separate lives, with high crime, and sporadic bursts of violence and protests.

I approach another couple. The husband says, "You should speak to my wife." I quickly see there is more to her than meets the eye. She's articulate, and she's on many committees, including for Boys Town, which is a home for abandoned and abused boys. "You have to give back," she says.

She also says that "There's a Girl's Town now too."
I ask, "Are they together?"
"Now that would be looking for trouble!"

Then I interview, ostensibly about wildflowers, but invariably talking about bigger issues, an Indian-South African couple, originally from Cape Town, but who have now emigrated to Canada.

"Where does all this violent criminality come from? South Africans are such good people," says Shobhna Gopal-Truter.
"Where is the country going?" asks the husband.
"I don't know," I say.

The thing is, I can't help agreeing with Shobhna. That there is a lot of good in South Africa. Yes, we are heterogenous and divided in many ways, but we are also united by this thing called nationhood. And I don't think the power of this identity can be easily underestimated—if it is harnessed. I think it's a fascinating country, and indeed, as Shobhna said, a beautiful one.

I also drive to the Biedouw valley for flower meadow shots. Following the particularly good rains of the winter, bright colours are seen across the pass. Capetonians, and people from towns, have come for the day, just taking in the sight, enjoying nature, and socialising.

CHAPTER EIGHT
The Mulanje Cedar

Malawi, where I lived from ages six to ten, is the last place where I can say I felt I fit in. After Malawi, my family went to Scotland, and I did not quite fit in there. After that, South Africa at the age of 14. Yet even after many years in "my country" I reached the point of realisation that I am only 60% South African. It is no surprise that I keep gravitating back to Malawi.

After several months back in Cape Town, working, and waiting for someone to buy my house so that I can become a full-time roving reporter and nomad, I need my "Africa fix." Using air miles I fly up to Malawi. Destination: Mount Mulanje, with some detours.

I am met at Blantyre airport by Carl Bruessouw, of the Mount Mulanje Conservation Trust. Just before travelling, in his last email to me, he warns me that we won't be going directly to Mulanje. Indeed, on arrival, we head north up to the lake for the weekend. It is quite a day, leaving my house in Woodstock, Cape Town at sunrise, and getting to Lake Malawi at sunset.

Carl is a third-generation South African in Malawi and lives in a large former tea estate house to which I am invited to stay. The sprawling home, with a view across to the Mulanje mountain, shows its age but is spotlessly clean, with a red-painted veranda floor so polished you have to be careful not to slip. The garden is lush and verdant, and Carl keeps a giant python in a cage next to the front door as a security measure—"Africans are very scared of him."

One more detour before starting my work is an evening out at the Mulanje Golf Club. Once upon a time when the tea estates around Mount Mulanje were run by Brits and expats, this was the main watering hole. The bar and club remain pleasant and well-kept. Along for the evening is David, a Brit who is looking at investing in a tourism venture in the Mulanje area. As Carl is the unofficial "mayor of Mulanje" David has come to him for advice. Over beers, David tells us about his life in London.

"I live next door to Madonna," he says breathlessly. "She doesn't trust anyone... A few times she lost trust in me. But then I tried again." I groan inwardly.
David asks me about my project. "Who's it for?"
"Associated Press."
"Oh and aren't they stingy with budgets?"
"I flew up here using air miles."
"Oh, well that doesn't make business sense."

That's what you call two people with two different ethos, having a conversation, and talking at cross purposes.

Carl turns to me: "You're in luck. Tomorrow we're going up in a helicopter."
"Sounds great." A good opportunity for visuals of the mountain.

Mount Mulanje is one of many inselbergs in the region. Inselberg means simply island mountain. Because of its elevation, and separation from the plains below, these inselbergs are home to a large number of endemic species: species that are found nowhere else. That's because, over time, these plants and trees evolved separately to the lowlands down below. There are thought to be over 250 endemic plant and wildlife species on Mount Mulanje. The most famous of Mulanje's native species is the Mulanje Cedar tree—actually a misnomer as it is a cypress. This, the national tree of Malawi has unfortunately been so heavily exploited that it is listed as endangered on the IUCN red list when I visit in 2007.

Early in the morning Carl and I drive out to the bright red helicopter awaiting us at the golf club. The pilot, Barney, a fair-haired, light blue-eyed African with sun-damaged skin, takes one look at me and my video camera, and says, "Hold on! Who is this for?"
"Associated Press, Horizons."
"No way that you include any shots of my helicopter."
"Okay."
Then he tells me why. "In the 1980s, when Robert Mugabe's [North Korea-trained] henchmen were carrying out the Matabele massacres, [where about 20,000 innocent civilians were murdered], I was commissioned to fly my helicopter for Associated Press, Roving Reporter. There were shots of my helicopter that were broadcast—and as a result, I was arrested and jailed for two weeks."
After giving us a moment to let this sink in, he adds, "And no, there was no buggery in the jail."
"No, for sure, I won't include any visuals of the helicopter," I say. "Of course, this isn't Zimbabwe," I add.
"No, this is colonial Africa," says Barney, acerbically, while climbing aboard his helicopter.

And so we ascend and I get some marvellous shots of the mountain from the helicopter. The mountain reserve covers 26 kilometres by 22 kilometres and Mulanje juts out dramatically from the plains around it, peaking at 3002 metres above sea level. From up here, I spot the last remnant pockets of forests, known as cedar clusters.

At the Mount Mulanje Conservation Trust, Conservation Biologist Julian Bayliss explains the appeal of the Mulanje cedar timber: "It's durable, it doesn't rot and termites don't eat it." Tourists buy wooden boxes and other trinkets made from the aromatic Mulanje cedar, whilst further afield the timber is used for making boats, and it is exported. Unfortunately, exploitation, which dates back to the colonial period, has been unsustainable.

The Malawi Department of Forestry together with the Mount Mulanje Conservation Trust has been trying to halt the timber trade with limited success. One of the methods has been to only allow the harvesting of dead mature trees. The result of that has been simply that the loggers ring bark mature trees, thus causing the trees' quick death.

The Mount Mulanje Conservation Trust has been very active in raising Mulanje cedar seedlings and planting them on the mountain, but they are fragile, take many decades to reach adulthood, and indeed few make it. I ask how many of the over 70,000 seedlings planted in the last five years have survived so far. "Frost this year killed off most of the seedlings," says the Mount Mulanje Conservation Trust's David Nangoma.

The next step for me is to get up on the mountain myself. There's a well-established set of trails with ten huts on the massif, meaning one can have a wonderful long hike and disconnect. Of course, I am not disconnecting—I am heading up to get visuals of Mulanje cedar and to search for the loggers. After a long day's walk, I arrive at Chitepo hut and have what must rate as one of the best showers of my life. An alfresco bucket of hot water crouching naked behind a rock. In the hut are an Israeli, an Austrian, and a Spanish woman, with conversations on various international issues, but just a bit too speculative for my liking. The next morning I tell them I am moving on as I don't have a lot of food supplies, though they offer to share theirs. "Good luck with your tree," says the Spanish woman a bit sardonically.

Walking along the trails on the plateaus of Mulanje, my guide is leading me to where we can hear the sawing sound of wood being cut. We approach some pit sawyers, sawing Mulanje cedar in holes in the ground, or pits. Winston Steve is surprisingly candid and I interview him on camera. He complains about corruption: sawyers who pay off officials to cut down cedars. He complains about unlicensed loggers. He also complains about timber thieves. Finally, there's a lack of law enforcement. All in all, it's a bad situation, and there are few mature trees left. That night I sleep at Lichinga hut avoiding a young radical student backpacker group.

Back down from the mountain, and in the town of Mulanje again, I need to interview the Malawi Department of Forestry to get to the bottom of the corruption aspect. Carl Bruessow, in his interview, has been diplomatic, speaking about the management situation needing to be turned around.

For seven years in the Cape Town film industry as a location scout, I had to find the right locations. Now I have to find the right people. Maybe all those years of scouting were of some use. I track down and interview Duncan Masonje, Mulanje District Forestry Officer, and he is surprisingly open, saying they are trying to halt corrupt practices and that three or four officers have been suspended.

It's too little and it's too late. In the August 2019 IUCN Red List assessment of the Mulanje cedar, it is now critically endangered, with only 49 mature individual trees left. The only hope is that some of the Mount Mulanje Conservation Trust's thousands of little seedlings make it into adulthood. Otherwise, the Mulanje cedar is functionally extinct.

Back in Blantyre, with the story finished and feeling more relaxed I go for drinks with some travellers. It is evening. The Spanish lady from the mountain, Dolors, and I are walking out the Mount Soche Bar. I want to take a taxi, but she is insistent on not spending the US$ 3. As we step out of the hotel entrance, a man comes out of the darkness, grabs her handbag, and runs away. I immediately run after him. I am fast and I am gaining ground. I shout at him, "I'm going to fuck you up." He drops the bag. I pick it up and give it to Dolores. "Can we take a taxi now?" I ask her. She concedes.

My 30-hour bus ride blur of a journey back to South Africa, which takes me through Malawi, Mozambique, and Zimbabwe doubles up as a further AP story: cross-border traders. The informal economy plays a large role in Southern Africa. Cross-border traders travel around the region buying and selling products. They are the entrepreneurs and nomads of Southern Africa. Cross-border trade accounts for up to 35% of the value of the region's formal trade according to The Common Market for Eastern and Southern Africa.

Before leaving I connect with Dexes Chanza of the Cross Borders Association of Malawi. The plan has been to travel with him by bus the 1700 kilometres to Johannesburg, interview him along the way, and get whatever other visuals. But on the morning of departure, he phones me to let me know he is down with malaria and is not travelling. At the bus, I find another trader but he turns out to be rather inarticulate so it's a disappointment. The most interesting part is getting a few shots in Zimbabwe. The country is at the height of its currency crisis, with denominations going into the trillions of Zimbabwe dollars. It is not a media-friendly country, but I get a few surreptitious shots. At the border, I cast about and seeing no one around I film the Welcome To Zimbabwe sign. It's pretty risky—just a week before an ENCA TV crew was arrested and thrown in jail by Zimbabwean police at the same spot.

Finally, at Johannesburg's Park Station, Emmanuel Chilemba offloads his Malawian cane chairs. Once he has sold these, he'll return to Malawi with clothing, electronics and shoes.

CHAPTER NINE
The rejuvenation of Gorongosa National Park

In early 2008 I sell my house in Cape Town. After settling the debt incurred from my first AP trip to Mozambique and Tanzania in 2006, with the remaining proceeds I buy my first professional video camera, a Canon A1. I am now a full-time vagabond. Wherever I lay my hat is my home.

In Johannesburg, I stop off at Southern Africa Direct, a TV channel that will turn out to be short-lived. But before their demise, I will sell them my first documentary that has been sitting on a shelf for nine years, the Dar es Salaam to Cape Town travelogue. I'll also sell them my Swahili Islands documentary, and my Long Street documentary. With the proceeds, I buy an ageing bronze-coloured Nissan Safari 4X4.

I also have my first meeting in Pretoria for the upcoming AP stories I have planned for Mozambique. Fossil fuels are an unsustainable source of energy and a major contributor to climate change through carbon dioxide emissions. An alternative to fossil fuel is biofuel—oil from plant, algae or animal waste. In 2008 the miracle biofuel crop is jatropha, a plant that grows to the size of an apple tree, and originating in Central America. Deulco, a South African company, is one of the many new players on the scene around Africa, clearing land to plant jatropha plants. The seeds contain up to 40% oil which can then be processed into biofuel, usable to run a diesel engine, and even as aviation fuel.

The project sounds promising: the jatropha plants grow in marginal soil where little or no food crops can be grown, are hardy, and require few inputs including little water and no pesticides. And if unused sandy land is being planted with jatropha that grows to tree size, as in Mozambique, then it's an afforestation project to boot. So when I meet with Deulco in Pretoria I am enthusiastic. Deulco tells me they'll be the largest jatropha plantation in Southern Africa within the next 12 months. And how big is that? 60,000 hectares are being cleared to make way for jatropha in Southern Mozambique, a massive amount of land.

In my communication with Associated Press, I am reminded to ensure that I also get a critical voice. For example, talk to the local communities. Good point. I head over the border to Maputo and start with an interview with Actionaid. Here Filipe Pequenino points out that in a country where 80% of Mozambicans are subsistence farmers it is inevitable that large-scale biofuel projects will become a source of conflict. I go to the ministry of agriculture and am told they can't provide a comment, and that I should approach the local government structure where the jatropha plantation is.

I start setting up my next batch of AP stories in Maputo. One of these sounds like it has a lot of potential—producing bread more sustainably in Mozambique. One of the legacies of Portuguese colonialism is that fresh bread is available everywhere in Mozambique. Unfortunately, the main raw material, or ingredient, flour, is not produced locally. That makes Mozambique susceptible to the vagaries of import costs for what is a staple food. According to the Food and Agricultural Organisation (FAO), Mozambique imports 100% of its wheat. But cassava is a crop that is grown locally, and the FAO are experimenting with substituting imported wheat flour with locally sourced cassava flour. That sounds brilliant. Especially as food prices keep going up. Unfortunately, when I finally track down a Dr Singh at the FAO it turns out the project is embryonic. Sadly even today this sustainable staple food project is yet to be rolled out. Come on FAO, with all your resources you can do better.

After the usual city time spent with logistics, I am pleased to be heading north once more. I have the biofuel story lined up as well as two stories at Gorongosa National Park. At Fatima's backpackers, a South African talking loudly on his phone bemoans how "backward" and "undeveloped" Mozambique still is. When one doesn't understand history, then one doesn't understand the present. There are many reasons for Mozambique's underdevelopment and they include corruption and mismanagement. But South Africa was directly involved in the war of the 1980s in which over a million people died and much of the country's infrastructure was destroyed.

It's time to get out of the city. Paul Theroux, writing in *The Kingdom By The Sea*, talks about travel fulfilling the fantasy of escape. Whenever he stays at another Bed and Breakfast and gets that, "staying at the in-laws feeling," he simply packs his bags and leaves early the next morning, walking away at a steady pace without looking back. And maybe sometimes we should allow ourselves to simply escape, especially knowing that the perspective gained from being away may well provide answers or solutions to whatever problems may be at hand.

And so I pack my car at Fatima's, and early the next morning drive up to Bilene, a small palm tree-fringed town idyllically situated at the edge of a lagoon. It's another place full of memories. I stayed here in 1993 with a group of university friends when it was a deserted and run-down tropical paradise. Maybe all these Africa trips of mine are simply nostalgic journeys—reliving happy childhood memories and that first adventurous student expedition, camping on beaches in a country without tourists and experiencing peace for the first time in three decades.

Unlike back in '93, Bilene is now, as it was in the colonial period, a (South African) tourism hot spot. I spend quite a bit of time going from hotel to hotel, but they are all simply too expensive for my tiny budget. Finally, in the evening I knock on the door of a semi-built hotel. Some rough-round-edges South Africans say, "No problem, we haven't finished building, so you can stay over for free."

That night at the bar, the burly South Africans are drinking rum and cokes with three Mozambicans. They ask me where I come from.
"Cape Town."
"Ah, you guys are more liberal down there. Us, we don't usually mix with Black people. But over here there's no one else, so we have no choice."

The next morning I am awoken by the sound of quad bikes screaming around town, and in the distance, jet skis howling back and forth on the lagoon. South Africans like their toys. My hosts tell me that several mega-tourism projects are being developed now at Bilene, including two five-star hotels, one with an eighteen-hole golf course. This is a US$1.5 billion investment by an Arab consortium, and one of 35 five-star hotels currently under development up and down the Mozambican coast. "When Bill Gates finds a cure for malaria, then tourism will really take off here."

I thank them and head over to the Bilene campsite. I have one day to kill before I start shooting the biofuel story, located nearby. At the campsite bar that evening, I play a game of pool with a musclebound 40-year-old guy from Johannesburg. His plump wife, which I'd place at half his age is sitting nearby tending to their baby. "My bru" (brother) tells me stories of drunken brawls in Johannesburg. And when he spots some 14-year-old girls he turns to me and in earshot of his wife says, "Nice and tight."

Early the next morning I head out to the site where Deulco is planting jatropha trees to produce biofuel. I meet former Zimbabwean commercial farmer Aubrey Dunn, another refugee from Mugabe's land reform next door. Jatropha as a biofuel sounds like a wonder crop: it reaches maturity after two years, and needs little water or nurturing.

Aubrey tells me the company has made a strong start towards planting 600 square kilometres of jatropha on, "marginal land." When ask what he means by marginal land, Aubrey shows me where they are planting the jatropha. Running his hands through the soil, it does indeed look practically like beach sand, unsurprising considering our proximity to the sea.

But when I meet the local Ndjeve community leader I am told that in fact, they had been growing various crops such as cashew, mango, pineapple and cassava in the "marginal soil." Community members agreed to be moved from their land to make way for the agribusiness to move in, after much negotiation with the government. Jobs are a carrot being dangled before the Ndjeve.

Moving people away from their homelands is the kind of thing colonial governments did, and that newly independent African states would ideally be wanting to avoid, however desperate they may be for development. And if biofuel, even if it is a promising alternative to fossil fuels, is being exported to Europe, then who is benefiting and who is losing? At least in Brazil locally-made ethanol biofuel is used in national fuel supplies.

Unfortunately, the African jatropha boom turns out to be a bubble. Many of the companies that set up shops across the continent proceeded to go bust, often after having cleared tracts of indigenous forest. The jatropha plant can indeed grow in sub-standard soil and survive on little water, but it won't produce many seeds in these conditions, and therefore will have minimal oil output. To get a good output the plant needs plenty of water, good soil, and pesticides to ward off bugs. That means it is not such a miracle plant.

According to a 2014 study published in the Sustainability journal, "In less than 10 years, tens of thousands of hectares were acquired for jatropha plantations and thousands of hectares were planted, most of which are now unused or abandoned."

It's a long drive north to Gorongosa National Park in Central Mozambique, but very good to be up here in the wilderness. Gorongosa was a renowned African national park before Mozambican independence in 1975, attracting international A-list celebrities. During the war of the 1980s, the park was the site of frequent battles between Renamo and Frelimo, resulting in carnage for the park's wildlife, which was hunted down for food or for ivory to trade, by soldiers. By the 1990s there was very little wildlife left, and the park was in ruins. This is where American Greg Carr steps into the picture. Carr sold his telephone voicemail system in the 1990s and turned to philanthropy. He signed a 20-year public-private partnership with the Mozambican government in 2008 to reinvigorate the Gorongosa National Park, an agreement that will later be further extended.

But it's not just a national park revitalising project. Jobs in honey, poultry, dried fruit, new schools and clinics, improved water supplies, and community-based tourism are some of the other initiatives. In other words, everything the state should be doing.

I set up camp in the far corner of the Chitengo campsite, where I'll stay for the next three weeks, my tent next to the fence, meaning I am centimetres from the wildlife of Gorongosa. In the night I hear the footsteps and scratching sounds of animals. In the morning I awake and peer out of my tent at the bushveld in dappled light. It's a perfect start to the day. Autumn here is lovely. The nights are crisp, the days are sunny and warm.

I'm producing two stories: the revitalisation of the park, and conservation at the adjacent Mount Gorongosa.

Joao Viseu is the park's business director, and he explains to me that the initial investment is 36 million dollars over the next 20 to 30 years. The investment goes into infrastructure, community development and upliftment, wildlife transfers from elsewhere, conservation and security. The pre-Carr per annum government budget for Gorongosa park was US$115,000.

It was the high concentration of wildlife that was one of the park's main attractions before the war. But by the time Mozambique's peace treaty was signed in 1992, over 90% of the park's wildlife had been decimated. At the time of my visit, one batch of wildebeest and two batches of buffalo have been reintroduced from parks outside Mozambique. Over the ensuing years, several more species will be reintroduced from other African parks. When I visit, there is a small skittish herd of elephants and low numbers of other key species such as hippos, impalas, and lions.

On a game drive, I spot oribi, reedbuck and waterbuck, and finally, in the distance the nervous elephants in a grove. These last surviving elephants lived through losing extended family members, and the constant terror of gunshots. Because so many of the Gorongosa elephants were poached for their tusks, these last survivors have a much higher preponderance of being born without tusks than normal. On another drive, we spot a pride of lions, looking comparatively relaxed, just metres from our vehicle.

The 4067 square kilometre park sits at the very tail end of Africa's Great Rift Valley. The parks consist of grasslands, savanna, dry forests, and rivers. The fever trees with their white bark are characteristic of the area. In the early days of European exploration in these parts, visitors and settlers found that they got ill with fever when near these trees. Hence they called them fever trees. What they discovered later is they were getting ill with malaria. But the connection is there. Mosquitoes that transmit malaria live in swampy areas where fever trees are found.

The peace of my campsite has been broken. Two South African registered Jeep Cherokees have parked, some distance away. Then another two South African 4X4s arrive. Why always in twos or groups? Safety in numbers in darkest Africa? Then another two 4X4's arrive, Johannesburg "okes" who are setting up camp just ten metres from me! My paradise bush tranquil has been broken. A poor night's sleep ensues, what with the snoring emanating from nearby, and their early wake-up.

Gorongosa Mountain is not part of the park, but as it is the source of water for the park's wildlife, what happens on the mountain directly affects the park.

What has been happening up on the mountain, as all over Mozambique and elsewhere in Africa, is deforestation. Local communities are clearing forests to make way for subsistence agriculture. As the trees on the mountain disappear, water flows off more quickly from the mountain into the park, and then drains and evaporates more quickly down in the park valley. Of course, there is also the issue of preserving the rich biodiversity of the mountain forests.

I set off for the mountain to see the indigenous seedlings being planted on the mountainside by park staff. Saplings of about fifteen species are being planted along river banks and steep slopes facing the brunt of deforestation and erosion. I also meet local farmers who the National Park is liaising with to establish organic farming as an alternative to slash-and-burn farming—which is cutting down trees and burning them to prepare land for farming. With organic farming, instead of burning old plant remains, these are mulched into the soil becoming a rich fertiliser. Properly managed organic farming land can be used productively, indefinitely, instead of the destructive slash and burn method which depletes the soil of nutrients within a year or two, resulting in the farmer moving on to find new land.

Before hiking up to the top it is necessary to ask permission from the spirits. This I do one morning early with a guide, at the village of Nhancuco. And we don't come empty-handed. I've been told to bring along red wine and a bottle of spirits. The *regulo* pours me, himself and several villagers some red wine each. This we drink. It is now 8.30 am. The regulo then pours some wine at the base of a tree. I then join in clapping and do my version of a Madiba shuffle (Nelson Mandela's signature dance) in a circle with the villagers. Together with my guide, we are then cleared to go up the mountain. Leaving I cast a look back to see the bottle of spirits being cracked open. Seems like the party is just getting started.

It takes a long time to get past the deforested zone, with its maize *machambas*. These are the plots of land forests are cleared to make way for subsistence agriculture. Then finally we enter the evergreen forest and it seems like the temperature has dropped about ten degrees. It is pleasant after the midday heat, and wonderful to be amongst these ancient trees. We keep going past a waterfall, and eventually exit the forest. Now we are nearly at the top of the 1863-metre mountain. Up here the vegetation is montane grassland with tree ferns and grass-like flowering plants like sedges. It's another world. I wish I could stay longer.

Deforestation on the mountain has already been extensive, so it is good to hear a few years later that the mountain becomes a part of the Gorongosa

National Park.

Back at Chitengo, the campsite all is quiet. The campers have cleared off, and it's just me, the staff, and the wilderness once more. In the evening at the restaurant, a few groups sit at different tables. I'm discussing conservation with a young Zimbabwean hunter, who says to me:

"Us hunters are the greatest conservationists of all! Hunting is a business and to be sustainable we have to ensure we only hunt animals that are more than what the ecosystem can bear."
"So hunting is like culling?"
"Yes!"

Killing an animal for survival I understand. And I get what he is saying, at a rational level, about the "sustainability" of well-managed hunting. Yet I cannot fathom what pleasure a person would get to kill an animal for "fun" or "sport." This thirst for blood is something I do not understand.

The reason a hunter has to justify his actions, and the only reason some national parks carry out culling is that we are too many people and there are too few wilderness areas. This trend only gets worse. Gorongosa brands itself as a "human rights park," investing in local communities as well as the park itself. That is laudable, but Africa's wilderness is sending out an SOS. And when a private foreign investor is financing and managing a national park, building schools and clinics, isn't a line being crossed?

The Gorongosa restaurant is a building with tall thatch ceilings. Suddenly there's a loud thunk. A snake that had been on a ceiling beam has fallen down to the floor. Everyone jumps up and dashes out. The snake makes its way to the next building and crawls into a gutter. The snake catcher is called. Minutes later he has caught a puff adder. I ask the snake catcher how dangerous is this snake.

"This will kill you in 20 minutes."
"Do you have the anti-venom here?"
"No"

And this is just one of several deadly snakes in these parts. Be careful where you step!

While at Gorongosa there is an upheaval taking place. Some Western conservationists are about to be shown the door. There were simply too many pale faces in an African national parks project, something Carr didn't take into account. One of the American conservationists, bitter at his exit, says to me, "South Africa will go down soon anyway and then the whole region will lose its tourism."

Further turbulence while I'm at Gorongosa is a wave of xenophobic violence in South Africa. Mobs have been attacking and killing African nationals in South Africa, with 43 dead so far, 23 of which are Mozambicans. Anger against South Africans in Mozambique is growing. Mateus and Regina from Gorongosa Park approach me looking visibly upset.

"After the long war which South Africa caused in Mozambique, now this? After Mozambique supported the ANC in exile, now this? Meanwhile, South African tourists are relaxing on the beaches here…"

I spend some time discussing it with them, but it's hard to intellectualise murder.

Dolors, the Spanish lady from Malawi visits me for a while. The relationship is not going well. Nonetheless, she wants a "takeaway baby." I just don't want to do that. I'm a bit traditional when it comes to these things. So in the end, I take Dolors to the bus stop at Chimoio, and we say our final goodbye.

My three weeks at Gorongosa soon come to an end. On my way out I stop again at the town of Chimoio and drop off my tapes at DHL to send to Associated Press. I walk in and greet the lady in Portuguese. I soon switch to English. She says:

"I thought you were South African because you are in a South African registered car."
Before I can reply she continues.
"Because we want to kick all the South Africans out of our country."
"I *am* South African," I tell her.
Her eyes widen.
"And *I'm* not doing it…. I feel bad about what's happening in South Africa. I don't even want to live there any more. It's a violent country."

After a return to Pretoria and Johannesburg, couch-surfing with family and friends, I soon hit the road once more. I arrive by bus back in Maputo and stay, as usual at Fatima's. There are no rooms available, so I have to make do with a bed in a dorm room. The only possibility that I will sleep in a noisy shared room is to prop up the bar every evening until late. After several beers, I will sleep. In between hanging out at the bar, I send off a few Malawi story ideas to Associated Press. This time I am without a vehicle and I enjoy walking the city streets rather than being insulated in a car. The relaxed vibe, the smell of the dust, exhaust fumes, walking the broken pavements, shoulder to shoulder with other pedestrians. And then there are the cops. Walking past the Egyptian Embassy on Avenida Mao Tse Tung, two of the AK47-wielding policemen stop me and ask me for my identification. Then, inevitably when looking at the notarised copy of my passport they create a problem.

"*Epa!*"
I stand my ground saying there is no problem.
They say, "This is out of date."
They are angling for a bribe, unsmiling, and aggressive.
On the edge of losing my temper, I take the paper from them saying, "Everything here is okay. Thank you very much. Goodbye." I turn and leave. My blood is boiling.

At Fatima's bar that night, I notice a South American brunette in a dark blue and white striped shirt talking about Mozambican politics. She looks gentle, smart and beautiful. She has developed some admirers. Fatima then makes a rare appearance, and surveying the scene says loudly and angrily, "Leave my girls alone." This doesn't deter the admirers. I manage a brief hello to the South American in the melee. The next day I walk across the road to the local restaurant. It is a busy Sunday afternoon, and I order Mozambique's famous peri-peri chicken. I overhear a Mozambican who has been wending his way between the patrons, and who is clearly in his regular bar, saying loudly, "But only until 6 pm. I stop drinking at 6 pm on Sundays," as if this strict rule shows just how responsible he is. Mozambicans are pretty good about drinking steadily and will do so all weekend, without appearing to reach the drunk stage, unlike other Southern Africans. Just then the South American comes in, with one of her admirers. She spots me, and I give a small wave. She turns to her admirer and asks if they should join me. Every bone in his body is screaming no, and he hustles her inside. There goes my last chance to talk to her, and all I can say that is positive is that she remains a perfect memory.

From Maputo I fly up to Tete in Central Mozambique. Tete airport is a good example of a small colonial-era airport that needed simply a coat of paint, rather than a fancy expensive new building being constructed. Not only that, but it is also a beautiful modernist building.

At the airport, I hail a taxi and travel 125 kilometres to the Malawi border. We're driving along the Tete corridor, a 260-kilometre stretch of road in Mozambique connecting Malawi with Zimbabwe.

I'm enjoying the air-conditioned comfort of what is the longest taxi ride of my life so far. The landscape is dry with intermittent baobab trees.

The Tete corridor was infamous during the Mozambican war of destabilisation as the "hell run." Truckers willing to risk transporting goods along this road were paid triple the regional rate knowing an attack by Renamo was a strong possibility. I remember as a teenager seeing magazine photographs of this highway littered with burnt-out trucks on either side.

Today, the risks are more prosaic. The Toyota sedan is continually slowing down and speeding up, and then slowing again to avoid, and sometimes crash into the numerous potholes, some as big as bathtubs. I catch myself taking a sharp intake of breath when the poor battered suspension crashes particularly hard.

"I'm sorry," says Patrick, the taxi driver. But I decide that Patrick is addressing the car rather than my mechanical sensitivities, so I say nothing.

Patrick is one of the many Zimbabweans who have fled the economic crisis back home to work in a neighbouring country.

I ask Patrick, "How is it that only five years after building a new highway, it is falling apart?"
"Mozambicans like their corruption very much!" says Patrick, smiling.
"From the top down," I say.
"Top level," He says.

By the time these roads are built, so much of the funds have been siphoned off that the tar is simply too thin to last for long.

As we slowly pull away after driving out of another crater of a pothole, we pass a woman walking on our right, laughing, stumbling and singing.
"What's up with her?" I ask Patrick.
"She is drunk!" he replies. He smiles broadly then continues, "women!" as if that explains it all.

More of Patrick's views of women appear soon.

I ask him, "With the Zimbabwean economic crisis next door, are there many Zimbabwean refugees in Tete?"

"No, but many Zimbabweans are at Zobue," the Malawi border town we are going to.

Patrick turns to me, and with a big smile says, "women!"

"Oh, prostitutes?" I ask.

Patrick lets out a slightly embarrassed schoolboy laugh.

At Zobue I catch a minibus taxi through no man's land, then get stamped into the country of my childhood. Another minibus taxi takes me into Blantyre where I stay at Doogles backpackers.

I hang out in Blantyre while arranging my national filming permit. Having lived in Addis Ababa in the late 1990s, eating lunch at an Ethiopian restaurant takes me back in time. The bright Ethiopian paintings, the smell of the coffee, the fresh fruit juice, the conversations in Amharic. Three English girls arrive and take a picture of themselves sitting at a table. The Ethiopian owner arrives, and angrily reproaches them, "Did I give you permission to take a picture?" The girls seem flummoxed. Understandably so. They converse and he seems to soften. But in that instant, I am reminded of the Ethiopian suspicion tendency. Whether because of the previous communist era or the country's mountain isolation or a combination, I don't know.

With my filming permit in hand, I take a minibus taxi east to the town of Mulanje, where I stay once again at Carl's tea estate house. I'm back at Mount Mulanje and the first of two stories I'll shoot is The Porter's Race. Malawi's only extreme sports event is a 26-kilometre run up and back down Mount Mulanje. Originally limited to mountain porters and guides, the run has become an annual fixture open to all, with local and international participants. Among the Malawian winners, some have gone on to represent their country abroad.

For Carl Bruessow, Mount Mulanje Conservation Trust Executive Director, the mountain run is also an opportunity to highlight the conservation of the mountain and its Mulanje Cedar trees. "This is a United Nations Global Biosphere Reserve, but we are facing multiple challenges: deforestation, invasive pine trees, and wildfire damage."

The steep route up begins in grasslands, passes forest, culminating in the afro-alpine zone. This year there are 272 participants. Most of the Malawian participants run barefoot. An average hiker, wearing hiking boots, of course, would take about 15 hours to walk the 26 kilometres up, peaking at 2500 metres above sea level, and then back down again. Today's winner is Malawian Francis Khanje. His record-breaking run is in just two hours and nine minutes. I interview Khanje who says, "I've been training this route every day." Khanje says he lacks the money to buy the correct gear such as running shoes, and that he'd benefit from a coach.

The second story I am covering is a project in Mulanje town. Deforestation is a major issue across Africa, partly the commercial exploitation of timber, and partly at the local level, where people cut trees to make fires to cook. Only 11% of Malawians have access to electricity, and wood is therefore what is used for cooking. Malawi's population as of 2019 is 18.6 million, compared to 2,8 million in 1950. That translates into a huge impact on natural resources. A 2019 study shows a drop in forest cover nationally from 66% in 1991 to 45.8% in 2017. The ramifications are many, starting with the basic ecosystem service of carbon sequestration and oxygen provision for the planet that trees provide. When the forests are all gone what is one left with? A desert. People don't survive in those conditions. A study of the history of civilisations shows the boom periods coincide with deforestation and the bust period occurs when these natural resources have been depleted.

Enter stage left the rocket stove. Developed in the USA in the 1980s this is a low-tech solution to mitigate deforestation in Malawi and similar countries. Utilising a design that ensures the optimum ratio between heat, fuel and air, the rocket stove aims to burn wood at the most efficient level of combustion. According to GTZ, the German International State Aid body now known as GIZ, which is implementing a Rocket Stove project in Malawi, this kind of stove can use 90 to 95% less wood than a conventional open fire.

The project, which is also being rolled out in eight other Southern African countries, has the goal of sustainability through training local producers. I meet Ken Chilewe of Ken Steel engineering, which is one of four companies now making rocket stoves in Malawi. Ken shows me how a rocket stove is made: insulative bricks at the bottom, insulative material along the combustion chamber, and steel on the outside. Ken tells me the temperature inside can reach 900 degrees centigrade. The rocket stove not only uses much less wood than an open fire, but it emits much less smoke—a health hazard for people cooking, especially indoors. Ken produces rocket stoves of various sizes. I visit some of the tea estates situated around Mount Mulanje, where rocket stoves are being used at an institutional level. Eastern Produce Malawi Lauderdale Tea Estate feeds approximately 1000 workers per day. Kitchen staff here remark on how little smoke is emitted from the huge rocket stoves which are used indoors.

It seems that foreign aid which is aimed at the grassroots level, building up small businesses, is far superior to throwing money at unaccountable governments. Ken Steel has gone on to be a successful business, producing rocket stoves on a large scale, selling especially well to foreign NGOs and UN agencies. So it's a sustainable success story... as long as the foreigners who buy the products stay in Malawi!

My time in tranquil beautiful Mulanje is over and I must return to Blantyre, and horror of horrors, pay for my accommodation. After a couple of nights in a musty, dank Doogles room, I move to Henderson's, a budget and basic local hotel.

I've got two more stories lined up. The first is on the Open Arms Orphanage. Malawi's HIV AIDS rate at the time of my visit is around 14%, which has brought the average lifespan down to 36, and this has contributed to a large number of orphans. To get more information I track down Dominic Misomali, District Social Welfare Officer in Blantyre. I ask Dominic about the orphans' situation, but first, he asks me for my filming permit, one of the rare times I am requested this document. He takes the paper from me and scrutinises it carefully for some time. It soon becomes clear why Dominic appears annoyed.

"I've been collecting dead Malawians at Chileka airport."
"Dead bodies? What happened?" I ask.
"Victims of xenophobic violence in South Africa. And I have to return these dead bodies to their home villages. And these people in isolated villages have absolutely no comprehension as to why their brother, son, or cousin has been killed. And what am I supposed to tell them?" he asks me angrily.
"What do you say?" I ask.

Dominic doesn't reply. Again, as when I was at Gorongosa in Mozambique, I try and struggle to intellectualise the xenophobic violence in South Africa.

"It could be connected to Thabo Mbeki's aloof leadership, South Africa's history of isolation, promises made in 1994 that did not materialise, a long history of violence." Or perhaps as political commentator Brent Meersman says it is, "economic competition at the grassroots level." Maybe it's all these reasons and more.

At the entrance to the ministry are a group of Malawians who are in the process of being repatriated. They appear sullen and exhausted.

Back to my orphanage story, Dominic has informed me that Malawi has 1.3 million orphans, in a country of 14 million. Many of these orphans are a result of the HIV AIDS crisis. Some organisations are working hard to care for these orphans.

There are two aspects to this story that bother me. They have to do with

Associated Press requesting me to include a reference to Madonna, who recently adopted a Malawian child. I understand that this is topical, she's a big name, and that it will help sell the story. I just find it unfortunate that stories out of Africa have to be framed by Westerners. This leads to my second issue. The young Western volunteers come to Africa to work at places such as orphanages. Why the phenomenon? Sometimes it seems to me that for Westerners Africa is just a continent to be saved, or to go on safari.

Sarika Bansal has written a book called *Tread Lightly: Notes on Ethical Travel*. She puts it like this: "Voluntourists' lack of self-awareness and perspective is seen as drifting into a toxic form of Instagrammable colonialism, often with more than a dash of well-meaning but ultimately damaging white saviourism." As Bansal says, voluntourism is incorrectly sold as an activity that will, "Change the volunteer's life and deeply impact the community they are visiting." They're playing God thinking they're going to solve a range of social issues in a foreign country during a two-week working holiday.

I meet Neville Bevis at Open Arms Orphanage. Open Arms isn't a traditional orphanage but rather a transition home. But a few adoptions have occurred from here. As instructed I ask Neville about Madonna. It turns out she'd been to Open Arms (sitting in the very seat I am in, gasp) and had met two youngsters who would have been more suited to adoption than the boy she did adopt as they had no family whatsoever, Neville tells me. Madonna will subsequently go on to adopt three more Malawian youngsters.

What is the motivation for going all the way to Africa to adopt a baby? Are there no orphans in the US? Is it because it is cool, trendy, or exotic? Is it because Africa's place in the world is something to be saved? If the 21st century is Africa's century to regain its dignity, as Yorick in Mozambique said, then that works two ways, for Africans, and for the West too.

Dominic Misomali has explained to me that non-Malawians who want to adopt in Malawi need to be resident for seven years. However, exceptions can be made. And with Madonna's influence and wealth, anything is possible, as it turns out.

Here at Open Arms, there are about 50 infants at any given time, most having lost one or both parents to HIV AIDS. I meet some of the young British volunteers, who after probably bonding with these infants will then disappear. I'm also invited to the lake with Neville, which is a pleasant interlude before producing my last story for this trip.

To offset my low-budget lodgings back in Blantyre, I enjoy coming to the four-star Mount Soche Hotel to drink some Malawi coffee in the quiet gardens. I usually pick up a local newspaper on my walkover. As I finish up, I briefly look through the last few pages with its advertising and tenders and I spot something interesting. UNICEF is about to distribute 1.1 million insecticide mosquito nets—nets used over beds for children and pregnant mothers living in malaria zones, to mitigate against being bitten by mosquitoes. Insecticide-treated nets, such as these, kill mosquitoes that land on them.

This sounds like a good story, and I immediately go to the hotel's office facilities and fire off an email proposal to Associated Press. I get a reply pretty soon with some requests, mostly to do with personalising the story. I'm asked to liaise with UNICEF as they are, "usually very media savvy." The AP medical writer also chimes in saying, "I am sure they will do whatever it takes to get the story done." It may be that the UNICEF New York office is efficient but that doesn't mean every UNICEF Communications officer in every country is efficient, or even helpful. My experience will prove to be not as AP described.

I get in touch with the local UNICEF Communications Officer, and after many emails, he agrees to let me join the mosquito net rollout event at the lakeshore. I explain to him that I need to also meet a recipient of a mosquito net and film at their home. "Okay," he says.

The day arrives and together with some Malawian journalists, I travel to the lakeshore in the UNICEF vehicle, a top-of-the-range V8 Toyota Landcruiser. Our UNICEF man laments that recently, "One of our vehicles killed a child pedestrian on these roads." Indeed there are many pedestrians on the roads in densely populated Southern Malawi. Strangely, the driver does not, therefore, take more care. Instead, we reach speeds of up to 170 kilometres per hour.

We arrive at the Lwanga Primary School in Mangochi where the mosquito net project is having its official opening. I check with my UNICEF contact one more time about finding a case study of a mosquito net recipient and dash around filming the event and getting interviews. There are speeches and there is drumming and dancing.

Africa carries a disproportionate share of the world's malaria cases and deaths—94% according to the WHO. "Malaria killed 409 000 people in 2019… most of them babies and toddlers in sub-Saharan Africa." In Malawi, 40% of all outpatient visits to hospitals are malaria cases. Some immunity gets built up if one lives in a malaria zone, but it takes ten years to build up this limited immunity—and thereafter people still get ill but it is not as severe. That is why children under five are most vulnerable. And pregnant mothers are also vulnerable, risking miscarriage, a premature born or stillborn child. These are the two groups being targeted by this UNICEF mosquito net roll out.

The event is drawing to a close, and I want to get my all-important case study now. I find my UNICEF contact.

"I'm sorry," he says, "But there isn't any time for that. We must return to Blantyre now."

"I just need 20 minutes with a pregnant mother and her young child."

"It's just not possible," he says.

But without the case study, my story falls flat. It simply won't work.

"I'm going to find a case study. I will meet you at your vehicle in half an hour," I tell him, before rushing off to find someone as quickly as possible.

The school helps me locate a young mother, and we walk to her home together. It feels like the clock is ticking, and thank goodness she lives nearby. I sit her down at the entrance to her simple mud hut and set up an interview. Asiyatu Amidu describes how debilitating malaria is: chills, fever and abdominal pains. She says she is grateful for the free mosquito net which she would otherwise not be able to afford.

I shoot a sequence with Asiyatu walking in with her child and sitting at the table, and also of her setting up her mosquito net in her bedroom. I have just shot the crux of the story in 20 minutes, and I dash back to the school for my lift back to Blantyre with UNICEF.

**

I have completed four Associated Press Horizons stories in three weeks which has been pretty intense. Back in the Johannesburg-Pretoria area, I set about arranging a Schengen visa for Europe, and West African visas, for my next travels.

I head over to the Moroccan Embassy in Pretoria. The office reeks of cheap aftershave. I approach the cubicle where the visa officer is shuffling through a pile of visa application forms.

I pass him my passport, and he starts to flip through. His demeanour changes. His head tilts to one side as if to say, "There is a problem."

I don't know what it is about my passport. Does he recognise my name from my Morocco documentary that aired in 2002, which I filmed on a tourist visa?

"What do you do?" He asks suspiciously.

Stupidly I say, "Film industry."

"So what do you do in Morocco?"

I explain that is just a holiday, but he is not convinced.

"I'm just transiting through Morocco to get down to West Africa."

After some back and forth, he looks me in the eye and says: "Sure you not going to work in Morocco?"

"Sure". I say, throwing my hands in the air, as I imagine a Moroccan might, "If I was going to work there I would get a work visa."

In between returning the next day to collect my visa, he calls again wanting me to bring more information—details of my Morocco contact person, my dates plus a ticket (which I don't produce), and a hotel I am staying at.

I return for the passport. He gets up and says, "Follow me."

We walk down a passage into the Embassy. Then we enter an office and sit. He starts questioning me.

"So you live next to the golf club?"

"Yes, above it," It's my father's address. I'm a nomad, after all.

"You been to Morocco before?"

"Yes, once in 2002."

"OK here is your passport with visa. But if you do something wrong, you will have the problem, not me."

"You have my word I am just going on holiday."

He throws his arms up in the air. I was right, Moroccans do throw their arms up in the air.

I say, "Thank you", and leave, feeling like I've just been unjustly interrogated.

The Burkina Faso Embassy makes up for the Moroccan experience. She is nice. Maybe my speaking French helps. But whatever the reason it only takes ten minutes, instead of a two-day service. I also get a Mauritanian visa. I am ready to ship out.

CHAPTER ELEVEN
Highway to Mauritania

I've got three stopovers in Europe before I cross over into Africa. In the UK I meet my Associated Press contacts in person, and I also meet with OBE TV, a Ghanaian-run Africa-themed TV station, but no business is to come of that, although it's great to spend time with the friendly Ghanaians for half an hour.

I got for a drink with a couple of Londoners I have met on my travels, and I am invited to a party but getting to the other end of London just seems too complicated and expensive so regretfully I don't make it.

Having lived in the UK from age 10 to 13 in some ways it feels like a homecoming. London feels dynamic and orderly. Clean and efficient.

I'm smoking a cigarette outside a pub and get talking to the bouncer. He says to me, "Careful where you throw out that cigarette. I chucked a cigarette out the window of my car. Then I pulled up at a garage. A man with a clipboard comes up to me and asks me to see him once I'm finished getting fuel. So, I go and see him, and he gives a fifty-pound fine for littering."

Is this the price to pay for safety and efficiency? On the tube, I read a newspaper. Across from me, someone is reading George Orwell's 1984. That seems fitting. In today's Daily Telegraph I read: "Children as young as eight have been recruited by councils to snoop on neighbours and report petty offences such as dropping litter… offered up to 500 pounds reward if they provide evidence of minor infractions."

Are these elements of control inevitable as political systems become more complex? Generally, in Africa, there is much more of a chaos factor, and when there is control it is somewhat cruder. Yet I have a taste of crudeness too, here. On my last day in London, walking through the crowds on Brick Lane, a man approaches me.

"Mate, give me 80p for a cup of coffee."
I kind of shake my head and keep walking.
"Come on mate, just 80p."
I turn and resolutely tell him, "I'm sorry, I can't help you."
"Mate, I don't usually beg. Just 80p for a cup of coffee."
I keep walking.
"Come on mate." He is relentless.
"Sorry, can't help."
His persistent implorations continue for another minute.

Finally, he turns nasty, shouting at me, "Fuck you and your mother."
I turn to glare at him but he's already gone. There's a fair amount of begging in South Africa but I've never been insulted.

After a detour up to Leeds, where my Shaw ancestors emigrated from circa 1849 to make a new life in South Africa, I head over to France to visit my sister. Near her house in Lyon, is the Lumiere Institute—the birthplace of cinema. The first film camera was invented here in 1895: the cinematographe, a camera/projector/film developer all in one. This is the origin of the word cinema.

Cinematographe number one is in the museum. This is the location of the first film ever made, in 1895: Workers Leave The Lumiere Factory (found on the aptly named Rue Le premier Film). The Lumiere Brothers sent out camera operators to different parts of the world to simply document life, which is quite telling of the late nineteenth-century era. These films are screened at the museum. For example, the French colonialist throwing crumbs of food to Indochina peasants who scamper about on the ground to pick them up, or the performing Africans on a London street looked on by bystanders as exotic curiosities.

Before hopping over to Africa, a stopover in Lisbon. After fifteen years of visits, travels and work in Mozambique, I am keen to see the former colonial power which has infused Mozambique with its influence. So I spend three days just soaking up the charming city's atmosphere. Certainly, money that came from the blood of the oppressed in their colonies abroad was spent on beautiful architecture. And the long Portuguese dictatorship of the twentieth century with its economic stagnation ensured the preservation of these lovely old buildings. Even the historic electric trams are still in operation.

My hotel room balcony overlooks the Praca da Figuira. In the twilight hour, skateboarders pull off stunts on the central square, while prostitutes saunter along the wide mosaic-tiled pavements pulling their tricks. A group of schoolchildren have been singing songs and drinking beers from the local bar for the last two hours. Middle Europe tourists gawk at their maps. A husband and wife have a screaming match at the entrance to the subway (or at least he screams at her). The taxis are constantly leaving and arriving at the rank. Here a driver gets out and slowly makes his way round to each of the other drivers, shakes a hand here, tells a joke there, pulls the one guy's cap down, a pretend punch to the ribs of the other driver... from up here on the fourth floor it all seems to be in slow motion.

The following day at dawn I get into one of the taxis on the Praca da Figuira and head to the airport. My flight takes me over to Casablanca, Morocco. My destination is the next country south, Mauritania, so I am in transit through Morocco. After a month in Europe arriving in Casablanca is like being thrown into the deep end of the pool.

The buildings are ramshackle, the driving seems chaotic, and the taxi driver, naturally has an angle. I tell him which hotel to take me to.
"That hotel is no good," he says.
"Yes? Why?"
"Very old. Not good."
This is where the taxi driver's angle comes into play.
"I know a good hotel. Good price."

Tired from a long day's travel I relent and end up in a tiny airless windowless room. And the taxi driver, no doubt, gets his cut from the hotel. I am back to travelling where you have to have all six senses on alert all the time.

This being Ramadan, finding food during the daytime is particularly difficult while travelling, so I soon learn to do as the locals do—eat plenty during the night, and nothing during the day.

It is possible to fly down to Dhakla but I don't fancy hanging around in Casablanca any longer, and the bus ride itself should be an adventure. The beauty of travelling like this is living simply. Every decision I make from what to eat or what bus to take brings me here to the present. I'm a free agent.

It's a 30-hour bus ride from Casablanca to Dhakla, a town in the disputed territory of Western Sahara. On the first evening, we stop at Agadir, a town I remember well from my Morocco travels of '02. The bus passengers join locals at a restaurant. As sunset approaches, tables fill up with food: harira soup, Arab bread, couscous, and more. Conversations become more animated until finally with the blast of a faraway horn known as the *zowaka*, everyone, including me, breaks the daytime fast. A dishevelled-looking man walks up to my table and gestures at my bread. Before I have time to indicate he can take it, he helps himself.

The next day we travel through the controversial territory of Western Sahara, which Morocco annexed following Spain's rapid withdrawal from its desert colony in 1975. Because of its contentious status, security is tight. There are numerous roadblocks where I, as the sole foreigner on the bus, have to go into a roadside hut and register my details in a log book, as well as answer questions. This is where I reinvent myself as a Professor of Sociology. Saying I'm a journalist here would complicate things. There's something to be said for reinventing oneself.

I spend the night in Dhakla. In the morning, while looking out the window at the goings on down below, I chat with a German, next to me.

"I brought a Mercedes 190D from Germany to sell here. People look at the car, but the price they offer, it's too little," he tells me. But I can't move my car further south from here. Customs problem. I must sell it here."

There has for a long time been a trade in second-hand cars from Europe down here. But over time this market has become more competitive and saturated.

I head over to the Morocco-Mauritania border in a Mercedes 190D shared taxi, and once through the Morocco formalities, we negotiate the badly rutted dirt road through no man's land. There are many wrecked and deserted cars on either side of the road, as well as the ubiquitous Mercedes 190D's being worked on by men in their flowing blue robes. Looking closer it seems that new number plates are being attached to the vehicles! It seems the German from Dhakla could have brought his car south by doing it the local way—changing the registration in a neutral zone.

The Mauritanian emigration official is standing outside his small hut. He pages through my passport until he reaches the Mauritanian visa I've been issued in Pretoria.

"This visa is no good," he declares. "It's a fake visa."
To be fair, the Embassy assistant in Pretoria who issued the visa made a mistake, scratched it out, and rewrote next to her error. Urgh!
"There's no problem with that visa, I got it from the Mauritanian Ambassador in Pretoria, South Africa. My voice is rising, and the French travellers standing next to me, watch with ever-widening eyes.
I pull out the Mauritanian Ambassador's business card. "Let's call the Ambassador," I say to him.
"I don't have airtime," he says.
I plead. Then I turn tough, telling him the Mauritanian Ambassador himself gave me the visa.
The French tourists look on wide-eyed as I argue with the man in the uniform.
Now what? I am literally in the middle of nowhere and stuck.
Then the official relents. He stamps my passport, and I can go on.

The journey continues in the shared Mercedes 190D taxi to the northern Mauritanian town of Nouadibhou. I see now that the 190D must surely be the national car of Mauritania—indeed this is where 190Ds come not to die, but to live on forever.

It is in such a car that I have my first unique Mauritanian experience. Only an hour into arriving in Nouadibhou, I take a private 190D taxi, whose driver, surprise surprise, doesn't know where any of the hotels are, so we take a long drive around asking for directions. As we turn one corner, a big 4 X 4 who must surely have seen us from a distance, proceeds to ram us in the side. The taxi driver gets out. He is not angry. Instead, he sheepishly approaches the driver of the other vehicle, and has a brief quiet conversation, as if this had been expected. The driver of the 4 X 4 and the passenger in the back remain impassively in their seats. A policeman and the taxi driver's boss arrive, and after a very brief discussion with the 4 X 4 driver, it seems the matter has been settled.

As we drive off I ask the driver, "Surely that guy saw us and drove purposefully into us?"

The driver points to his shoulders and says, "He's military, he can do what he wants."

Indeed, following a coup d'état two and a half months ago, this country is run by its military. In fact, the country has been under the control of the military for most of the post-independence years, and the recent democracy lasted only about a year. When I ask the taxi driver about the coup d'etat, he replies nonchalantly, "Yes we get them from time to time."

The last leg down to the capital city is, naturally, in a Mercedes 190D shared taxi, in which two passengers share the front seat, and there are four in the back seat. The passenger shoehorned in at my left in the front seat tries to get the radio to work, but to no avail. So he breaks into Islamic incantations for most of the way, through the intense heat of daytime Sahara, the road leading us through this vast expanse of nothingness, that is compelling for that exact reason—its raw simplicity. Or maybe it is just the adventure of it all that is so compelling. Between the enervating heat and the slow progress through the desert I struggle to keep my eyes open.

Then the taxi driver pulls off the road and stops next to a nondescript mud house. I drag myself out of the Mercedes, and enter the cool darkness, flopping down onto a carpet. In silence, a boy brings me tea. It is the ubiquitous mint tea of the region and it is loaded with sugar. I am revitalised.

Finally, Nouakchott, Mauritania's capital. When this country was colonised by the French it was known as *La Grande Vide* (the great void) because it is mostly Sahara desert. The French ruled from St Louis, south of the Senegal river, which is France's oldest settlement in Africa. St Louis became part of Senegal at independence, so a group of Mauritanian elders chose the location for the new Mauritanian capital in the late 1950s, which is Nouakchott. So it is a post-colonial capital city if you like. And a pretty nondescript city it is too.

But Nouakchott is replete with the textures, craziness and chaos factor that one finds in Africa, but not in Europe. Driving is a great example. It seems like anarchy on the roads. At the auberge I am staying I ask Mohamed, who is a Scotsman who has chosen to live in Mauritania, about the driving:

"It really seems to me that there can't possibly be a driving test, because there don't seem to be any rules."
"No, you simply buy your driver's licence," Mohamed says. It shows.

Day two in Nouakchott and I am involved in my second car accident. This one is comparatively minor—a traffic bump. The two drivers shout at each other for about ten seconds, then we drive off.

City public transport is in shared cars, mostly Mercedes 190Ds, that follow no particular route. The rather fluid system means the driver will go to each passenger's destination in the order that they climbed in. This means one should expect various detours before getting to where one needs to be.

Before I can start my Associated Press work in Mauritania, I head over to the South African Embassy.

I'm in a little private taxi. There's just been a brief downpour, leaving the streets largely flooded. The driver of this ageing Peugeot is a Ghanaian, so we switch from my halting French to English. He's been here for 15 years. As his run-down car slows to a spluttering halt and he pumps the accelerator trying to restart it, he tells me in exasperation about life in Nouakchott.

"Everything is imported. For example, all fresh food comes from Morocco. This is despite the natural resources and low population density."

The country has iron ore, as well as other commodities such as copper and gold, fisheries, and a population of three million. And because almost everything is imported living costs are expensive.

The car gets going again, but before long it starts spluttering. The driver keeps talking.

"I could write a book about these people," he says. "Trying to operate or own a business here as a foreigner is impossible." The car has crawled to a halt at a garage, but the attendants indicate there is no petrol. The driver tries to start, and revs, but the engine dies. "The first problem is racism. The second problem, is the Biden (moor) keep all business amongst each other."

"Why don't you go back to Ghana? Things are going well there," I say.
"Yes, that's what I'm working towards." A pause. "Home is home."

I imagine he always planned to return to Ghana as a rich man, and that he now has to face up to that not happening.

The car has started. He has managed to coax it alive with just the right combination of revving and clutch slipping, and off we go navigating our way around the dirty puddles of the Ghanaian taxi driver's city of broken dreams.

The South African Embassy is an office with two rooms in the Hotel Tfeila. I meet Ambassador Sam Kotane, with an introduction from my father, who in South Africa's 1990s transition period was a colleague of his. How does it feel to be welcomed by Kotane? Humbling.

Among the small staff is a Mauritanian, Mohamed Weddady, who works as the Embassy's communications officer. I inform the staff of my work plans in Mauritania, and Mohamed offers to help me through the media accreditation process. It's the first and only time a South African Embassy does something like this for me. After all, it is not within their ambit. Together we take a drive to the Ministry of Communications. And once there we go straight to the top.

"I was at university with the minister," says Mohamed.
Now that is a good contact!
We are ushered into the minister's office. Mohamed introduces us.
"I was Ambassador in South Africa," says the minister, who for some reason gets it into his head that I am "Rhodesian."
"You are from Rhodesia?"
"No, South African."
"Not originally from Rhodesia?"
"No, always South African." He turns away, looking unconvinced.

We then shuffle about from one office to the next, shadowed all the time by an unsmiling soldier, perhaps to remind us of who is in charge of this country.

When it comes to filling out the forms for the accreditation, it turns out there's a 500 Euro fee.
Okay, I think to myself, *tomorrow I go south to Senegal and sit on a beach*.
Mohammed asks, "Is there something wrong?'
"Unfortunately with the budget I work with I just can't afford to pay 500 Euros."
Together with Mohamed, we pay another visit to the minister, who with a

wink of an eye, makes the payment disappear.

Shortly afterwards I have a signed and stamped filming permit in my hand.

Leaving the ministry, Mohamed and I discuss making a documentary about African migrants taking boats from Mauritania across to the Spanish Canary Islands. This is a topic that has been well covered and I can kick myself much later when I realise a unique documentary was staring me in the face in the *auberge* I am staying at. Mohamed the Glaswegian, tells me his story over the weeks I stay there on and off, and yet I don't click that this is a great film—until later.

"I raised my son alone, back in Scotland. I kept telling him what I want to do is lead camel caravans through the Sahara. One day he snapped back at me, "do it then!" So I left everything at home, and this is my new life, here in the Sahara." Mohamed will go on to tell me anecdotes about the dangerous characters who are out there in the desert, and about survival in the Sahara.

Back to the present, and the Associated Press projects I have lined up. I may have a national film permit, but now I have to do the leg work of locating all the interview subjects and arranging the logistics for shooting the stories. And I am operating in French, which I don't speak well.

The first of the two stories is Mauritania's famous iron ore train. I make my way to the National Mine and Industry Company's office in Nouakchott, where I meet with the director, Mohamed El Moctar Ould Taleb. He tells me that at two and a half kilometres long, and 22,000 tons in weight, this is both the longest and heaviest train in the world. It transports iron ore from the mines located deep in the Sahara Desert at Zouaret, 700 kilometres to the port town of Nouadibhou, for export. There are six trains every day. That's a whole lot of iron ore.

I'm led from here to the workshops where I meet the engineers.

"Back in 1982 when we first started operation with these diesel-electric locomotives, sand worked its way into the engines and destroyed them." The engineers worked with General Motors in the US to develop additional filters to prevent sand from entering the engines. Locomotive engine cooling systems also had to be upgraded to suit the high temperatures of the Sahara. And sand ploughs, adapted from snow ploughs, have been attached to the front of the locomotives to push away any sand that has blown onto the railway tracks."

Before I can make my way back north, to experience the world's longest train for myself I need to set up my other story. In the days of the Sahara camel caravans, trade and ideas were transported around the Arab world. In this far-flung Western edge of that region, ancient libraries from this period still exist, famously at Timbuktu. One of the other Sahara library towns of the region is Chinguetti. My mission is to visit this town and see what condition these manuscripts, some older than 1000 years, on mathematics, science, astronomy, and literature are in.

I make my way in a shared taxi to the Mauritanian Institute of Scientific Research (IMRS) in Nouakchott, which is in charge of preserving the country's approximately 40,000 manuscripts. I am ushered into an office, and I explain who I am and what I would like to do. They ask to see my film permit, which is scrutinised. I am told that their organisation is not listed. This seems rather pedantic as "Chinguetti manuscripts" is clearly listed and the IMRS is the overarching government body responsible for this.

My diplomatic skills go down the toilet as I plead and persist, and persist some more until I am eventually shuffled out of their office.

I return the next day, having phoned a contact who has called a contact. This time I am sent to someone else with the promise of an interview.

With few resources at its disposal, IMRS admits that too little is being done to conserve the country's manuscripts. "So far we have catalogued 30% of the country's ancient manuscripts." These 3700 manuscripts make up the country's largest collection. One of the conservation methods they have utilised is putting plastic covers over the pages, which keeps human bacteria off thus slowing the deterioration. Many of the private owners simply don't want to hand over their family heritage. I'll meet some of these soon.

Being an Islamic Republic, Fridays in Mauritania are like Sundays in the Christian world. But I am now working seven days a week. In between arranging the two Associated Press stories, I am looking into two further potential stories on dolphin beachings, and customs of local fishermen. Neither of these comes to fruition due to production costs. I am also re-editing the three travel documentaries I have sold to Southern Africa Direct channel—working on my laptop in the *auberge*. It is with some relief that I head back north in another shared taxi to Nouadibhou once more to shoot my two Associated Press stories.

The highlight of taking the world's longest train is hanging out with the train driver and engineer up front, until the evening. They share endless glasses of mint tea. With temperatures exceeding 50 degrees here in mid-summer, the sugary beverage is a godsend.

Empty, the train trundles along at 60 kilometres per hour. The driver,

Selemtou Ould Mohammed Abderrahmane, tells me that one of the ways they deal with shifting dunes which move onto the railway tracks is to plant dead tree branches into the sand to stabilise them. Looking back through the diesel exhaust smoke and Sahara dust the train appears endless.

Later I transfer to a sleeper. The train's primary function is transporting iron ore. Passengers, and their comfort, are a secondary consideration. But at least I get to sit in a proper seat in a passenger wagon. Most passengers taking this cargo train have to make do with empty iron ore wagons going east, or sitting atop a pile of iron ore, heading west. That's roughing it.

The final destination is the edge-of-the-world feeling mining town of Zouerat. At the hotel canteen, I meet a French woman, clutching a carton of Camel lights and chain-smoking her precious cigarettes. She tells me she's an explosives saleswoman. My mining company escort arrives and takes me on a tour of the operations. Mauritania is Africa's second-biggest producer of iron ore after South Africa. Desert mountainsides are gouged out in the quest for the metal. I see the valuable resource loaded onto the train. From Nouadibhou the resource is shipped to China and elsewhere around the world.

Leaving Zouaret, I travel back to Choum by train. Here at two in the morning, I meet a Mauritanian student returning to Cuba from a home visit here in Choum. As well as getting to see pictures of his Cuban girlfriend, he goes out of his way to find me transport to take me on to Atar. These small acts of kindness, of hospitality, is what make travelling worthwhile, and sometimes when it's rough going, make it manageable. One hopefully then reciprocates when meeting foreigners in one's own country.

From Choum a dilapidated Landcruiser takes me to Atar from 2 am to 8 am through the Sahara along a piste. This is a surreal experience with a full moon lighting up the barren Sahara landscape. First light and sunrise are magic.

In Atar, I spend the night in an auberge. I must appear quite travel-weary because as I walk in the French owner takes one look at me and says, "It's always harder when you're alone."

The next day I travel east to Chinguetti. Established in the eighth century the Saharan town of stone buildings was once a thriving trade centre with a population of 20,000. Today only 1500 people live here and it seems the town is in danger of being engulfed by the constantly shifting Sahara desert. In its time Chinguetti was a centre of Islamic religious and scientific scholarship in West Africa. Pilgrims returned from the Middle East with manuscripts, and many were written by Mauritania's historians, scientists and poets.

The dry climate of the desert has been good for the preservation of the Chinguetti manuscripts. Much better than a humid climate, for example. But there have been other issues such as poor storage, rain damage, and termite damage.

With its palm trees and ramshackle stone buildings, the town has a distinctive look. Avoiding the drifting sand dunes, I search for the Habot family library. This is the most renowned of the town's 12 libraries. Indeed this is the best-organised library and houses the largest collection of manuscripts in Chinguetti. I track down Mohamed Koulame who first asks to see my media accreditation which he carefully peruses before we can proceed.

I enter the cool interior and Koulame opens a metal cupboard to pull out some of the ancient manuscripts. He tells me subjects range from mathematics, religion, and literature to astronomy. The oldest manuscript is an explanation of the Koran and dates back to the 11th century. I'm also shown a 15th-century manuscript indicating the moon's waxing and waning, and other phenomena such as lunar eclipses. Another manuscript I am shown is half eaten away by termites. The entrance fee and occasional outside funding are not enough to properly conserve these cultural treasures. And few visitors make it here. It is out of the way, and with Islamic extremism, many parts of the Sahara are not considered safe these days.

I also visit Saif Ahmed Mamoud of the Ahmed Mamoud family library. Mahmoud shows me a sixteenth-century Arabic grammar book while lamenting the costs of maintenance of a centuries-old building made of clay and stone, as well as the issue of termites.

Departing Chinguetti, heading back south in another shared taxi, we travel over a desert mountain pass into the Adrar range. The best comparison I can think of is the Orange River area in the South Namibia/Northern Cape province of South Africa. Once upon a time, the Sahara was a verdant region with giraffes, elephants and much more. All this changed very rapidly due to climate change about 8000 years ago. But this dry terrain still harbours life. It would be fascinating to investigate what lives in this barren landscape today. Aside from trees like the date palm and acacia, there are nocturnal reptiles, and animals like the addax antelope, the fox, and so much more.

Foreigners in Mauritania need to register at the military post at the entrance to every town and city. On some routes there are many. From Atar to Nouakchott there are over 15. On this particular hell ride, with a speeding driver in an overloaded vehicle, we once more come to a halt at a post. The soldier disappears with my passport to fill in his logbook. He returns to the car, passport in hand, which clearly says on the front: South Africa/*L'Afrique du Sud*, and he asks me, "Your nationality?"

And I'm like, "um, er, hmmmmmm... South African?"

Back in Nouakchott, I am finally getting close to finishing editing not only my two Associated Press stories but the three documentary re-edits for Southern Africa Direct. It's a challenge working in a basic room seven days a week in an auberge where everyone else is on holiday. But finally, the end is near and I can DHL off the tapes.

It is a late Friday afternoon and I take a breather. I leave the *auberge* to get something to eat. Being a Friday, most shops are closed. The light is getting softer, summer is turning to autumn, and the weather getting a bit milder. The city feels at peace, and I take a seat at the new Lebanese shawarma joint. My Guinean friend walks by and we talk about his dreams of going to Cabo Verde, "Where life is chilled, the beaches and the girls are beautiful." The owner of the Shawarma joint joins me and extols the beauty of his Moroccan homeland. And he tells me about the West African countries he has visited, and how, "Travelling is like a second school."

"Maybe it's like the first school," I reply.

I am also guilty of dreaming of somewhere else—I'm looking forward to when I finish up my work, cross south into Senegal and take some time off.

I pay up and stop off at the corner shop for a cold juice. Even this shopkeeper is friendly for a change.

What a peaceful afternoon. I hope the mood lingers. The next morning I stop off at DHL and then catch a *grande taxi* south to Rosso where I cross the Senegal river into my next country. And who would have believed that leaving Arab Africa and entering sub-Saharan Africa would be so clearly delineated as this river crossing? Well, that is exactly how it goes. On arriving on the southern flank of the river I am back in my region. I am welcomed by a young hustler who attaches himself to me:

"Mister, I'll show you."
"No thanks."

But he just stays with me no matter what I say. I enter the immigration building and while I am again telling this teenager *"Non!"* and getting exasperated, the immigration officer is watching. I hand the immigration officer my passport which he duly stamps, and then literally flings it back at me. That's the second time I've had my passport thrown at me. I exit the immigration building and keep walking, following the crowd. The teenager is still sticking to my side. Finally, I get to some waiting vehicles. When I refuse to give the teenager any money, he throws a tantrum and then sulks. I relent and give him a small amount.

I am seated in the third row of a Peugeot 504 station wagon, next to a woman in a soldier's uniform. She is forthright and wants to invite me to an event. Mohamed the Scotsman from Mauritania had warned me that women in Senegal can be "predatorial." I just didn't expect to be hit on by an Amazonian female soldier 15 minutes after arriving in the country.

Soon we get to Saint Louis, Senegal's historic French colonial town. I check out a couple of places to stay at and go for the cheapest. It also happens to have no other tourists. It is quiet. Too quiet. In the evenings I prop up a bar in town. The only friend I make turns out to be yet another hustler.

Eventually, I move out of Lonesome Street Hostel into the slightly more expensive *Auberge de Jeunesse*, where my life changes fairly radically. I join "the crew" comprising various European nationalities on beach trips, and bar trips and culminating in an all-nighter in a local nightclub. This is the holiday I need. Two weeks later I head down to Dakar and catch a flight back to South Africa.

Having produced some Associated Press stories in South Africa, I hit the road to Mozambique in my Nissan. North of Maputo, I am stopped by traffic cops. One approaches me at my window and another, armed with an AK47 stands unsmiling staring at me from the passenger window.

"What items are you transporting?"
"Everything I have has been noted and stamped on the manifesto."
I do my version of an unsmiling heavily armed traffic policeman as I give him the document to look at.
"What is inside there? I want to see," he says.
"It's all on the document."

I wonder if my talking at cross purposes helps me get out of these situations. I also wonder why it appears like I have entered a war zone. I haven't of course, just a crooked cops zone. Finally, I am waved through.

The next traffic cop to pull me over alleges that I was speeding. 68 km/h in a 60 km/h zone.

"That's not possible." There is no way I am relenting. And as much as he continues to insist I continue to put my foot down.
"Okay," he says, finally admitting defeat. "Give me a cold drink."
"I don't have a cold drink."
"I'm a traffic policeman!" He says to me in exasperation.

I tell him I have not broken the law, and I leave. Later I wonder if the large after-market tyres and wheels on my car possibly changed the gearing, and hence the speedometer reading! Maybe I was in the wrong after all!

Two days after leaving Maputo, I arrive at Envirotrade's project next to Gorongosa National Park. Envirotrade works in the carbon trading sphere.

The burning of fossil fuels as a result of vehicle, aeroplane, cargo ship and coal power are some of the major sources of carbon emissions into the atmosphere. Deforestation is also a major contributor to growing levels of carbon dioxide. This is because trees store carbon which gets released into the atmosphere when they are cut down. These ever-escalating levels of carbon emissions are what are leading to climate change. The earth is getting hotter, with more extreme weather conditions.

With carbon emissions credits, a country or polluter can pay for the right to emit carbon, and that money is sent to the developing world to conserve forests and plant new trees.

Critics say carbon trading doesn't do enough to address over-consumption in developed nations. In other words, rich countries get to maintain their levels of consumption, including carbon emissions.

On arrival, I meet Envirotrade Mozambique Country Manager Piet van Zyl, who is ex-South African military.

"I was in the SADF, and later I was a mercenary. I designed the buildings you see here in the same layout as our military base in South West Africa during the [Angola] border war."

After being shown my tent, I am then introduced to Gary. Gary's a former Zimbabwean forestry farmer, now working here after having lost everything to farm invasions over the nearby border in the eastern highlands of Zimbabwe. The first thing we do is set off on a long hike. Fortunately, I don't have a problem with long walks through the Southern Africa bush—quite the contrary.

Gary intimates that every newcomer to the Envirotrade project is sent on a long hike. It's a military initiation.

As we make our way through the bush, Gary says to me, "We used to take people on much longer hikes." Considering we've been walking for a half a day I wonder how long they used to walk for.
 We approach a village, and Gary turns to me and says, "Whatever you do, don't take off your shirt."
"Why is that?" I ask.
"In colonial times Portuguese men would often go about shirtless. And on entering a village, they would take a woman. That memory lives on."

We stop at a village bar and Gary orders a beer. And another. "Back in Zimbabwe I only ever drank on Saturday nights, and then it was just about six beers." Now beer is his lifeblood as I am to discover—and can see on his drinker's nose. "The other day I bought a crate of beers and invited a few of the guys from the village. They came over, quickly polished off the beers and left. Didn't even say thanks." Once a month Gary drives over the border to Mutare in his trusty Landcruiser to visit his wife who still lives in Zimbabwe.

We're still sitting at the village bar, and Gary has opened another beer. "We had a high-level delegation of Mozambican ministers visiting here. They were taken on a guided tour of the project. When they got to me, they asked, who are you? I said to them "Sou deslocado." That means I am a refugee, and all the government people immediately were very sympathetic." Mozambicans with their history of war know what it is to be a refugee.

My old Nissan has developed various mechanical problems including a shock absorber that has popped out of its socket, a rough running engine (as usual), and the starter motor has packed up. Fortunately, there is an on-site mechanic who sets to work on the vehicle.

At the project offices, I talk further with Piet. Because forestry projects are not yet included in the carbon trading scheme, participating companies do so voluntarily. Companies like the Man Group and Creative Artists Agency Foundation in Hollywood have bought carbon credits to offset their carbon footprint or for corporate social responsibility reasons. The project has also had EU funding and the University of Edinburgh scientific support.

This, one of three Envirotrade projects in Mozambique, covers an area of effectively 30,000 hectares. In the six years leading up to my visit, a claimed 230,000 trees have been planted here, and farmers are paid for taking care of the trees. One of the agroforestry strategies utilised is inter-cropping, meaning tree saplings such as the *faiderherbia abida* (white acacia) are planted between rows of food crops. Falling leaves create a natural compost for the crops.

This is a preferable alternative to the typical slash-and-burn agriculture, which entails clearing a forest, burning the undergrowth, and planting crops until the soil is exhausted three years later. And then moving on to clearing the next forest. According to the World Bank, although 43% of Mozambique has forest cover, 0.79% of it is lost annually. And 65% of that forest loss is caused by slash-and-burn agriculture.

Forestry has great potential to combat climate change because trees absorb and store carbon dioxide. Although difficult to quantify, Envirotrade says the carbon credits sold up to 2008 are equivalent to 150,000 tons of carbon dioxide, or 1.26 million dollars.

If it all sounds so great, why am I being treated with suspicion? Gary for example told me he had to give feedback to Piet on what he thought of me. Well, dig a little deeper to find some issues. A recent Sunday Times article states that the carbon sequestration claims are exaggerated, not to mention that the EU has just suspended its final funding payment of their total €1,587,000 project funding due to poor reporting, and unsubstantiated claims about carbon emissions offsets.

In the evenings, I have dinner with Piet and his traditional Afrikaans family. "Gary doesn't eat with us anymore," I am told. Then I retire to my tent for the night, and to be honest I don't remember being bitten quite so much in my life. Rich biodiversity is a beautiful thing, but this is what it means up close to it: I have welts, itchy bites, scratchy rashes, and lately a swollen foot. And in the summer the heat and humidity are enervating.

I am shooting not only for Associated Press but also a separate story for a South African environmental TV programme called 50/50. This entails constantly changing tapes and shooting formats and keeping my head about me as I juggle between the two separate stories.

While I am on-site, the company's Chief Executive Officer arrives. Charles Hall is an ex-US diplomat. "I took early retirement. What's the point of eventually becoming an Ambassador that no one in the Embassy really likes." Later, while scrolling through Envirotrade's website I notice how a community member is featured on the opening page, standing in a field, shirtless. I send Charles an email asking if it wouldn't be more dignified to have these community members dressed in clothes. I do not receive a reply.

Piet arranges for me to be shown around other aspects of the project. Farmer Chitambe Joao Jorge tells me that he used to live in a thatched hut, but that he used the money he was given for planting trees to build a house with a corrugated iron roof. He now considers himself a medium-sized farmer with many fruit trees that he can bequeath to his children.

Piet tells me, "We're helping improve food production, the road network has improved, and we've built a school." I am taken to the communities that have benefited from Envitortrade's largesse. Indeed two new schools have been built in the Nhambita area. He also mentions challenges such as alcoholism in the communities, and efforts to address this. But where does one draw the line with social upliftment? Is it not the Mozambican government's responsibility to develop these sectors and assist communities? It's hard to reconcile foreign capitalists with a developing country's domestic governance.

The last evening is the highlight of my visit. I am taken on a bike ride with the three Afrikaans farm girls on their two Chinese motorbikes. The last of the day's sunlight is flickering between the green foliage, one of the girls has an eye for me, and one of these days I'll be too old for girls to have an eye for me. It's exhilarating being taken on this little *alfresco* journey through the bush and it ranks up there with the three Italian girls who invited me to their home to make me spaghetti al pesto in Calabria, Italy, many years ago.

How did the Envirotrade project pan out? Well, three years later, in 2012, the Mozambique Bulletin reported that "Tree planting is too expensive and the idea of advance carbon sales has failed." According to REDD Monitor, an online portal that "explores the contradictions and controversy behind the harebrained scheme to allow continued greenhouse gas emissions from burning fossil fuels by offsetting these emissions against "avoided deforestation" in the Global South," stated that not enough carbon credits had been sold to make the project viable, local farmers were not being paid, and that the project has failed.

The fundamental flaw in the carbon credit concept is that the world's richest countries get to keep polluting the planet, which is precisely what needs to be brought to a halt. Green New Deals in the US, the EU, China and elsewhere in the industrialised world make more sense as they now attempt to reduce carbon emissions at their source—from those regions emitting by far the most carbon dioxide.

With my newly repaired Nissan, I head north. Soon the engine is running roughly again, and I stop off in Nampula at the Nissan garage where they clean out my carburettor. I receive the compliment I get at every petrol station, "Strong car." Yes, and thirsty, and unreliable. Nampula is in my experience not a safe little town, and once again I fall victim to criminality here. Returning to my car in the town centre I see the back window has been bust open. I can't find anything missing. I head over to Pemba to produce my next story on a conservation project grappling with illegal logging.

According to the Food and Agricultural Organisation (FAO), 420 million hectares of forest were lost globally between 1990 and 2020—the size of India and Egypt combined. Clearing forests for agriculture is the main cause of deforestation globally, according to the FAO, and Mozambique is no exception as I just saw down at the Gorongosa Envirotrade project. But commercial logging is a further key driver of deforestation, and Mozambique is again no exception.

A 2006 report entitled "Chinese Takeaway" funded by Christian Aid, NOVIB and HIVOS explores the illegal logging of hardwoods in Mozambique's Zambezia province, destined for China. "Asian timber buyers, local business people and members of the Government of Mozambique and their forest services are colluding to strip precious tropical hardwoods from these slow-growing, semi-arid and dry tropical forests at a rate that could see the resource exhausted in 5-10 years."

Dominik Beissel is a German who was exploring Southern Africa's wilderness areas in the 1990s. He came across the Mareja area in 1997, "When after very slowly making my way through quite thick forest, I hit something hard." Getting out to take a look he realised his vehicle had hit an overgrown building, which turned out to once have belonged to a German aristocrat.

Dominik stayed on to create a 35,000-hectare conservation area. He has restored the farmhouse he drove into, and offers accommodation in separate buildings. It's a community-managed conservation project where visitors can go on guided walks with the local Makua people.

In the early morning, we head out for a hike, climbing one of the inselbergs that so characterise northern Mozambique. As far as the eye can see it is dense miombo forest, with early morning wisps of mist hanging over the treetops. However, looks are deceptive. There is plenty of illegal logging taking place under that green canopy.

Dominik explains to me that working through local loggers, Chinese operators arrive from time to time to load up timber onto their trucks. This is even though Mareja falls within the Quirimbas National Park, a protected area. Having an international port nearby makes the area particularly attractive for illegal logging.

Dominik and the community rangers have already stopped these activities several times. Walking through the forest with community ranger Juma Anibal, Dominik points out a tree stump where he and his team saw some action. "An amazing time Juma and I had here where we captured a whole group of loggers in their logging truck with a load of logs. We made a battle plan because it was going to be two of us against sixty people very keen on getting their product out of the forest. Juma is a man of unusual courage so I thought with this guy we can probably manage to hold them off until we radio for help. We made little fires, we pretended to be many: Juma was walking with his hat to the front, then he was walking with his hat to the back, and then he took his hat off. The Chinaman who was in his truck kept saying, "I don't know anything…" That's the only thing we could get out of him. It got pretty hairy, and then our rangers arrived." The timber, which filled two trucks was confiscated. Despite these rare victories, logging continues in many different parts of the park.

In his Nissan Patrol, Dominik and I continue our *bundu-bashing* (off-road through the bush) tour of Mareja. We stop and take a walk to a river where we sit under a beautiful large old riparian tree. I am again shooting two separate stories, one for Associated Press and one for 50/50, so I am constantly changing tapes and shooting formats, and staying abreast of two separate but similar stories.

Miombo forests hold about 150 types of trees, and where any one specific species is logged the entire forest structure is weakened. Beisel says a recent study produced in conjunction with the IUCN indicates that 60% of this forest, "Has insufficient regeneration to sustain itself." When trees are logged, grass and other combustible material fill the gap. Thereafter fires become much more damaging than they would otherwise have been—for the entire forest.

In the car with Dominik, the occasional branch knocks against the vehicle. A couple of colourful spiders fall on my lap. I brush them off very quickly. This is what rich biodiversity means close up. But it is sad to think these forests and the life they house are disappearing. And when they're gone, it's forever. And this is not just about the loss of wilderness, and climate change. Several studies have linked deforestation and monoculture plantations (such as the palm oil plantations in Asia that replace indigenous forests) with outbreaks of epidemics. Much of the biodiversity is lost but generalists such as rats and mosquitoes flourish and spread pathogens to humans. Natural disease regulation is lost. If climate change and the loss of wilderness areas don't bother you, what is your opinion on pandemics? Are we as humans engineering our demise? After all, we're not aliens dropped onto the earth, but an integral part of the ecosystem and if that system is out of balance, nature will find a way to re-balance it.

Back in the town of Pemba, I also interview Jose Dias dos Santos Mohamede, Chief Park Warden of the Quirimbas National Park, within which Mareja falls. Jose explains that there was a bust recently at Pemba harbour. Containers full of logs destined for China were confiscated. "Some game scouts from the Department of Agriculture who were involved were suspended." And, he says, six park wardens were recently dismissed for taking bribes from timber operators. Jose seems friendly and willing to talk, and rather than having the large belly of one who is "eating much" he is thin as a rake. With corruption so rampant it is hard to know who to trust and who is simply saying whatever sounds good to a journalist. In an All Africa article written by Mozambique expert Joseph Hanlon on the untimely death of Jose in 2020, he wrote, "Dr Dias was one of the few national directors who was not corrupt and was able to make a difference even under the existing corrupt systems." Rest in peace Jose.

There have been dramatic developments since my travels to the northern Mozambique region in the 1990s and 2000s. A violent Islamic insurgency started in 2017 and has caused much death, instability and a humanitarian crisis. It is worth noting that the discovery firstly of ruby precious stones, and then vast amounts of offshore gas coincided with the violent uprising. Once it became clear that the wealth was not for the benefit of the general population, extreme elements started taking action. The paradox of Africa is although being a continent of great natural wealth, it is the poorest continent in the world. And the countries with the highest concentration of natural wealth, for example DR Congo, Sudan, Chad, Nigeria are amongst the poorest and most unstable. This is sometimes referred to as the "resource curse." To manage natural wealth well, one needs strong governance, and post-colonial Africa, with some exceptions, still needs to attain that. Africa needs strong institutions, and that is the primary challenge for the continent.

According to Mozambique expert Joseph Hanlon, "The result [in Mozambique] is a failing, resource-curse state with increasing poverty and inequality, but with profits and jobs for foreign companies and money for key people in government and Frelimo [the ruling party]."

As of 2022, Mareja, where I spent eight days with Dominik Beissel in 2009, is closed following a "devastating robbery," and Dominik is in Europe with his family. Does he rue the fateful day that he drove into the ruins of a big old house that had once been a European settler home, and decided to stay? He did much work to create a community conservation project, fighting not only illegal loggers but also poachers. And now that old colonial house is being reclaimed once more by the forest.

I have one more story to knock off before leaving the region. It's a short hop over to Ibo island on a small plane and the smallest airport I have ever landed at: a field with a ten-square-metre building serving as the airport. Here I meet Rebecca Marques, a Brit who is Tourism Officer for Querimbas National Park. She acts as a guide and interlocuter as I set about a quick shoot of an "alternative tourism" story.

Homestays on historic Ibo island are an opportunity for those tourists wanting to get some insight into the local culture. Instead of staying at a regular hotel, you get to stay with a local family, interact with them, and eat with them. I stay with Mariamo Amisse, one of three homestay options on the island. I watch, and film, Mariano as she makes bread using coconuts. It's really enjoyable, and when I hike the Indian Himalayas the following year I choose the homestays there too.

Ibo was one of my "Swahili Islands" that I travelled to and filmed just three years earlier, so I already know some of the island's history: as a slave entrepot and Portuguese colonial commercial centre. Historian Joao Baptista tells me the island's decline set in when the Portuguese authorities moved the regional capital from here to Pemba in the 1920s. Hence the ghost town feel of the place. Joao is old enough to have been an adult during the colonial period. Not only that but he was one of the very few "assimilados" (assimilated) in the country, and had a civil service job.

To become an assimilado, a Mozambican had to satisfy several criteria, such as fluency in Portuguese and taking on a Western lifestyle. Considering that a minuscule number of Mozambicans attained assimilado status and that their civil rights were never on par with Portuguese citizens (many of whom were illiterate), it can be argued the assimilado category was nothing more than a publicity stunt by the

Portuguese government. "Look world, we're progressive colonisers!" Obviously, that is a contradiction in terms. There is nothing progressive about imperialism.

Joao is nonchalant about having been an *assimilado* and of the Portuguese as colonisers.
"What was it like, working with the Portuguese?"
"They treated me well. I never had any problems."

Leaving Pemba I head back west to sketchy Nampula. This time I stay at a safe motel called Complexo Nasa, a little way out of town. But I do go into the town centre for coffee and cake while keeping a beady eye on my vehicle, parked at the same spot it was broken into two weeks before. I make sure the rag-tag motley collection of "informal car guards" know I mean business when I leave the car. Then when I return I give the leper, who by virtue of having no hands is the only person in Nampula unable to break into my car, five meticals.

The following day it's a 12-and-a-half-hour drive west over the border into Malawi. The only traffic cop halt on my route through Mozambique is a brief and friendly stop. Yet the guy selling third-party vehicle insurance on the Malawi side of the border seems intoxicated and is trying to overcharge me. Talk about turning things on their head, considering I always talk about Malawi as benign in comparison to Mozambique.

Installed in a musty, dingy dark room at Doogles Backpackers Lodge in Blantyre, Malawi, I set to work editing while Saint Patrick's Day festivities can be heard from the bar. As usual, I am hard at work in a place full of holidaymakers.

I've got a couple of AP stories lined up in Malawi, and I am keeping an eye open for more.

Recently, in Cape Town, I produced a story on recycling. It was an eye-opener in many ways, including visiting one of the last remaining landfill sites near the city that still has space for rubbish. Before visiting the landfill sites, I hadn't given much thought to where the waste we generate—what we throw into a bin—goes. Landfills are massive holes in the ground where human rubbish is dumped. That's right, it has to go somewhere! As activist Mary Murphy points out, nature knows no waste, and only humans have developed this concept. In Cape Town, only 14% of waste was recycled in 2007 when I produced that story. Little has changed since then. Mary's motto is to reduce, recycle, and reuse, and she says 80% of what we throw out can be recycled.

I had also seen how on the Cape Flats, the sandy area outside Cape Town and home to some of the poorest inhabitants of the city, composting organic waste allows some of these communities to grow their vegetables in the otherwise very poor quality sandy soil. Turning waste material into a valuable commodity—compost—is both efficient and brilliant.

Mia Nesbitt is a Glaswegian fashion designer based in Malawi. She has created a unique fashion style that is also environmentally friendly. She recycles second-hand clothes into designs that also utilise traditional African cloth.

In throwaway Western societies, huge amounts of clothing are chucked out, often after brief usage. Many of these end up on landfill sites. Some second-hand clothes are donated to charities in the developed world, and end up for sale in developing countries like Malawi. Critics say this trade undermines the development of the local clothing sector in the developing world. It is also something of a strange business where Westerners' donations end up for sale elsewhere. "These donated clothes should be given for free to people in the poorest countries," says Mia.

Reuse and recycle should be the catchphrases for all societies, but particularly the West which generates the most waste. Mia's fashion line aims to get people thinking about the throwaway society we now live in.

Baulking at the US$100 fee, I don't have a national filming permit, so when I go with Mia to Blantyre's Mbayani market to film her picking out the second-hand clothes, I use my little palmcorder rather than my Canon A1 professional video camera, to keep a low profile. Mia picks out items from the piles of trousers, bras, shirts and various other cast-off western clothes. She then buys some colourful African cloth. Back at her studio, she cuts out pieces of material according to her designs, creating an amalgam of "traditional textiles interspersed with rough and ready street styles." The designs are sewn together at a local tailor, back at the market. "Each of my designs is unique," says Mia. Finally, a fashion show is held at Doogles Lodge, with models showing off Mia's fashions.

My TV news feature works well because the visuals tell the story, and the text merely supports it. I wouldn't want to compare my news inserts with the work of Alfred Hitchcock, but it is interesting to note that he made his start as a filmmaker during the silent film era, and he remained grounded in that tradition of visual storytelling throughout his career, well beyond the advent of the "talkies" in the late 1920s. It is said that all his films can be understood without understanding the dialogue. This is the fundamental aspect of filmmaking—to tell a visual story.

As for the future of second-hand and recycled clothes, closed-loop production is the goal with clothing, and indeed all production. The same materials being used over and over at an industrial level sounds idealistic, but it is not impossible and is more and more entering the mainstream discourse.

When we as humans see our place in the world as an intrinsic part of nature, and not as superior and technologically advanced, then maybe we'll respect the environment enough to ensure its, and our own, survival. But in more simple terms, recycling is simply about efficiency.

At this stage, I have had enough of staying at Doogles, with its constant flow of backpackers, its noisy bar, and my dingy room. Taking into account my small budget, I seek out a quieter hotel. Wanela Family Lodge is a short distance on the dusty bumpy suburban backroads of Blantyre from Doogles. It is a low-budget hotel whose walls are smeared with dirt, but it is quiet and cheap.

Fortunately, I soon hit the road out of the city, and head over to the lake. I am about to shoot a story on an elephant translocation. Surprisingly, for a relatively densely populated country that has little wildlife left, Malawi has a herd of about 60 free-roaming elephants in the Phirilongwe area. Less surprisingly, human-elephant conflict is a problem. For example, elephants raid people's crops and people retaliate with snares, bullets and arrows. "Some elephants have had their trunks amputated by snares set by local villagers, while others are suffering from wounds caused by bullets, arrows and nail-embedded planks as well as poisoning," says IFAW (the International Fund for Animal Welfare) who are involved in moving these elephants away. According to the Department of National Parks and Wildlife, 14 people have been killed in this elephant-human conflict.

Now IFAW, with the Malawi government, is translocating these free-roaming elephants into a game reserve in the south of the country. And not just any game reserve, but Majete, which is probably the only functional protected reserve in the country.

Via one of my Malawi contacts, it is suggested I speak to a local businessman and politician. I meet up with Ismail Khan who is trying to stop the elephant translocation. He wants an existing forest reserve at Phirilongwe to be fenced so that the elephants can remain locally, where they are a "tourist attraction." Khan has started legal proceedings to stop the elephants from being taken away. "There has been no consultation with local communities, and there is no environmental or wildlife assessment."

In the evening I meet the IFAW team. I am greeted with a general air of suspicion. Why? Any animal translocation is somewhat controversial by nature. No matter how much it is couched as being in the best interests of the animals, the truth of course is these translocations are in the best interests of people. The elephants are being moved elsewhere so that people can live peacefully. The following is a description of how a group of 60 elephants are moved 300 kilometres away.

In the morning together with a handful of other journalists, we have made our way to a meeting spot in the bush. A red helicopter is the centrepiece of this rendezvous. The helicopter pilot is non-other than Barney who I went up with over Mount Mulanje a couple of years before. There is a call for a journalist to join in the helicopter. I raise my arm and step forward before anyone else. The helicopter rises off the ground. We are hovering only about 50 metres from the ground and the pilot is manoeuvring backwards. This makes me nervous because there are treetops around us. Sure enough, the rear rotor hits a tree top. Bang! The whole helicopter drops but then the pilot regains control. This is not a good start.

The helicopter is then used to locate, and herd the elephants towards the waiting trucks and ground crew. This can't be much fun as an elephant, to be harassed like this. Then, using a rifle, the veterinary doctor fires tranquilisers down into the elephants. The pilot continues his elephant herding. One by one the elephants fall to the ground. The helicopter lands near the prostrate elephants. I alight and walk through what looks like a killing field. Elephants are lying on the ground left right and centre. Their breathing sounds like V8 engines. The ground team is moving the elephant trunks to ensure that they can breathe freely. Cows and their calves are numbered to ensure they match up at the end destination. With their legs tied together, the elephants are lifted, upside down, onto trucks. Tranquillised, in metal containers, in the heat of the day, they are transported on trucks for eight hours to the south of the country. Eventually, as they awaken, the steel door opens, and they can stagger out to a new and unknown place. How would you like to experience this in the name of "human welfare?"

Ismail Khan who had started legal proceedings to stop the elephant translocation has now mysteriously halted the legal action. According to an Open Democracy article, "Those who were campaigning against the transportation and seeking the injunction were intimidated with threats of violence and death." Why not invest in fencing the existing Phirilongwe Forest Reserve so that the elephants could remain in their area? Indeed such an upgrade had been discussed for several years, including an EU study and possible World Bank funding. This is where everything gets murky, and any further understanding of this elephant translocation is difficult to reach conclusively. What is for sure is that earth is the human's domain, and in its quest for development, in its money-centredness, and its population expansion, it is human welfare that comes first, not animal welfare.

***

When I lived in Malawi's capital city Lilongwe as a child, my family would go up to Kasungu National Park on weekends to enjoy the bush and wildlife. Since the 1980s the situation with Malawi's national parks and its wildlife deteriorated to the extent that these conservation areas became known as "paper parks." That is parks on paper only. This happened due to a lack of resources and funding, and rampant poaching.

I drive back down to Majete Game Reserve, where the Phirilongwe elephants have been translocated to, to produce a story on this reserve's renaissance. Suffering a similar fate to Kasungu and the country's other wildlife reserves and parks, Majete lost all its elephant, sable, zebra and many other species to uncontrolled poaching in the 1980s and 1990s. Six years before my visit, in 2003, African Parks, a private parks management institution based in South Africa, started their work to turn around Majete's fate. Now electric fencing encircles the entire 700 square kilometre park, over 2000 wild animals have been reintroduced, poaching has been brought to a halt, and the wildlife is thriving for the first time in decades.

I ask assistant parks and wildlife officer Harvey Mtete how the turnaround has been achieved.

"Resources. In the past, the reserve was heavily under-resourced. You can't achieve anything in that situation. We were on the verge of total collapse in 2003."

I have some wonderful wildlife encounters at Majete. Driving around the park, I get video footage from my driver's seat, including a rare daylight sighting of a hippo that scuttles right past the front of my car. They seem rather innocuous, like cows, but are one of the most deadly of Africa's wildlife. As a child one of my school friends was killed by a hippo at the lake—bitten in half.

But I most enjoy the elephant encounters. Noticing some elephants just ten metres away I stop and turn off the engine. I slowly point my camera and shoot. As I do so one of the elephants walks closer and closer. Finally, her face is just a metre from mine. She is looking right at me. And I am trying to remain calm. This is a wild animal after all. Finally, she moves off.

That night, I awaken to rustling sounds. I get out my bed and walk to the tent's opening. In the moonlight I see two elephants eating right outside my window. I could practically lean out and touch them. A tent seems rather flimsy in those moments.

Finally, on the last day at Majete, I join a walking safari. We get to within 50 metres of a herd of elephants. It's thrilling but a year later I am told by contacts in Malawi that a person was killed during one of these walking safaris, and these activities were then halted. In the course of my research, I also read about a safari vehicle being overturned by an elephant at Majete. There is anecdotal evidence that the translocated elephants are aggressive, after all these intelligent and sentient creatures experience trauma and have memory.

Meanwhile, African Parks is continuously expanding its footprint, revitalising reserves and parks around Africa. This entails restocking parks depleted by poaching and improving infrastructure. In 2017 150 elephants were translocated from Majete's burgeoning population up to Nkhotakota in central Malawi, now also experiencing a rebirth thanks to African Parks. Another forced emigration for these elephants.

Back in Blantyre I am lodging in the dank and musty rooms at Doogles. Having finished my Majete story, I go for some beers at the bar, and get talking to an Afrikaans guy, who is disgusted that a Malawian man is chatting up the European girls! Shock and horror! Inter-racial socialising! The power of apartheid ideology lives on for some.

I take a friend, Gudula, to a Frenchman's house, as she is looking to buy a car. This fellow who is from Corsica ("Oh no, I am not a Parisian", he says, making the distinction clear) tells an amusing anecdote.

"I met some Afrikaners. And I asked them about South Africa and being African. They looked at me quite shocked. We're not Africans! We're Afrikaners!" That reply is so loaded with meaning but most of all it is just ironic, because of course Afrikaner means African, in Afrikaans. To be fair, there are all different kinds of Afrikaners, including progressives.

Meanwhile, Gudula, who is German but is following the maxim when in Rome do as the Romans, starts breastfeeding right there. The Frenchman's eyes nearly pop put his face.

The next two stories I am covering are a highlight of my travels and experiences. They will also result in a shift of gear in my career. It's also a case of being in the right place at the right time. Ecologist Dr Julian Bayliss is someone I know socially in Malawi, and he has recently made a pretty big scientific discovery. While looking at google earth Julian came across unknown dark patches in adjacent Northern Mozambique. Zooming in he realised what these dark patches are: large unchartered mountaintop forests. There was little scientific work conducted by the Portuguese colonialists, and then the long war hampered any such scientific work post-independence. Many expeditions—all the first of their kind—to these mountain forests will ensue following Julian's google earth discoveries, and I am fortunate to go along on two of the earliest of these trips.

Mount Mabu's massive 7880-hectare rainforest is the gem of these mountain forests—this has now become known as the largest rainforest in Southern Africa. Remarkably, it was discovered on google earth in the 21st century. To get there, I join a convoy of vehicles that depart in the early morning from Mulanje town in Malawi. Over the border in Mozambique, we negotiate some pretty bad secondary roads, until we are forced to a halt at a heavily damaged bridge over the Lugera river. Soon villagers arrive. Some negotiations take place and they start carting rocks onto the bridge, effecting a repair. An hour later we make it across and head to our first night's stay, camping at an abandoned and asset-stripped Portuguese tea estate home.

There is a small group of journalists. In the evening we ask each other general knowledge questions. BBC journalist Jonah Fisher is good. Jonah makes a point of wearing normal clothes: smart trousers and a clean shirt, even though we are hiking up a mountain. He reckons people who get dressed up in khakis look daft. I take his point.

Before we can proceed up the mountain, we partake in a local ritual. A man slowly pours flour and then a bottle of beer at the base of a tree. Meanwhile, in his indigenous language, Chinyanja, he asks the spirits to allow us to go up to the mountain and back without any harm befalling us. "Please welcome them," he says.

It's a long hike up with porters carrying all our food, equipment and camping gear for a week. We set up camp in an idyllic clearing amongst the giant trees. Julian is brimming with enthusiasm at the untouched state of the forest. He suggests I go out with Steve Collins, a lepidopterist who is the director of the African Butterfly Research Unit in Kenya. I traipse along with Steve who is carrying his net and finally get to some net traps he has already set. "How extraordinary!" he says as he approaches one of these traps. He has spotted a new butterfly species.

"Butterflies are a good indicator of biodiversity." That means finding five new species here is a positive sign for the state of biodiversity. "It's great fun when you're going out to this kind of area and finding new butterflies," says Steve. "It's very special for us to find a piece of a forest as big as this. In the mountains of Eastern Africa these days, due to population pressure most of them are under severe threat. Here you have a magnificent piece of forest that is really pristine... We have to find a way to find some conservation strategies with the government to make sure this is saved."

Botanists, herpetologists and other scientists are also making discoveries every day. I ask Julian about this. "Mountain areas are like islands. But instead of being surrounded by the sea, they're surrounded by the lowland African plains." The lowland forests disappeared about 10,000 years ago due to climate change, and the mountain forests became separated from each other. Since then unique species have evolved in these isolated mountain forests.

In the evenings I join herpetologist Bill Branch. "There are many pygmy chameleons around the camp area. They're only found in the mountains in this type of forest. Not in the savannas between the mountains." During the day Bill sets up traps by making a long barrier that reptiles and amphibians walk along until falling into a bucket. Bill also turns over logs in his wildlife quest. Several new species are discovered at Mabu, most significantly a new forest viper. Bill Branch passed away in 2018. May he rest in peace.

In total ten new species of plants, mammals, butterflies and reptiles are discovered at Mabu.

Just as it all seems like we have stepped into a garden of Eden, we face a reality check. The magic spell of the idyllic forest is broken by an encounter with some hunters. The forest, though pristine is not unspoilt, as hunters do visit. Julian questions them and discovers that they trap bushbuck, blue monkeys, rock hares, rock rabbits, and klipspringer. But it seems the level of hunting is low because the population density around Mabu is low. "The greatest threat in the future for this forest will be logging if it is not protected," says Julian.

A week later we are back in Malawi. Soon I join one of the subsequent expeditions, this time to Mount Inago. It's always good to get back to Mozambique. There's just something about this place. At least partly it is the wilderness and open spaces, which Zambia also has. Sadly, these days parts of Northern Mozambique are unsafe due to extremist Islamic violence.

We leave our vehicles in the town of Malema once all the permissions to go up the mountain have been finalised. Don't try going up these mountains without permission. I've heard of foreigners being arrested. Then 15 people and 30 porters trek up to the plateau in the heat of the day. We set up camp next to a patch of riverine forest, and that river will be where I have my chilly and rejuvenating wash at the end of each day's long mountaintop hike with different scientists.

Speaking of scientists, Lincoln Fishpool is a bird specialist, Bill Branch is a herpetologist, meanwhile, most butterfly collectors are men, and primate specialists tend to be women. Is that all clear?

Julian tells me, "We're the first scientists to Inago. We know this because there are no biological records. And that generally holds true for all the Mozambique montane areas."

Finding new species in these forests can be a case of stretching out your hand and seeing where it lands. That's what happened to Julian when he came to Inago on a preliminary scoping trip the year before. "I was crossing a tributary to this main river and it was covered in algae and moss. I slipped and fell on my back, and as I put my hand down I put it on some water weeds, and underneath that was a freshwater crab. I collected it, and it has turned out to be a new species. So based on that accidental discovery I am collecting some more now which I'll send down to Professor Savel Daniels at Stellenbosch University in South Africa." Savel will go on to identify four new crab species from Inago. All the river crabs collected at each of the mountain forests Julian visits are new to science. Amongst the many other new species found are bats. At night, Julian collects bats in a net strung out across a river and sends them down to Professor Peter Taylor in South Africa. Four new species are declared.

In the evening over a cup of tea at the campsite, Lepidopterist Colin Congdon tells me that he is finding new butterfly species every day. Colin bemoans, "Where I come from this is usually beer time."
"Me too!" I reply.

In his mid-seventies, Colin says "I had sixteen years of marriage, and even that is a pretty good accomplishment... oh well, hope springs eternal in the loins!"

But while scientists are making discoveries on Inago, the situation is very different to Mabu. Inago has felt the impact of human encroachment and the forests here are disappearing to make way for agriculture.

On a long hike with Julian, we come across a blue monkey that has been caught in a gin trap (known as a bear trap in the north). It consists of two metal sides with sharp teeth that snap shut if triggered. The trapped blue monkey, next to a maize field, is frantic. His hand is caught in the trap. It is difficult to try to help it, as the monkey is aggressive and dangerous. In fact, it is very hard to open one of these traps at the best of times. For locals, monkeys are a source of food. But traps are cruel—animals can stay there for days in agony, waiting for the hunter to return, often dying a slow painful death. "As it happens our guide is a hunter and probably a friend of the person who set the gin trap. So we are not able to release the monkey and the hunter kills it. It's a very difficult situation and not at all nice to witness," says Julian looking downcast as I interview him on camera.

On another day I go out with Ornithologist Lincoln Fishpool. "What little forest remains seems to be disappearing quickly. This expedition is something of a requiem for the forest birds and other fauna and flora that live within it. My feelings are mixed because I hope I don't find something too special because how would we protect what we found?" Lincoln talks to me while he measures an East Coast Akalat that he caught in a mistnet—a net set up to capture live specimens. This is one of two globally threatened bird species Lincoln finds here.

Despite human encroachment several more new species are found including a new butterfly and a pygmy chameleon.

If a significant aspect of making these discoveries is that these areas need to be conserved, then the expeditions have been a failure. I do interview the Mozambican government on plans to conserve these mountain forests, and they talk about the importance of doing so. But several years later, in 2021, by which time Julian has led scientific expeditions to about twenty of the Northern Mozambique forests, all replete with new species, nothing has been done. As he points out in a Mongabay interview, "The forests only have the protection of traditional district authorities with limited enforcement abilities and not the government of Mozambique. Basically, there is no one there to stop [deforestation]."

In Blantyre, I fetch a friend's brother from the airport. On the road back to town, I start saying:
"Malawi is Africa for beginners," because it is one of the easier African countries. But no sooner have I finished my sentence than a convoy of military Landcruisers appears on the road, hooting, armed soldiers waving other traffic off the road. I move over to the dirt next to the road. Okay, well, everything is relative.

***

Five months after leaving South Africa, I drive back to Cape Town. While producing the two Associated Press news features on Mount Inago and Mabu, I also worked at the same time on something bigger, by shooting extra footage, because I know this is worthy of a larger project. I try with 50/50, a nature and conservation programme in South Africa, without success. Then I approach Carte Blanche, which is South Africa's leading investigative television programme, in the vein of 60 minutes. A contact there passes on a DVD to their Executive Producer and I get a response showing interest but, "Please cut down your 30-minute documentary to 10 minutes." I spend the Christmas holidays at the Transkei coast working on that edit, to be in time for when Carte Blanche reopens in early January. That includes working on Christmas Day and New Year's Day. I send my ten-minute cut by courier on a DVD at the start of January, as this is before internet speeds become fast enough for uploading and downloading video. I receive an email saying they want the insert and please deliver within a few days.

Producing for Carte Blanche is a good step forwards, although the editing process is not without stress. I approach the editor who helped me for free back in 1999 with my first documentary. It seems only right to go to him now that I have a budget. A word of advice—use an editor or cameraman who is already experienced in the format or programme you are working in. I have already done most of the editing when I take my project for post production. We mainly just "assemble" it, and record the voice over. Unfortunately, we are working to a deadline, and his computer freezes. It takes ages to get it working again, and then we still have to output to DVCAM tape. Meanwhile, the courier guy is standing around tapping his feet, waiting for said tape. Finally, we get it sent off, and Carte Blanche complains that the audio levels are all out. These inserts need a professional final mix, which is where the audio is cleaned, levels balanced, and music added. Carte Blanche do what they can to fix it, and the story is broadcast. Despite a bumpy start, I am in with Carte Blanche, and I set about looking for more stories for them.

CHAPTER THIRTEEN
My year of living dangerously

Antananarivo, Madagascar's capital city, reminds me at first glance of Addis Ababa: cool climate, ramshackle buildings, similarly sing-song-sounding language, hills, and even ancient taxis whose doors sometimes open when the drivers take corners. On my first evening, I meet for dinner with Erik Patel, who will feature prominently in my TV production about illegal logging in Madagascar. I don't have a film permit, which costs 2000 Euros and can take months to arrange. A member of the anti-rosewood logging network had advised me not to come without this permit, but Erik had said, "It's okay, we'll take precautions."

So here I am, feeling slightly nervous about working here as a journalist without accreditation. Rosewood logging is a sensitive matter not only because it is illegal but also because government officials have been implicated. A peace corps volunteer was evacuated from Madagascar after threats to his life following filming the rosewood logging. A TV journalist based here recently left the country after receiving death threats because he had filmed rosewood logging—the friend who stayed on his house was shot dead, with two bullets to the heart. Erik himself has experienced all kinds of threats, but he is a sanguine character. Later, I will come to a different conclusion about working in Madagascar on such a story without a permit—that indeed perhaps keeping an ultra-low profile is the best way to go. But that revelation will come later in 2010, my year of living dangerously.

Madagascar is renowned as being replete with unique species. That is because as an island, fauna and flora evolved separately from the African mainland. Human impact has unfortunately been heavy. Until about 2000 years ago, Madagascar was an Eden without people. Then the human immigrants arrived from Asia and the African mainland. Elephant birds, giant lemurs, dwarf hippos and many other species were quickly hunted out. Almost all of Madagascar's different types of forests have been destroyed. A few protected areas hold some of the last tracts of unspoilt rainforest. Or at least that is how it should be. The reality is that since the coup d'état of early 2009, a year before my visit, foreign aid has been frozen. Timber barons, with links to politicians, are selectively cutting down valuable rosewood in national parks, and exporting it to China. The rosewood is Madagascar's cash cow.

A short flight takes me up to Sambava, a town in the north-east. I walk off the airfield to the little airport and wait at the carousel for my luggage. And wait. And wait. After some time I am informed that "The plane was too full, so those items will arrive on tomorrow's flight." I take a taxi with a driver who has been sent by the anti-rosewood logging network, a somewhat androgynous fellow. "Air Mada no good!" he (she-he?) says when I tell him what happened. In the evening, wearing the same clothes, but thankfully after beer number one, I watch the passing parade of Malagasy. It is hard to believe that the country is in such turmoil. Following the coup d'état, apparently, the state coffers will run dry in three months. There is even a risk of flights to South Africa (that's me, folks) being banned as a result of the military takeover. And yet here in Sambava life seems to go on. It's often like this. Seems worse from far away.

My first port of call is the anti-rosewood logging network. I am taken, with our special taxi driver, to the house of one of the most active members. I am surprised to see it has been built from rosewood timber. That seems ironic. Nevertheless, this network documents illegal logging activities and disburses the information as far and wide as it can. "So far we have managed to stop all four international shipping companies from exporting rosewood from Madagascar," the activist tells me.

I ask him about some of how they gather information about the rosewood logging activities. He gives me an example. "I go to the internet cafe and work at a computer." Sooner or later one of the logging mafia guys arrives. "I stay there until he leaves. Then I move to his computer. There I open word, and click recent documents." And that is how he finds detailed information about their logistics, and plans, including shipping the timber.

"The loggers and collectors are dangerous. Be careful. If they're on to you, they could shoot you. That is in the forests. Or if they are on to you in a city like Antananarivo, they could send a decoy to occupy you, then break into your hotel room, and destroy your tapes and laptop. I think you should courier your tapes back to South Africa as soon as you have your footage."

That evening, wearing fresh clothes from my baggage that has caught up to me, I watch a stereotypical scene in the hotel restaurant. An elderly Frenchman is dining with a young Malagasy woman. They sit in awkward silence. He cleans his glasses. She scratches her ear. A brief stilted conversation. Could this be love? No, it is sex tourism.

After a fortuitously pleasant short two-hour drive in a private vehicle, I make it to Andapa the next day. Andapa is next to Marojejy National Park, where I will soon be shooting.

I meet another contact here, Eric Mathieu who is amongst other things, a guide. It is pouring down in buckets when I visit Eric at his house which is behind the car parts business he owns. Eric is another expat character who enjoys the simpler way of life in rural Madagascar. He is married to a

Malagasy and has a daughter but with the political situation being as it is, he is considering taking his family elsewhere. He points out the "Frogs in New Zealand" website he is checking out, a guide for French people emigrating to New Zealand. In the three racks of bookshelves behind him are many gemstones, a woollen hat, and a model of "la quatrelle"—the Renault 4, or Madagascar's national car. On the wall are political icons like Nelson Mandela and Mahatma Ghandi, and musical icons like Jimmy Hendrix and Janice Joplin.

Eric fills me in on logging, conservation, politics and deforestation.

Concerning my safety, he waves his hand and says, "Don't worry, This is not Central Africa!"

That's when I spot the Dalai lama and Buddhist doctrine on the wall.

Hoping that I have imbued a bit of Eric's Buddhistic approach, I head over to Marojejy National Park.

I meet scientist Erik Patel at the park entrance and together we start the long hike up to his camp, leaving behind the rice paddies and entering the rainforest zone. For some reason unknown to me, perhaps to do with taking a Buddhistic approach, I don't pay for my park entrance. Maybe in the back of my mind, I think that because I am with Erik, who is a long-term scientist in the park, I don't need to. Well, the following day, just after packing my camera gear away under the bed, who should appear but the park director. He opens my simple little canvas-walled chalet door unsmiling, without a word, looking around carefully and then asking why I didn't pay the park entrance fee. He has walked half a day just to check out who the suspicious character is. And I am indeed a suspicious character, filming without authorisation! Erik calms down the director and I promise to pay my fees when I exit. That was a close call.

Marojejy National Park is one of the last rainforests in good condition left in Madagascar and is located in dramatic mountainous terrain. The region has very high levels of biodiversity, including eleven lemur species. Erik is studying the critically endangered silky sifaka, a rare white lemur. It is one of the world's 25 most endangered primates. Of course, the threats to the last silky sifakas are a worry to someone who has dedicated his life to studying their behaviour. Aside from hunting for bushmeat, here at Marojejy, the rosewood trees are being cut down in the habitat of the silky sifaka, thus threatening their already precarious existence. Erik has taken an active role in working against rosewood logging, at great risk to himself.

I join Erik and his colleague Desire Rabiry on a mission through the rainforest in search of the elusive silky sifakas. This is not a pleasant jaunt along paths. This is cross-country *bundu-bashing* (walking with no paths) through dense mountainous rainforest terrain. It's tough going, muddy and wet. It is all worthwhile when we spot lemurs. Being accustomed to the scientists allows us to get quite close to the silky sifakas, and I get some good shots. I even have time to have a look myself, away from my monitor and have the real experience!

On another hike with Erik and Desire we search for signs of rosewood logging. A few hours in, we come across paths that have been made by loggers. We follow a trail and it leads us to a makeshift shelter, used recently by rosewood loggers. Near the huts, we find a clearing, with some rosewood tree stumps in the middle. Many more trees have also been cut down in the area so that the loggers have space to work, multiplying the damage to the forest. I shoot some interviews with Desire despite the cacophony of forest sounds and get some visuals of the destruction.

Within two days I have most of the footage I need, so for the remaining time, I can explore the park further and get some "beauty shots." I'm keen to get to the highest point, so I hike up, tagging along with a Spanish tour group. The highest peak is at 2132 metres above sea level. The final ascent is the highlight. Waking up in simple huts in the pre-dawn, then making our way through the mist, suddenly exiting the rainforest zone to enter the Afro-alpine zone, the sun burning through and the mist clearing up finally as we make it to the peak, the rarefied atmosphere at the top in that montane scrub, the grasslands like clouds above the earth, distant jagged mountain peaks, the rainforest down below.

On the last night at the camp, I walk into the open-sided eating/kitchen area and exclaim "No rain! What's wrong?!" Some laughter. Then Erik suggests a night walk. We go out with torches to search for nocturnal creatures. The most amazing find is a leaf-tailed gecko that looks rather like a small dinosaur. After a while, I leave the group and sit on a rock next to the river, which is coincidentally known as "foreigner on the rocks," and just enjoy the moment. A two-thirds full moon, many stars, perfect temperature, gurgling river and the mountain's silhouette.

The next day I walk down the mountain together with Erik and Desire, holding some interesting philosophical discussions on the way down. I spot three snakes during my hike and wonder what this could mean, as snakes symbolise metamorphosis. At a more prosaic level, coming from mainland Africa, it's pretty interesting to note that Madagascar has no dangerous animals. The same goes for snakes. There are many species but none are poisonous.

I have a lot of great footage, including Erik and Desire working on educating children at schools surrounding the park. What is missing is shots of rosewood loggers and the transport of this timber. Back in Sambava, I meet an anti-rosewood logging network contact, who will put me in touch with Augustin Sarovy.

An official parks guide and a musician with three albums to his name, Augustin also runs his own NGO. His mission is environmental education, and he does so by carrying out concerts and spreading environmental consciousness. He also documents the illegal rosewood logging, sometimes taking along journalists, and disseminates the information to the anti-rosewood logging network.

Augustin has a genuinely sunny disposition. Indeed Augustin neither looks like nor acts like a Malagasy, who can be a bit surly compared to mainland Africans. He is liked by all—except the timber mafia (and his wife who left him because he put all his energy into his activism). He can only eat at certain restaurants as the risk of being poisoned by the timber mafia is too high.

As well as being my guide, I think Augustin will make a great protagonist for a documentary, and I shoot a short clip to try to sell the idea to Al Jazeera Witness. I've been sending them ideas over the last couple of years, but I think this is a strong one. The catch is, what happens to Augustin after he is shown on television criticising the loggers and the government? My contacts tell me he would simply have to leave the country as it would no longer be safe for him to stay in Madagascar. So would a budget need to be set aside for him to be able to leave the country? These are hurdles to jump later.

Walking through the streets of Maroanstra where I meet Augustin, he says to me:

"Slow down! You need to behave and look like a tourist, and tourists are never in a hurry!"

So we trudge slowly through the streets strategising our trip. Augustin is a certified guide, so on the face of it, I am simply a tourist visiting the natural beauty sites of Madagascar. We travel by pirogue to a nearby conservation area where I film a short clip of Augustin explaining the rosewood situation, and playing his guitar. I also get some shots of rosewood logs and a waiting boat, but my attempt to shoot loggers loading rosewood with my camera under my rainjacket fails. It is simply not safe to film these characters openly.

Then, the big adventure. We leave the end-of-the-world feeling town of Maroanstetra and travel all day down the coast to Ranta Bay, each of us on the back of a small Chinese 125cc motorbike on some of the most atrocious roads you can imagine. But what an experience, with some absolutely lovely scenery between wave-pounded, palm-fringed, boulder-strewn beaches on the left and thick rainforest on the right. This mode of transport is all I can afford with my budget, but it doesn't hurt to appear as much as possible like a low-budget backpacker, a hippy in search of adventure (which is of course what I am) when covering delicate stories like this. In the evening Augustin and I eat at a small local restaurant: rice, with water which the rice was cooked in to drink. They love their rice in Madagascar.

Just then tragedy strikes. At our basic little hotel, Augustin receives a phone call. His mother has just passed away. He must return to his home village, and being Madagascar, the funeral is likely to last four days. This is frustrating as Augustin has become a character in my production, so I will need to rethink the storyline. But there's no point getting too upset. After all, Augustin's mother died of high blood pressure. So, try and stay calm, Neil.

Augustin sets about finding me a local guide so that I can still go on my rosewood mission. Unfortunately compared to Augustin the guy has zero charisma, and seems rather indifferent and rude, for some reason. Augustin and I say our goodbyes, and I set off with the new guide on a long arduous mission in search of rosewood activity. The trails are steep, the humidity is high and the guide is unfriendly. I am also stressing about my story and that it is not coming together. That night we stay in a little village in the hills above Rantabe. I sleep on the wooden floor of a basic wooden hut on stilts. I get a real sense of the poverty in these parts the next morning. Turning my head as we head further inland, I see two villagers scurry over to my empty tin of tuna and scrape what little remains inside. Desperate.

We continue the hike, crossing rivers on pirogues, walking up steep paths, sometimes wading in the deep river instead of a path, and slowly getting closer to the Makira forests. By now, I am starting to wonder if I have missed the rosewood activity. The area has been very busy recently but perhaps there has been a slowdown in the logging.

When it comes to rosewood as a product, it's the villagers who do the grunt work, and they get paid a pittance for it. In difficult economic times, in a poor country, they are easy to recruit. We do what we can to survive and have a plate of food. These villagers get paid about 2 US$ per day to illegally cut down the trees and float them downriver, or drag these heavy logs to the coastal towns. Middlemen buy from these guys and a handful of dollar multimillionaires export the timber to China. The trade is supposed to be illegal, yet the government, desperate for revenue collects taxes on rosewood export.

Not quite in the Makira forests yet, we suddenly come across what I am searching for. Villagers haul rosewood logs up a steep hilly path. My guide talks to them, and they say they are okay with being filmed. I get some good footage of the rosewood transportation and even interview one of the loggers who bemoans how little they are paid for their hard labour. Trying to film this rosewood at the coast or with the middlemen and export traders would be disastrous for a journalist. Possibly deadly. But today, fortunately, these villagers didn't care either way. Now for the long haul back to civilisation.

Returning to Rantabe, I insist on stopping at a local clinic so that someone can have a look at an ankle wound that appears to be infected. With all the precision and empathy of a brick, the male nurse scrapes the wound clean. The pus out, the wound open, he puts on a purple ointment. And as with pretty much every other African hospital and clinic experience I have had, I am put on a course of antibiotics. But thank God there was a hospital in the middle of nowhere. The following day, after negotiating a payment, I get a lift up to Maroansetra on the back of the Rantabe mayor's motorbike. This is a step up as it is an XL125, which has the right suspension for these terrible roads. It's also convenient to be waived through the police checkpoints. If the mayor only knew my true mission... after all you can't be sure which official is in cahoots with the loggers around here.

Back in Maroansetra I reinstall myself back at the Coco Beach Hotel (no coco and no beach), enjoy the luxury of a bed, and a cheese omelette with coffee for breakfast. The simple pleasures.

The road is long but the end is near. Back in Antananarivo, I meet up with Erik Patel.

"So did it ever seem like you were being followed?"
"Not that I noticed."
"Well, it's really only here in Antananarivo that you could expect problems."

Great, thanks, that's reassuring.

That evening I gobble down my delicious and expensive steak with mashed potatoes, to get back to my hotel room and keep an eye on my precious tapes. Just before leaving the north-east, I was warned by someone in the anti-rosewood logging network about beautiful Malagasy women seducing me in bars, while my room would be searched and tapes destroyed.

In the morning my nerves are not in good shape. The hotel wifi is not working so I go out to a nearby internet cafe. Slightly paranoid after Erik's warning, I keep a lookout for suspicious characters. A guy is sitting on the other side of the road. I stop to take a look at him. He looks down at his cell phone. Am I being watched?

I finish up at the internet cafe and head out to the WWF office, with my gear and my tapes. The interview with the country director is the final piece of the puzzle of my TV production. The interview with Niall goes well, and he predicts that if things go on as they are, Madagascar will end up like Haiti, devoid of forest and biodiversity.

In that upbeat tone, I explain to Niall my next step is to get the tapes couriered to South Africa, and he helps arrange a courier pick up immediately from their office. TNT arrive, and off go my tapes and notebook. I can relax because my precious cargo is safe en route to South Africa.

The following day I go to Ivato airport for my flight back to South Africa. I pass pretty easily through immigration and customs, where the official, taking note of my Malagasy hat, says:

"You look like John Wayne."

The first friendly jocular Madagascan—as people are in mainland Africa.

"Except I don't have my guns."
He laughs heartily.
"Maybe next time you will have your guns."
"Oh no, I'm not allowed that!"
He laughs heartily once again.

I am high in the sky, safely out of Madagascar. It is probably safe to say I kept a low enough profile to have stayed off the radar of the government.

Soon after getting into Cape Town, I am struck with a mysterious malady. I edit the Madagascar insert, doing most of the work myself while staying in a dodgy apartment room which reeks of a stale restaurant in central Cape Town. I also manage to get my audio fixed by an expert. My audio equipment is below par at this stage, but the expert manages to improve the quality. Hearing the croaking temporary voice-over recording that I have sent as the first edit to Carte Blanche, Managing Editor Jessica Pitchford asks, "Did you pick up a lurgy?" I sure did. I have aches and pains and have no strength.

In retrospect, the mystery illness could simply have been a result of a stressful month. It will take a month before I have my health back. Developments back in Madagascar are firstly that Al Jazeera expresses strong interest in a documentary about Augustin. But then their investigative thread People and Power run a Madagascar documentary exposé, that touches on the logging issue. My story being too similar means Al Jazeera are no longer interested. Then I receive more dramatic news. Augustin, after receiving death threats has fled Madagascar, and is in Europe. He is still there today.

***

I receive good feedback from my Madagascar insert, one of the Carte Blanche staff comparing it to the Last Chance To See BBC series on highly endangered wildlife. What story should I do next? Sipping a coffee at the Daily Deli in Tamboerskloof, Cape Town, while reading a newspaper (remember those?) I come across a two-page spread on the South African government's plans to build new nuclear power stations. And about the opposition to these plans by environmentalists. It's the first time I have thought about nuclear power and don't have an opinion about it. That will change in due course.

Having just wasted eight billion Rands (about one billion dollars) of tax payer's money on pebble bed nuclear technology, the government has decided to scupper this project as it is unproven technology. Yet more wastage of tax-payers money. Instead, the government is planning to build three new nuclear power stations using proven technology. The waxing and waning of new nuclear build plans is described to me years later by anti-nuclear activist Peter Becker as possibly an opportunity for the consultants to make money irrespective of any actual nuclear build. That and kickbacks, or potential kickbacks.

The story is commissioned, and the shoot goes well. My crew and I travel the country visiting the three potential sites, and talking to local communities and activists, as well those in the nuclear industry. There are many reasons to be concerned about nuclear power. If something were to go wrong, no matter how small the chance is, it is a big disaster. We know that from Three Mile Island, Chernobyl and Fukushima. There is no solution for nuclear waste, which has been accumulating globally for decades. The proposed sites for the nuclear plants in South Africa are biodiverse zones. Local communities and businesses are opposed to these kinds of developments.

Once again I work alone on the edit, and I try to be as balanced as possible. I send in my "cuts" to Carte Blanche, but they are not happy with them. I am almost literally pulling out my hair trying to think of how to make the editing work, in my little rented flatlet in Tamboerskloof. This goes on for months until I disappear off Carte Blanche's radar. Eventually, I arrange a meeting with George Mazarakis in Johannesburg. For the first time, I get the low down on the Carte Blanche formula: two case studies, with experts woven in between them. "You need to develop an argument, and take a position," he tells me. "You need a progressive narrative structure." When I tell George I have been editing myself, he says: "What?! You need to get an editor." I find the foremost Carte Blanche Editor in Cape Town, Dan Clayton, and he helps me rebuild the story, which then finally gets finished, months later.

***

Then, Earth Touch, a wildlife television production company in Durban get in touch with me. "We watched your Madagascar Carte Blanche insert, and we'd like to fly you up to Durban to discuss a similar project." So, off I go to Durban, where I meet the people at Earth Touch. The company is going through a consolidation process, and the owner's accountant is currently running the show. They are planning a blue chip feature-length documentary on the plight of the silky sifakas lemurs at Marojejy National Park, and the impact rosewood logging is having on their habitat. This is a production with money and a crew including a Director of Photography. My role would be to find rosewood loggers and shoot their activities. Naturally, I agree.

At Marojejy camp, the Earth Touch crew of three, together with me and Erik Patel plan the silky sifaka shoot. I won't stay long, as I will go on a mission to various places to get rosewood logging footage. We are lucky to spot a fossa one evening lurking under the main wooden kitchen/eating area. This feline-looking carnivore is the only predator in Madagascar.

I also stay long enough to witness a prototypical White South African scene. The South Africans, needing to get their clothes washed, simply approach a member of the camp staff, and tell them to wash their clothes. Erik hears about this and is furious. "You cannot expect anyone to wash your clothes for you." Anyone with black skin is obviously a worker to do your labour. I remember a friend telling me about some South Africans who on setting off on a holiday to the coast during the apartheid era, grabbed the nearest black man, and he became their labourer for the next few weeks. That is nothing less than slave labour. Is it any surprise there is anger bubbling under the surface of the "rainbow nation"?

Travelling with guide Desire Rabary we find the container ship The Kiara moored near the town of Ampanafena. We believe it has rosewood on it, and manage to get some shots from a quiet area after driving around looking for the right spot. Near the harbour, in town, is a large stockpile of rosewood. Desire finds an acquaintance and asks him to stand near the timber. We tell the acquaintance we want to take a photo of him. He complies. He seems bemused. But it gives me a chance to get some shots of the timber stockpile. In the evening I transfer footage over to a hard drive and also take a look. It is risky working with a video camera one is not familiar with. Most professional camera people will refuse to do so. I would now. But not then. The Sony EX3 I am using has a design fault. The monitor's screen knobs are easily adjusted accidentally. This is what happens to me, and as a result, what had seemed like correctly exposed shots are over-exposed. I re-shoot some, but I know the editor can most probably work with the shots.

From Maroanstetra I retrace my steps down that idyllic tropical coastline to get back to the Makira area and hopefully get some rosewood logging footage. The difference is this time, with a bigger budget, we travel in a 4X4 vehicle, which certainly handles the terrible roads better than little Chinese road motorbikes. We also have the 2000 Euro national film permit, so I feel fairly confident about our mission. From Rantabe, together with guide Armand, we begin the long hike inland. Two nights later we are camping on the edge of the Makira forests. The day starts early once more. There's not a breath of wind. Smoke from a fire inside a hut filters ever so slowly through the thatch roof and floats up into the still air. It is sunrise in a Makira village. Blue skies hold the promise of another beautiful day. The chickens peck on the ground around me, the village scavengers. The first light of the day casts a soft warm glow on the forested hills.

We set off into the trees. Armand has been in contact with his network, and after many hours of trudging, we come across a logging scene. It is tricky to shoot. The forest is very built up, so it is hard to get a wide enough shot of their activities. But I do what I can and get the classic tree-falls-down-having-been-chopped shot. Now for the long haul back to the coast.

At Rantabe, the guide, driver and I eat lunch at a local joint. Rice, naturally. A man in a uniform gets up and as he walks past, he gives me a big smile. But it is not a friendly smile. I don't think too much of it at the time, but it is a red flag. An omen.

Our entourage hits the road back up to Maroansetra. The Toyota Hilux double cab diesel slowly negotiates the terrible road, the driver constantly shifting from low-range to high-range four-wheel drive, the boss' son doing his best to delay the journey so that we will have to pay for another day. It seems interminable. But finally the mud, then dusty tracks make way for tarmac. It is now evening and we are approaching Maroansetra town. I ask to be dropped off at the pedestrian bridge from where I can walk to the

Coco Beach Hotel, where I stayed a few months before. The guide, Armand, seems slightly reluctant, but unable to say why explicitly. Just then another vehicle pulls in front of us, blocking our way. Our driver seems confused and frozen. The driver of the other vehicle barks some orders. I catch the word *vazha*, the foreigner. I get back into the Toyota when told we must follow this policeman to the police station.

"What's going on?" I ask Armand.
"I don't know. Let's go to the police station to find out."

When we get there they make a point of getting the driver to bring the vehicle into the police compound. Inside the Commissariat's office are three other men, all dressed in civilian clothes. I'm told these are senior ministry of environment and forests, and police officials. News has gotten out that a foreigner is filming rosewood in the town of Anandravola. They tell me that to do that one needs special permission. I show them my national permit. They indicate that means nothing to them.

At first, the local police chief is fairly friendly and tells me I'll sign a letter stating I'll delete the images of the rosewood, and then go and do it. I almost smile with relief. But then the good cop-bad cop routine gets started. The men in plain clothes start screaming at me.

"You'll delete all your video here, now."
Then on cue, the police chief dials it down, saying, "okay, okay, it's okay," and gesturing with both hands in a calming way.
Then the "bad cops" start their tirade, shouting at me in Malagasy and French, their words echoing off the bare cement walls.

At this stage, I wonder what will become of me. Perhaps they'll lock me up and throw away the key? The good cop-bad cop routine goes on for a while. Then a young guy arrives. He is the village IT specialist and is here to check I delete the images. I start deleting, but only a handful. Then I am told to wait. Sometime later in the night, they return with a document stating it is not legal to film any hardwood in Madagascar! I sign it. I am told to hand over my passport, and I leave in the early hours of the morning with Armand to a small cheap local hotel. Armand deems this hotel safe (assuming even he is trustworthy), and indeed, the owner knew about the police preparing to arrest us, and had tried to phone Armand during our drive there, but Armand's battery had gone flat!

I don't get much sleep, as is usually the case when my passport has been confiscated by corrupt officials in a country with an illegitimate government. In the morning I call the South African Embassy. They seem to think that complying with the police would be best.

At five pm, I go back to the police station with Armand. I am ushered into the police chief's office, who, being the "good cop" that he is, somewhat farcically says, "Excuse the mess!" It seems they are satisfied that I deleted the images, and I am given my passport back. Armand says the alarm was raised by the mayor of Anandrivola, who is implicated in the illegal logging. But it's a moot point. Unlike my first trip where I kept a low profile travelling like a backpacker, this time we made a splash by being part of a team in a 4 X 4 vehicle. And the national filming permit wasn't worth the paper it was printed on. Although I saved most of the footage, I lost the key chopping down the rosewood tree footage. Looking back I wonder why I didn't just try and get similar footage elsewhere, in another forest. Maybe it was decided with the Earth Touch team that *le jeu est terminé* (the game is up)? I just don't recall.

Back in Durban at the Earth Touch offices, I wait expectantly for a debriefing. An opportunity to discuss what happened. The clock ticks and there is no meeting. How strange, I think. Perhaps they had just written off the whole incident and were making some other arrangement to get the requisite footage. Is it maybe because the accountant now running the company is still new, and not a film person? Or is it an Anglo thing where confrontation is avoided? Good leadership means taking responsibility. But I take part of the blame for not having spoken up and said let's discuss what happened. Hopefully, I learn a lesson there—to always be proactive.

In Madagascar, the political crisis ends in 2013. Unfortunately, rosewood logging continues unabated despite various attempts to curtail the logging and confiscate the timber. Almost all of the rosewood ends up as *hongmu* furniture in China. Of course, it's a finite resource which is being depleted. So the outcome is obvious.

***

I meet the Carte Blanche Executive Producer in Johannesburg and pitch a story in Zimbabwe. There has been a lot of media attention on the plight of the white commercial farmers kicked off their land, but what about the wildlife? After all, Zimbabwe is renowned for its nature and animals. Over and above high levels of poaching out of the national parks, most of the privately owned game ranches have been seized by the government. What has happened to Zimbabwe's wildlife in its ongoing crisis? I don't appreciate at the time how good I have it to meet the Executive Producer, or EP, in person and get a story I want to make commissioned, just like that!

"Yes, it's about time we did a Zimbabwe story." Then the EP adds, "You're

brave."
"Not really." I don't consider myself brave at all.
It is made clear to me that I should not expect to be baled out if I have any problems there, but that is the lot of the freelancer.

Working as a journalist in a non-democratic country like Zimbabwe is tricky! But, the situation in 2010 looks slightly better. Small democratic concessions are being made thanks to the current Government of National Unity, in effect a coalition between ZANU PF, in power since Zimbabwe got its independence from the UK in 1980, and the opposition party MDC. This coalition will be short-lived. Soon wily president Robert Mugabe will eat up his coalition partners and spit them out for breakfast.

In the interim though, I can get a national film permit, which is a positive development. I'm advised by an activist in Zimbabwe to tell the government I am producing a story on tourism and wildlife. This subterfuge does not sit well with me, but sometimes it's the only way with these investigative stories. Following all the usual bureaucratic logistics, as well as arranging my storyline, protagonists to interview, and locations to visit, I leave for Zimbabwe.

At Johannesburg's O R Tambo airport, I call one of my Zimbabwe contacts. While talking I realise someone has sidled up to me. As soon as I turn the person disappears again. There have been reports of Zimbabwe CIO (police intelligence) operating within Johannesburg's airport. Going through official channels for a media visit may offer some protection (but not necessarily as I discovered in Madagascar), but it does also mean one is on said government's radar.

Sitting on the tarmac, the pilot announces a delay. Dammit, I think. I have a tight and busy schedule. Finally, we get going.

On arrival at the Harare airport, I proceed to the immigration officer.

"Your job?"
"Producer."
"Producer? You mean journalist?" he says looking irate.
"Yes."
"Well just say so!" He snaps at me.

I pay a customs deposit for my camera at the airport.

My first stop is to the government media office to get my media accreditation. I am a bit stressed because of the flight delay, and I need to get this sorted out today.

"How are things now in Zimbabwe?" I ask the taxi driver.

"Well, we now are using another country's currency, so that is a bit better." But the way he says it, it's clear this is a disappointing development in terms of national pride. To try and survive an economic meltdown which was precipitated by the loss of the commercial farming sector, the government simply printed more money, and hyperinflation was the outcome. At its weakest, the Zimbabwe dollar was being printed in 100 trillion dollar denominations. That's fourteen zeros. When I arrive, the government has given up on their currency and introduced a basket of foreign currencies, dominated by the US dollar.

I make it to the media office just as they are closing, and fork out US$ 200 for a national film permit.

I then head over to my protagonist's house, from where we will leave together early the following morning. Johnny Rodrigues is a wildlife activist who runs the Zimbabwe Conservation Task Force. And he has paid dearly for being an outspoken defender of wild animals and the environment. He had his trucking business taken away. The goons arrived late one night and took everything including his fleet of trucks and his home. That was for speaking out against the poaching of wildlife and the degradation of the environment. And he continues with his mission. This he recounts to me in the home of his daughter and son-in-law where he lives.

Referring to the government I say "these ZANU PF guys are just terrible."
"Your lot's just as bad," says Johnny's son-in-law, testily.

Well, maybe in terms of corruption, but the ANC are not as vicious as ZANU PF. And South Africa's saving grace is a lively civil society, not to mention stronger institutions.

Actually, I have a soft spot for Zimbabweans, Black and White. I find that White Zimbabweans are much more African than White South Africans, and I find Black Zimbabweans well-spoken and friendly. The climate and landscapes are also fantastic. If only it weren't for the toxic politics.

In the morning, Johnny and I set off before sunrise, and drive to Bulawayo, Zimbabwe's second city.

Johnny is a no-nonsense, gruff fellow, an ex-soldier. But he is also a fighter for a good cause.

He has been travelling the country documenting poaching and other wildlife injustices for many years. These range from the exporting of baby elephants to Chinese zoos, to mass wildlife slaughter in national parks to feed soldiers.

"You realise how dangerous what you're doing is?" Johnny asks me.
"Yes," I say, without really knowing exactly.

"They've tried to kill me four times. By driving me off the road. High-speed chases. I seriously damaged the transmission of my Landcruiser by driving at 180 km/h for an extended period. Another time I was nearly pushed off the road by two vehicles near Victoria Falls. I'm lucky to be alive."

And it's not just the Zimbabwean government's ire he has raised. South African hunters taking advantage of corrupt officials in Zimbabwe to shoot trophy animals in protected areas have also been named and shamed by Johnny.

"I was once in a bar in Tzaneen, South Africa, near the Zimbabwe border. A South African hunter comes up to me and asked me:
"Are you Johnny Rodrigues?"
"No, I replied, I come from Maputo, Mozambique."
As soon as I could, I got out of there, using the back entrance."

It is now dawn, and we are on the outskirts of Harare. Suddenly we have a flat tyre.

"Here on a new tarmac road," exclaims Johnny. While he changes the tyre he says, "Notice how quiet it is around here. There used to be many dogs in this area. Now there are none. It was the Chinese who built this road. Not only did they eat all the dogs, but it was also how they killed them. They'd hang the dogs from a tree. For them, the meat tastes better when there has been a rush of adrenaline in the dog just before it dies."

On the drive south, Johnny fills me in on some statistics. "Over the last ten years, we've lost about 40% of our wildlife within the national parks, to poaching." Most of the private game ranches, as with the commercial farms have been violently taken by war veterans and the government.

Later in the day, on arrival in Bulawayo, the first port of call is refuelling the vehicle. No need to ask Johnny why—the country has experienced serious fuel shortages, so you fill your tank when you can.

Our next stop is a vehicle swap, for safety reasons. In the quiet suburbs of Bulawayo, we pull into a house and Johnny parks his car behind the house. Here I meet an activist, who will drive Johnny and me all the way south to the Beit Bridge area. We get talking, and hearing that I am half "Anglo" South African and half Afrikaans, my contact says, "Ah so you're a real South African!" Later, I think to myself, Not really. Maybe if I also had an infusion of Zulu! I'm also told, "You look like us, so you blend in easily here in Zimbabwe." Turning to each other they bemoan the British female journalist they recently helped, who with her strange clothes, pale skin, and aggressiveness, simply stood out too much.

We head south. It is September and it must be pushing 40 degrees. We've changed vehicles. Now we're in an ancient Land Cruiser. Our contact says, "I used this to ferry drums of petrol from neighbouring Botswana during the fuel crisis. Until I was arrested and spent a night in jail. I stopped after that."

There's a loud whirring sound. Eventually, I ask Johnny, "What is that sound?"
Johnny doesn't hesitate. "Propshaft coupling."
Our contact doesn't look too pleased at my critique. But then says: "I'm going to keep driving this until it falls apart."
"It won't fall apart. It will just keep going," says Johnny.
Yeah. Toyota Land Cruiser—king of the road in Africa.

Finally, we make it to Denlynian private game ranch near the South African border. In normal times, it would have been well stocked with wildlife, hunters would visit and pay to shoot animals, and the owner would ensure the hunting is carried out sustainably. That is to say, wildlife numbers remain at the carrying capacity of the ranch. That is no longer the case.

Between 2000 and 2010, Zimbabwe's private game ranches decreased from 645 to about five. Most have been grabbed by government cronies. Denlynian is one of the last five in existence. The situation is fragile. Alleged war veterans (from the 1970s independence war) have entered the property several times over the last few years, on the pretext of using it for agriculture, but hunting out the game instead. Most of the wildlife, such as impala, eland and zebra have been poached out.

Johnny explains to me that as is often the case it is the ruling ZANU PF behind the land grab, and although they will say they are taking the land for the people, it is a handful of people in power who benefit. "Behind the war vets here, is the local Member of Parliament, Kembo Mohadi." Later, back in Cape Town, I manage to phone Mohadi who says he has no comment. Soon thereafter he will become vice-president of the country.

Johnny and I meet up with Justin van der Merwe, who runs the Denlynian anti-poaching unit. Justin, who is the last man standing at Denlynian, takes us for a drive around the ranch. There are animal carcasses everywhere. But it's only the hides that have been taken. The rest of the animals, including the meat, is left to rot in the sun. There are also signs of deforestation.

Justin explains to me that most of the fencing has been stolen. This wire is being used to make the snares that kill wildlife.

"Let's go meet one of the war vets," says Justin.

Staying in what would once have been a lodge for visiting hunters, which has been largely gutted, Justin confronts a man. All he says is, "All things have an ending." I am surreptitiously filming, and I ask the man what the situation is on the ranch. He tells me that he'll only talk, "If you come here with a policeman." He gets angry that I am filming him. I tell him I'm just a visitor. This moment is what I would call being at the coal face of Zimbabwe politics, which is to say decolonisation. The price for colonialism is being paid, and it is a messy business.

Johnny is also filming at Denlynian. As part of his mission to document the wildlife and environmental injustices in Zimbabwe, he has been amassing a library of video footage that he hopes will one day be used as evidence against perpetrators.

As Johnny has pointed out, the political and economic chaos of the last decade has not only resulted in almost all the private ranches being taken from their owners. Poaching, both at a commercial level where ivory and rhino horn gets sent to China, and bush meat or local level poaching has increased dramatically, out of national parks and reserves. He gives examples of 600 buffalo killed in one go in the Kariba area, and elephants being poached to feed soldiers due to a lack of beef. "Law and order is the problem." Having visited a private ranch, I'm on my way to a national park next.

Saying goodbye to Johnny in Bulawayo, I take a bus to Victoria Falls. At one stage a policewoman sitting behind me smiles at me and says, "Welcome! Zimbabwe is safe!" I find it hard to smile or say anything in concurrence. Considering all this subterfuge, risk, and information I have about the situation, I can't find a positive spin right now.

Zimbabwean Charles Brightman runs the Victoria Falls Anti-Poaching Unit. We meet for a coffee in Victoria Falls town.

"Do you have all the necessary permits to film in Zimbabwe?"
"Yes, I have the national permit, and I will get the national park permit before I film you."
"Ok. I had another journalist here, and I answered some of his questions. Then sometime later, in the early hours of the morning, I was awoken by loud knocking. It was CIO (police intelligence), and I was harshly interrogated in my home. I don't want a repeat of that. I have a family."

I get my national park permit (official video production topic: "tourism") and meet Charles again to interview him. His anti-poaching unit works within the Victoria Falls National Park to halt the illegal hunting of wildlife. In the last decade, his team have removed 20,000 wire snares used to trap animals and has caught over 550 poachers, both bush meat poachers who hunt for meat for local consumption, and rhino horn and elephant ivory commercial poachers. His team hands over poachers to authorities, but conviction rates are low. According to Traffic, the wildlife trade monitoring network, only 3% of rhino poachers in Zimbabwe are sentenced.

Charles' team works together with the national parks to fight poaching. I join an anti-poaching patrol within the Victoria Falls National Park. It's a good time of the year to be on a foot patrol here. Coming to the end of the dry season means the vegetation is at its thinnest (the trees have no leaves), so the visibility of wildlife in the bush is excellent. Just after dawn, we set off on a foot patrol, and soon I am rewarded with an elephant close encounter. We get to within 20 metres of her. What an experience.

Continuing our way through the dry bush, the team stop and examine the dust. Footprints. These are poachers, and the team can estimate how recently they walked here and in which direction they are going. We keep walking through the bush, stopping when the team find wire snares. These they remove and take with them. The snares have been set recently, and maybe by the poachers whose tracks we are following. Wildlife that gets their legs caught in a snare suffers from a slow painful death unless the team find them and can save them.

Later I will get some good footage from Tom Varney, a filmmaker based at Victoria Falls. It is disturbing footage of wildlife that has been caught in the snares that Charles and his team collect in the bush. It is very unpleasant to see an elephant or a giraffe trying to walk with most of one of its feet hanging by a thread. Previously animals found like this would be shot to be out of their misery. Now Charles is working with veterinarians to save these creatures, if they are found staggering about, still alive.

The team find more snares and collect them. We are still tracking what we assume to be a poacher. Everyone suddenly crouches. Then we stand and run. The team reaches a man who they handcuff. His wife and daughter are nearby. The man claims to have been cutting firewood only, itself an offence. It is not clear whether he has been setting the snares we found en route to him. He vehemently denies having set snares. He says he has no electricity and needs firewood which cannot be found in the areas outside the national park where he lives. His reason for entering the park to search for firewood is quite simply poverty.

Having copied over my footage to Tom Varney's hard drive at Victoria Falls, so that I know I have a backup in case I experience any problems, I head for the border into Zambia. Now I can breathe a sigh of relief! All that's are two flights back to Cape Town, and editing the insert.

Soon after I visit Denlynian Game Ranch where we confronted the alleged war veteran who had moved onto the private property, Justin van der Merwe is arrested, and thrown in jail.

While editing the story, Charles Brightman phones me, sounding anxious. He asks me to please be careful about not having him be critical of the state. "I'll be careful," I assure him.

Once again I miss the boat for a great documentary opportunity. It takes me a few years to realise that Johnny Rodrigues could be an excellent protagonist for a documentary. This is not only because he is such a fearless crusader for environmental injustice in a non-democratic country. It's because he has 30 hours of video footage he has been recording for his database. A few years later I get in contact with Johnny. His news is that after another attempt on his life he fled Zimbabwe with a suitcase and is in Portugal, from where his parents had emigrated when he was a toddler. Johnny is open to the idea, and I start pitching the documentary proposal. When I finally get some interest, I get back in touch with Johnny. No reply. Then I manage to get hold of his daughter, now also in Portugal. Johnny has passed away from cancer. He was in his 60s. Rest in peace Johnny. You made a difference.

***

But why stop at one investigative piece on Zimbabwe?

The Marange diamond fields in eastern Zimbabwe are well-named. A diamond rush to this area by thousands of artisanal miners seeking their fortune made some people very rich from the easily accessible precious commodity found near the earth's surface—literally diamond fields. The bonanza was brought to a violent end by the state. In a country lacking good governance, the potential wealth did not and has not benefited the nation. More's the pity considering the desperately broken economy. Dubiously registered Zimbabwean government-allied companies extract the mineral for the benefit of a handful. Considering the Marange diamond fields are said to contain 30% of the world's supply, the impact it could have had is enormous were it not for Zimbabwe's extreme level of corruption. I am telling the Marange diamond story from the perspective of small Mozambican town, just across the Zimbabwean border, booming thanks to the illicit flow of diamonds over the porous frontier.

Before leaving South Africa, I buy a hidden camera that looks like a pen, and if it is placed in one's top pocket, the tiny lens points forward, and you can film the person you are looking at. This I plan to use to get footage of the diamond dealers. I buy the hidden camera pen in a camera shop in Sandton City, Johannesburg, I have also arranged to meet Andrew Cranswick of African Consolidated Resources, here. We have a coffee. His lawyer is present. A beautiful brunette walks past. Andrew turns to his lawyer:

"Arrange me one of those."
African Consolidated Resources was initially licensed to excavate at the Marange diamond fields, but in 2006 this licence was cancelled by the Zimbabwean government, and a free-for-all ensued. Then in 2008, in its effort to gain control of the wealth the military massacred hundreds of these artisanal miners. Many of these innocent civilians were killed by being fired at from helicopters, and some by dogs let loose on them. The dodgy diamond companies were installed, ensuring a steady flow of money to the small ruling party elite and its cronies.

Andrew tells me he has footage from the area that I can make use of. Unfortunately following the meeting, Andrew no longer responds to any of my follow-up enquiries. Perhaps his lawyer advised against this kind of media exposure.

From Johannesburg, it's a short hop over to Maputo. Armed with a national Mozambican filming permit I take a flight up to Chimoio. This is where I produced a news feature on the Zimbabwean commercial farmers trying to start over, three years earlier. I am back and dressed in my hippy clothes, with my camera gear in a backpack. I am shooting on a Sony palmcorder, not a professional camera. Strolling the streets of Chimoio who should I bump into but Piet van Zyl from the Envirotrade carbon credits project, with his wife and daughters sitting in their Toyota Landcruiser.

"Hello Piet! How's life?"
"Alright. I'm not with Envirotrade anymore."
Oh, what are you up to now?"
"Consulting."
A nebulous reply such as that deserves an understanding nod and a "Have a good day!"

I meet the first of my contacts here in Chimoio. A South African involved in the diamond trade, who used to be based in Angola, renowned for its conflict diamonds—places where the diamond trade fuels conflict. Quite candidly he tells me:

"When I left Angola, I came down to Cape Town with a suitcase full of cash. I thought, hell man, I want to buy a property but how will I get it right with cash, no questions asked? It was so easy. I bought a house in Constantia (one of Cape Town's most upmarket suburbs)."

My contact, looking at my hippy clothes then asks:

"Do you know how the diamond trade works?"

"Not really," I say, as I am flying on a wing and a prayer here.

Getting serious he says, "This is like the cocaine trade. This is dangerous." He waits for this to sink in, and then adds, "Last year someone was snooping around in Manica, asking about diamonds, and the Nigerian traders didn't like the look of him. They cut him right open, thinking he was a diamond mule who had ingested diamonds. Dead."

"Oh." Manica is the Mozambican diamond boom town where I am headed. There are said to be around 300 West African, Lebanese, and Israeli diamond traders who have set up shop there, dealing in diamonds from over the border in Zimbabwe.

I hail a taxi to take me the 70 kilometres to Manica town which shows some signs of new-found wealth. Freshly painted buildings, and many high-end vehicles. The municipal swimming pool has just been renovated by some of the diamond traders. But I am keeping my visits to town short. I am staying at a bush camp hideaway, in a very simple room, about 30 kilometres out of town. I have a contact across the border in the Zimbabwean town of Mutare. He is an activist who will prove crucial to my production. Let's call him Dan.

Dan crosses the border and meets me at my bolthole. He brings with him a Zimbabwean diamond smuggler. I bring out my small video camera and start the interview, hand-held. It's just me with a little video camera and this helps a lot to keep people relaxed, and for me to keep a low profile. I will blur the diamond trader's face. It is simply too dangerous for his identity to be revealed.

After paying soldiers to have brief access to the diamond fields across the border at Marange, the independent smuggler, known as a "sniper" heads to Mozambique.

"Manica is a cool place! Selling diamonds in Zimbabwe is very risky. And prices offered here are higher."

"How do you get the product over the border?"

"If it's a small amount, I can carry it on me, and cross the border normally. If it is a larger amount, I bypass the border post and cross into Mozambique by walking over that mountain."

"Is that dangerous?"

"Yes. There are thieves. I travel very early in the morning to avoid them.

Also, there are military around, but I always buy them cold drinks. The traders who are new risk being stopped by Mozambican police and having their diamonds confiscated. Once you get into Mozambique, you have to travel with the right taxi driver only. The taxi driver takes a commission. But you're safe."

Taxi drivers take a 5% commission, and the taxi driver I meet tells me he has already bought two more taxis from the trade.

"And the diamond buyers here in Manica?"
"I know which ones offer the best prices. Some of them have opened normal shops: hardware stores, and grocery stores. You go in there and make the transaction right there. They all have tight security. Guys are armed with AK47s."

The diamond traders have licences to deal in gold, not diamonds. After all, Mozambique doesn't have diamonds. One can assume that the local authorities turn a blind eye with some financial inducement. I do get to interview a Mozambican police spokesperson later, who says one person has been apprehended so far but that, "It's difficult to find these people and this type of mineral."

It's October, "suicide month" in these parts. The daytime high pushes 40 degrees centigrade. It's not a problem, as long as one drinks a lot of water. And it's dry heat, not humid, thank God. At dusk at my bush camp, I walk up the nearby koppie and watch the sun go down. In the distance are the Vumba mountains, forming the border with Zimbabwe. Another colonial relic as the people on either side speak Shona.

The next time I meet my Zimbabwe contact Dan, it's in Manica town at the Flamingo Bar. I'd like to see how he can assist me with the rest of my shoot. Together with Victor, our trusty taxi driver, we cruise around town, and I get all sorts of surreptitious shots of signs of the boom town: flashy cars and newly painted buildings. Dan says he knows someone in Harare with footage of the diamond fields for US$200. I say, okay, but let's try to talk him down. Footage from the diamond fields is crucial to my story. And as a militarised zone, not easy to access.

While we wait for news about the footage, Dan and I agree to start visiting some of the diamond traders. These are the guys who operate much like the cocaine industry, as you might recall.

Dan, myself and of course, our trustworthy taxi driver Victor take a drive through what was once a Portuguese colonial suburb. Now the 1950s and 60s distinctive square-shaped houses are spruced up, many hiding a furtive diamond trade.

The diamond traders export to places like Dubai, Tel Aviv and Antwerp, and there is no way of knowing where the diamond that you as consumer purchases, comes from—from a legitimate source, or a conflict or blood diamond.

We approach the first diamond trader's house. I switch on my hidden camera that looks like a pen in my shirt pocket. I walk up to the front door and knock. An Israeli opens wide and lets me in. He leads me to a backroom. He puts on a small light. It is too dark to get visuals with the little pencam.

"Buying or selling?"
Good bloody question, I definitely could have been better prepared for this.
"I'm looking to buy. My brother sent me here from South Africa to check out prices."
"Depends on how much."
"Ah"
"How much?" he asks a bit testily.
"To start with just a small amount, to.. um… check the product."
He looks at me quizzically. After a pause, he says "when you know the quantity, come back."
"No problem."

I leave. The footage is no good anyway.

We drive around until Victor stops at another house. I go up to the door and knock. This time a Lebanese opens.

"What do you want?"
"To buy"

He looks busy and says I should come back.

Victor and Dan say we should go to the Nigerians. The very same ones who murdered someone snooping around here recently. There is a large group of them standing around outside. We park nearby, I put on the pencam, and approach one of these traders. I shake hands with one of the guys.

"I'm here to buy," I say.
"We're not ready now. Do you know John?"
"Ah no."
"He's coming now. He has everything. All grades, all qualities. Later today."

These visuals at least come out well. Victor and Dan take me to my fourth diamond trader, in one of the newly painted houses. I walk up to his door and knock. A Middle Eastern-looking man arrives and looks at me suspiciously. Indeed I don't look like a typical diamond seller or buyer! I don't have a good feeling.

"What do you want?" he asks aggressively.
"Ah, I'm here to check out your prices."
The guy looks at me, looks at my pen, and then looks at me again. "No." he closes the door. I turn around and say to Dan "it's okay, I have enough. Let's get out of here. Now!"

The taxi driver takes us out of the diamond trader suburbs, and back onto the main road. We drop off Dan and keep going the 30 kilometres to my bush hideaway. Only then do I relax.

I hang out here, staying in contact with Dan, over in Zimbabwe, trying to arrange the enigmatic footage. Eventually, it becomes clear that I am not going to get my hands on existing footage. Dan makes a new suggestion. He has a contact who used to be a labourer in one of the Marange mines. He lost his job due to, err, diamond theft. But he still has his work access ID. If we can get my pen camera to him, he's willing to go to the diamond fields and shoot some undercover footage. For US$400. It sounds risky. A gamble, really. Just what I like! So I said to Dan, "Let's do it!"

The following day, my taxi driver, Victor arrives. We're heading for the border to meet Dan so that I can hand over the pen camera. In Manica, Victor veers off the road.

"I want to stop for a Red Bull."
"Just keep driving to the border. You can get a drink later." I want to spend as little time in Manica as possible, especially after having met a few of the diamond traders. We keep going until just before the border. And there sure enough is Dan. We turn around and find a quiet spot to park. I give Dan instructions on how the pen cam works.

"I'll go right back now, and give the pen cam to my contact. I'll let you know very soon."
"Thanks Dan."

On our way back to my hideaway, Victor again veers off the road in Manica town.

"Where are you going?" I ask, impatiently as he turns into a side street.
"To get water."

"Please, I don't like this town, I'd like to move on."
Victor ignores me. Then examining the bottle of water a pavement vendor has given him says, "This is not real water! It's too cheap to be real water." He gives it back to the vendor.
Oh my God, I say to myself, as Victor continues to a little supermarket. Knowing I can make the purchase quicker than him, I say, "I'll go in and get it." I walk in, grab two bottles of water, and pay. Then, who should walk in but Victor.
"I want a Red Bull."
Oh bloody hell, I think to myself. I exit the shop. Outside, I can't get into the locked car. Just then a sleek tinted window top-of-the-range Toyota sedan pulls up. Two guys get out. *F"*&!* These are the Nigerian diamond traders I met a few days ago. As calmly as possible, I sit on the hot concrete, and sip my water, looking at the sky, and ignoring their presence.

After a short eternity, Victor arrives, clutching his precious Red Bull. He fumbles with the keys. Then he opens up and we leave, me saying *"Vamos!"* Surreptitiously I look into the side mirror as we depart, but the diamond traders are inside the supermarket.

I wait at my bush camp for news from Dan. Communications are tricky. I don't have internet access, and phone calls to Zimbabwe rarely work. But finally, I get a message from Dan.

"I have it! I'll meet you tomorrow at 10 am."

The next morning I go to the meeting point with Victor the taxi driver. 10 am comes and goes, and no Dan. I try to phone him, but the line is dead. I am getting convinced he is up shit street without a paddle. Finally Victor, irate, calls a friend of Dan's over in Zimbabwe. Apparently, Dan's wife is giving birth to a baby. He'll be here at 13H15. That sounds like a very specific time for these parts. It is only later in the afternoon that Dan arrives.

"The childbirth thing was just a story. I was stopped by Zimbabwean immigration and interrogated for three hours. They wanted to know why I cross into Mozambique so often. They searched me, but they didn't look at the pen camera twice. Here it is." In total, the footage has cost me US$500, but it is well worth it, illustrating the Zimbabwean mining operations and the roads in and out of them.

I have everything I need, and I am out of here, backtracking to South Africa via Chimoio and Maputo, to edit the insert. I stay in touch with my contacts to make sure they are all safe, which they are.

In 2017 Zimbabwe experienced a coup d'etat and Robert Mugabe is usurped after 37 years at the helm. Any hope for an improvement in the economic or political situation (broken economy and no democracy) is quickly dashed. Former Zimbabwean Finance Minister Tendai Biti in 2021 calls the country a, "Fully fledged kleptocratic state." Only when the ruling ZANU PF is ditched, and people with integrity take power, will the country have hope for renewal.

In 2011 I zig-zag from South Africa through Swaziland, Mozambique, Malawi and Zambia to Tanzania, over six months, covering many stories both for Carte Blanche and Associated Press. I shoot, produce and do either all or most of the editing of these projects. The journey is in my elderly Nissan Safari, sometimes camping, and travelling with Nicole Mccreedy, who is writing articles and keeping up a blog.

In the north of Mozambique, I cover two eco-lodge news features for Associated Press. "Eco-lodges" are the phenomena where five-star prices are charged for a hotel made cheaply of local materials, thus being sold as "sustainable." "Community participation" is another buzzword. The "Eco Lodge" will tick that box by providing outreach programmes to the local communities such as skills training (usually skills the communities already possess, such as sewing or jam-making), or health aid, such as malaria education. Because a village in tropical Africa has probably never heard of malaria. Hotel guests, who have paid exorbitant amounts of money for a bamboo shack go on a "poverty tour"—which is to say they get to see how their hard-earned money is "uplifting" local communities (who may even sing and dance for them) and they can go home not only suntanned but feeling good about themselves because after all, they have made a difference to the lives of the world's poorest.

For some reason, the traffic cops are not stopping and harassing us. It is smooth sailing through the back roads of Northern Mozambique. That is until Praia de Zalala.

After all the busy resort towns of Southern Mozambique, I am keen to find an authentic beach experience. The evocatively named Praia de Zalala is reached following a long palm tree-lined potholed road from Quelimane, and it fits the bill. We are the only tourists around in the sleepy village. We make a deal to camp on the grounds of a half-complete hotel, and just metres away, beyond the pine trees is a deserted beach that goes on for miles in each direction. We set up camp.

It is low tide. We are on the beach under an umbrella. There is no one else. Nicole stays on the beach and I head into the sea. This is a painstaking exercise at low tide. About 800 metres into the sea I am finally waist-deep in water. I plunge into the water, a respite from the heat and humidity. By now Nicole is almost a dot on the horizon. *But wait, what's that?* A man is running up to her, grabbing something and running off. Nicole, facing the front is oblivious. I am running back to the shore now. But between the sense of dread and the fact that I am trying to run through water, progress is slow. The guy has headed off to the north, and I can't see Nicole clearly. I keep "running" through the water. Slowly I make progress, my legs thrashing through the sea and gradually the level drops and I can run faster. I get to her. She's unaware that anything happened. I look around and see what he got—my sunglasses. It doesn't sound like much, but they were a really expensive pair, still brand new. My only luxury item. And it's the principle. Don't touch my stuff!

I say to Nicole, go back to the campsite. And I start running. And running. I am on a mission to retrieve my sunglasses. After about two kilometres north along the beach, I cut inland. I lost track of the guy when I was still in the sea, but he has a red t-shirt. I am running into the village now, wearing only my swimming trunks and no shoes. I am getting a serious amount of exercise. Some guys ask me what's up. In my broken Portuguese, I explain that I am looking for a thief who stole my glasses. They say "Just glasses?" I say "special glasses." They help me by running through the village with me, asking people if they have seen a guy with a red shirt come through. No one knows anything. We run over a little hill to the next village, asking around. No one knows anything. By now I am also concerned about Nicole who I have left alone. I thank the guys by buying them a coke each. I walk back to our site. Along the way, I pass the police station. The policeman is sitting in front of the little building. This is rural Mozambique. It's an outlying outpost. Things are very quiet here. He knows there's a ruckus in the village. He asks me, "What's up?" I explain about my "special glasses." He doesn't have any suggestions. My expectations from these cops are very low to zero. I continue to the campsite. That evening I am still quietly fuming. It's just not acceptable. There must be another way. Then it strikes me: when in Rome, do as the Romans do.

I head back to the village, this time wearing clothes. I find one of my accomplices from the chase. And I ask him:

"Do you know where I can find a *curandeiro*?"

A *curandeiro* is an African shaman. I am taking things to the next level.

"Let's go," he says.

We walk to the second village, on the edge of the coconut grove. I am led to a mud house, and my accomplice knocks. An old lady opens up, and through a slow process of broken Portuguese, I inform her what happened.

"I will come this evening to the place where you are camping. Get the following items for me: a conch and a bicycle tube."

"Okay, and thank you."

My accomplice and I locate a large conch, and I buy a bicycle tube in the village. True enough, as the sun is setting the *curandeiro* arrives.

And so begins the procedure. I write what was stolen onto a piece of paper. She places this paper into the conch. Then she speaks in the local language and starts pumping up the tube.

"In one week I will return here, and we will see about the stolen item."
"Oh. Um, we're leaving tomorrow."

The *curandeiro* looks exasperated.

"That's the problem with you White people," she says, "You're always in a hurry."

Only later will I fully understand what the ceremony means.

***

Also in Northern Mozambique, I set about producing an investigative insert for Carte Blanche on elephant poaching. To introduce my protagonist Koos Von Landsberg, let's first step back in time… to the 17th century. The Afrikaners of South Africa, descendants of Dutch and German settlers but with various other unacknowledged bloodlines, were living a fairly free lifestyle until the British arrived in South Africa. After all, before the British arrival in the late 18th century, the Cape was not a fully-fledged colony with all the rules that go with that, but an outpost of a Dutch trading company. Afrikaners, particularly farmers in the Cape hinterland, were left to their own devices for one and a half centuries. The British annexed the Cape in 1795, and the Afrikaners, unhappy about becoming British subjects, not to mention no longer being allowed to keep slaves, departed northwards. The Great Trek in the 1830s was a mass migration of those Afrikaners who chose to seek out new lands. Following conflicts with indigenous inhabitants, because there were people already living there, the ironically titled Orange Free State, and the Transvaal Republic were established. The Afrikaners had their republics now, and all went reasonably well until the discovery of gold in what is now the area in and near Johannesburg. The British in the Cape, feeling confident about the might of the British Empire, decided to take the Afrikaner republics, and thus the gold. It was a bloody three years, which the British shamefully put Afrikaner women and children, and Black South Africans, into concentration camps. 48,000 people died in these camps. The British were the victors and the year was

1902. Once again, some Afrikaners were unwilling to live under British rule, and set off further north, this time to Kenya, where a large community farmed in the Eldoret area. Most of these Afrikaners "returned" to South Africa in the 1950s during the violent Mau Mau Kenyan independence uprising.

Koos von Landsberg's family are of the Eldoret Afrikaners and he returned to South Africa as a child. But, as a child of Africa. In the 1980s Koos worked for Tiny Rowland's multinational Lonrho firm which had many business interests in Mozambique, such as agriculture, and kept them running throughout the war with heavy security. During that time, Koos became intrigued by a distant koppie, and when the war ended in 1991, he made it to his koppie, Taratibu, where he established a nature reserve. Later his reserve was to fall within the Querimbas National Park, established in 2002.

I drive over from the town of Pemba to Taratibu to meet Koos, and shoot the story. Koos is around 60 years old, bearded, trim and in military fatigues. Taratibu is set in the shade of a grove of tall trees next to the koppie. "We are just under 70,000 hectares," which is within the 7500 square kilometres Querimbas National Park. "We've built 250 kilometres of bush road. We do our anti-poaching even though we are only allowed an old Mauser rifle."

An anti-poaching unit is the first clue to the problems faced here. Despite the global ivory trade ban of 1990, elephant poaching is ongoing, and indeed increasing in these parts. My experience of this issue during this visit in 2011, is one I will see again and again. The demand from China is strong. "The tusks from an elephant are worth US$30 - 40,000," says Koos. That is a big incentive. And a locally employed poacher may get 25% of that, which is a small fortune to a Mozambican villager.

Capitalism demands a price tag for all resources. Gold and diamonds are just shiny minerals yet thanks to the value placed on them countries like South Africa industrialised. Ivory is just bone and rhino horn is keratin, like our nails, but their commodification means elephants and rhinos are disappearing off the face of the earth. And what for? To make chopsticks, rings, and ornaments out of ivory, and rhino horn powder in traditional medicine with no scientific basis. The end buyer is China and Asia.

"How is the poaching carried out?" I ask Koos.

"They are armed with AK47s or 357 rifles." But you need to shoot an elephant in the right place, the heart, or otherwise, it takes many shots to try and fell one of these behemoths. Koos has found dead elephants with over 20 bullets in them, and that's a long slow death.

"Or the poachers make a hole in the ground. The elephant steps in. Then they make a fire on top of him. Burn the animal alive."

Poachers also use planks with nails sticking out. The elephant steps on it, it is hurt, and his mobility is limited. This gives the poachers a chance to poison the elephant which takes two or three days to die. Another method used is agricultural chemicals placed in bread or fruit, thus poisoning the elephant in that way.

Aside from commercial ivory poaching, the other threat to elephants is conflict with humans. As with all national parks in Mozambique, people live within Querimbas National Park. 100,000 people. This throws up certain challenges, as it does with the majority of African national parks that have people living within them. After the war ended in Mozambique in 1991, the landmines and gunshots disappeared, and gradually elephants began to move around more freely. Locals retaliate when elephants enter their fields of sorghum, maize and pumpkins to eat these crops.

"They make fires, they throw fire and they bang drums. They antagonise the elephants, and every year two or three people are killed by elephants." Elephants, usually with the biggest tusks, are then killed as retribution. That is where things start getting complicated because of the high-value ivory. Corrupt district police chiefs are allegedly supplying arms to villagers to kill "problem elephants."

"There have also," Koos says, "been cases of people dying of old age, and then an elephant is killed in retribution. I think as many as 90% of the elephant killings are fake. The meat is used for food, and the tusks are sent to the district-level officials."

"I've paid communities to not kill elephants," says Koos, who has also developed an explosion system for the communities to ward off elephants. Koos has trained locals how to use oxygen acetylene, which is usually used for welding, to set off small explosions. 1.5 litre plastic bottles are planted in the ground, and a small fire is made on top, resulting in an explosion. This reminder of war deters elephants from entering the area.

While at Taratibu I also go on long hikes, in search of the elephants. In a clearing, I get stopped in my tracks by the guide just five metres from a cobra. They spit their venom up to three metres away. There is no serum here. We slowly backtrack and walk a long way around.

Since my visit, the jihadi insurgency of northern Mozambique has destroyed tourism, which was one of Koos' income earners at Taratibu. It has also made the area much more unstable. Leonard Cohen said, "I've seen the future and it is murder." Well, when poverty leads to terrorism then that murderous future is the present. And as terror and organised crime become interconnected the fate of the region's wildlife is even more parlous than before.

***

Between the Carte Blanche investigative stories and the Associated Press news features this road trip is a pretty busy working trip. On the shores of Lake Malawi, we camp for a week at Nkhotakota. The campsite is a well-manicured lawn with shade provided by palm and sausage trees. I work on my laptop using a cellphone internet connection. We are self-sufficient and vervet monkeys are our only companions. In the afternoons the skies darken and then the summer rains come torrenting down.

When I say self-sufficient, I don't mean the classic South African overlander who has packed every single item of food needed for his journey north of South Africa, including often a fully loaded four-wheel drive trailer behind the expensive Land Rover (because aside from the Brits, only South Africans buy Land Rover's despite their questionable dependability. Japanese vehicles are generally the way to go), as if it is a journey into the African interior circa 1700. Aside from the ubiquitous well-stocked South African Shoprite supermarket chain (found throughout Southern and East Africa, and beyond), in every village one can find the basics such as onions, tomatoes, green peppers, eggs and bread.

Roaming away from our beach camp, I watch CNN at the nearby lakeshore luxury lodge. The crowds are building up at Tahrir Square in Cairo. And then President Hosni Mubarak is deposed. The Arab Spring is well underway, and I wish I am not sitting at the Malawi lakeshore but the coalface of global events in the Middle East. Be careful what you wish for.

***

The capitalist model which most of us blindly accept as being the only economic model presupposes that production must take place at a large scale to be profitable. That model turns us into consumers who must in turn find ways, whether or not satisfying, to make money. And so the machine keeps purring. The alternative is... self-sufficiency. This is anathema to governments that must collect taxes, and to the powerful multinationals and corporates whose goal is to amass profits.

The commercial jatropha biofuels boom ended pretty dismally as I discovered three years earlier in Mozambique. This had to do with the plants needing much more input than had been initially thought. The fact that clearing land for jatropha results in large-scale deforestation is not helpful.

Yet next door to Malawi, in Zambia, I find an alternative model. It's another option for both clean energy production and an alternative to the convention of mass production, consumerism and profit. The Sherriff family are resourceful ex-South Africans who have made a life for themselves in Zambia. They were part of a group of South Africans who were given land in remote Central Zambia. But whereas most of those South Africans were focused on partying, the Sherriffs buckled down to work, and to make the most of the opportunity given. A few years later, they are the only ones left. The Sherriffs grasped an opportunity to start over with lots of land in a country with plenty of sunshine and water. When they arrived they planted 40 hectares of jacaranda and mahogany seedlings. This was met with much muttering and pooh-poohing. Yet now these are nearly fully grown and will soon be harvested, and the timber sold for a tidy profit.

But it's their small-scale 200-hectare jatropha plantation that I am here to produce a story on for Associated Press. The Sherriff farms are far from anywhere, surrounded by African bush. We pass the timber and cattle operations on our way to the jatropha plantation. I have contracted malaria, and it is thanks to the sugar in the coca-cola that the Sherriffs kindly give me, that I can move around slightly, and keep working. At the jatropha trees, one of the first things Peter Sheriff tells me is, "There was a misperception that this is a lazy man's crops. But it needs inputs just like all crops do. It needs fertiliser. It needs irrigation for worthwhile yields."

Peter's son, Roger Sherrif, a trained mechanical engineer, is getting a ton per hectare of jatropha, from which he produces about 7500 litres of oil per year. Using methoxide, Roger processes the crude oil pressed from the jatropha seeds—this removes the glycerines and gives them a near-diesel consistency. This biodiesel they use to power all the tractors, generators and some of the diesel vehicles on their farm, Now that's what you call self-sufficiency. You don't have to be a happy drone consumer. Governments and corporates beware! With "waste not want not" his motto, Roger has yet another side business selling soap made from the glycerine by-product of the bio-diesel from jatropha process.

On the outskirts of Lusaka, Zambia's capital city, we meet Professor Sinkala, who is also dabbling in small-scale jatropha. Sinkala has taken jatropha to the next level by creating an integrated farm system. Aside from the biodiesel potential from the jatropha seeds, goats have been introduced to eat the weeds that grow between the jatropha plants. Goats multiply and can be sold. Instead of using pesticides, chickens, which are a further and significant source of income, eat termites and other bugs around the jatropha bushes. These chickens, goats, and even cattle provide natural fertiliser for the jatropha. Sinkala has also put up a beehive—bees pollinate the jatropha plants and produce honey, another source of income. When oil is pressed from the jatropha seeds, a by-product is seedcakes, which Sinkala uses as a natural fertiliser on his farm. Sinkala says that all told, one can make a tidy living from his jatropha integrated farming system. Why are not more people doing this? Because farming is not sexy, and cities are the magnets for the youth. Because commercial farmers think "monoculture." Because we are locked into thinking the traditional capitalist consumerist system is *the* system. It's not. I think what Professor Sinkala is doing is great and I try pitching this as a documentary to Al Jazeera, to no avail.

Later in the year, when I am back in South Africa, I produce an Associated Press piece on rooftop gardens. This is an innovative way to turn cities from food importers into food producers. Many cities have unutilised flat roofs. I visit The Greenhouse People's Environmental Centre's pilot project atop the AFHCO building in central Johannesburg. Volunteers grow vegetables ranging from spinach and spring onion to garlic and beans, without the use of any chemicals or pesticides. As the volunteers are unemployed, they keep much of the food for themselves, but surplus produce is sold on the street's pavements. There have been similar pilot projects in Cape Town, but for some reason, this just hasn't taken off yet in South Africa.

***

The "Great North Road" leads us from Lusaka up to Tanzania. Driving at night is not recommended, and we are reminded why when we continue past sunset. Suddenly in front of us, the Nissan's headlights illuminate an overturned truck blocking the whole highway. Thank goodness my Nissan is slow. I see the obstruction in time to stop and slowly drive around it. Finally, Dar es Salaam, Tanzania's de facto capital city.

When Tanzania got independence from the UK in 1961, the population was ten million. Julius Nyerere, a former teacher would preside over the country for the next three decades. By the time he stepped down the country was an economic basket case, but he did succeed in uniting the disparate ethnic groups. He understood the importance of nation-building in a geographic area comprising many different ethnicities that were only recently and randomly placed together by European colonialists. It was a success when you consider Tanzania has always been at peace. Compare that to the ethnic strife experienced in neighbouring Rwanda, Burundi and Kenya. Nyerere was also an environmentalist, and his government greatly expanded the country's natural protected areas in the early years of independence. National parks, for example, grew from one to nine in the first decade. Fast forward to 2011 when we arrive in my Nissan Safari. The country's population is 45 million, and the protected areas are under threat from the government's desire for development at all costs.

The Serengeti is the jewel in the crown of Tanzania's wildlife areas. Aside from beaches, which are a dime a dozen globally, tourists come to Tanzania to see wildlife. The annual migration of around two million wildebeest that loops through into Kenya's Masai Mara National Reserve is a spectacle that draws people from all over the world. The wildebeest's epic journey sees them under attack from lions, crocodiles and indeed poachers. But now they face the existential threat of... a highway. In its wisdom, the Tanzanian government has decided that a new highway from Tanzania's coast to Lake Victoria and the landlocked Great Lakes countries of Rwanda, Burundi and Uganda should run right through the Serengeti National Park.

It seems President Kikwete made election promises to develop rural areas, such as the North Serengeti region, and he intends to keep to his promise. It makes me wonder, what's the point of being a UNESCO World Heritage Site if the national government can willy-nilly destroy said area of "outstanding universal value?"

An Environmental Impact Assessment for the trans-Serengeti highway estimates 800 vehicles driving through the park every day by 2015 and 3000 per day by 2035. In the course of my investigations, I speak to those both for and against the highway. Hussein Kamote of the Confederation of Tanzanian Industries cites Mikumi National Park as an example of how to manage a highway through a national park. The busy east-west Mbeya-Dar es Salaam highway bisects Mikumi National Park. It is where in 2006 I nearly got rear-ended by a Mad Max long-haul bus, while parked on the side of the road getting free wildlife footage. But Richard Rugemalira of the WWF says Mikumi is a bad example, as a huge amount of wildlife does get killed here by vehicular traffic, despite the speed bumps. Also, the wildlife density in Serengeti is much higher than in Mikumi.

There are many more voices against the highway, and I speak to a few of them, such as the Frankfurt Zoological Society which has a local presence, the German Ambassador (Germany is a significant donor to the Tanzanian state) and local NGOs near Serengeti. I have the (US$ 1000) national filming permit, but as I know from my Madagascar experience this neither guarantees there'll be no problems and indeed puts one on the radar of the government that one is looking at critically. Tanzania, like most African countries, does not rank well in press freedom or freedom of speech.

I also meet a Frenchman I had met a few years before in Dar es Salaam, who owns a media company. I am in his office asking him about the Serengeti Highway. I can see he is a bit nervous. "Next time let's meet somewhere else," he says. Wow, is he concerned about the government listening in, at his office? He changes the subject.

"My parents were archaeologists: Roman Empire specialists. I spent my childhood travelling the Mediterranean region and I ended up living in the Middle East. Came to Tanzania on holiday and saw the economy was liberalising and there were many opportunities."
"Interesting to have had that exposure thanks to your parents."
"Yes, and I often say, the areas in the former Roman Empire have a lot to be thankful for to the Romans. They introduced plumbing, roads, and so much more."
"True."
"And it's the same here in Tanzania. The British built infrastructure where there was none. Infrastructure that is still in use."
"It's too soon here to talk about it impartially like we can talk about the Roman Empire," I reply.

Having met and interviewed some of the key players regarding the planned Serengeti highway, we drive up to this world-famous park. Compared to South Africa's parks, such as our Kruger National Park, I find the Serengeti very expensive, the roads are terrible (I suffer a destroyed tyre), and the campsite is basic to the point of disgusting. My work done, we leave.

As with most African countries, the traffic police's main mission in Tanzania is to make your life miserable. The Tanzanian traffic cops are among some of the more hardcore. There are many roadblocks on the national roads and highways. They ask to see your driver's licence, temporary import permit and third-party insurance. And then they start looking for "problems."

"Windscreen wipers." I am being asked to demonstrate that my windscreen wipers work, and to spray the windscreen with water. Naturally, on my old car, these don't work well.
"Lights... Indicators." check.
"Fire extinguisher." What?! Apparently, in Tanzania, all vehicles must carry a fire extinguisher. Let me tell you, you have got to do some serious talking to extricate yourself from receiving a fine. And again. And again.

Finally back in Dar es Salaam, I head straight to the city centre Kisutu area where back in 1999 I managed to track down replacement mini DV tapes, this time to buy a fire extinguisher. Needless to say, I am never asked by a traffic cop to see my fire extinguisher again. And it's 5300 kilometres to get home from here.

In 2014, the East African Court of Justice rules against the plan to build a highway through the Serengeti. Pressure from foreign governments, the UN, and civil society wins this particular battle.

But the threat to Tanzania's protected areas continues unabated. By 2020, the country's population has risen from 45 million during our 2011 visit to 58 million. Population pressure is undeniably a factor in the environment, but so are commercial foreign interests, such as poaching for ivory and rhino horn. The Selous Game Reserve, one of the largest protected areas in Africa, is a 50,000-square-kilometre wilderness in central Tanzania that few tourists make it to. I was there in 2006 producing my Selous-Niassa Wildlife Corridor feature for Associated Press. Like the Serengeti, the Selous is a UNESCO world heritage site. Since 2014 the park has been classified by UNESCO as a "world heritage site in danger." Yes, it's in danger alright! A corner of the reserve has been de-gazetted to allow for uranium mining, a hydro-power station is being built within Selous which will include the flooding of 1000 square kilometres and the building of access roads, the reserve has now been split into two, and there is talk of mining within this massive protected area.

There's always going to be a conflict between development and conservation. I am here to ask, isn't there a better way?

It's not like the Selous didn't already have problems. According to the WWF, its elephant population has been, "Decimated by industrial-scale poaching." Elephant numbers dropped from 110,000 to 15,000 over the forty years leading up to 2016. The critically endangered black rhino has been nearly entirely wiped out. So the area needs more protection, not de-gazetting, splitting up, and industrial development within the reserve.

From East Africa, it's a long journey back to South Africa. The engine has been guzzling oil and fuel at an alarming rate, so I first get the engine overhauled at the Nissan dealership in Dar es Salaam. This sets me back several weeks. Fortunately Zanzibar with its cheap hotels, Stone town and beaches is nearby—an ideal spot to wait out the mechanical work. Finally, when I return to Dar es Salaam, I'm told they can't get the rebuilt engine to run smoothly with the Weber carburettor and so they source the original carburettor. The car is now significantly slower and guzzles as much petrol as before.

On the way south in Mozambique, I stop off at Praia de Zalala, to look up the *curandeiro* with whom I am still halfway through a procedure to get back my stolen sunglasses. Unfortunately, she is away from her village.

The full meaning of the interaction will be revealed to me later.

Meanwhile, the Nissan, with its straight-six petrol engine, has such a high petrol consumption, that I find myself two TV news features to produce for Associated Press en route through South Africa to fund my petrol bill back to Cape Town.

CHAPTER FIFTEEN
Elephant dictionary

In the 1980s, Dr Katy Payne discovered that elephants are making infrasonic calls to each other. Infrasonic sound lies below 20 hertz, which is under the threshold of human hearing. Payne, "Sensed a thrumming vibration in the air," while viewing Asian elephants at the Washington Park Zoo in Oregon. Payne had experience in tracking this level of communication in whales and made the species jump to pachyderms, setting up the Elephant Listening Project at Cornell University in the USA. Later Peter Wrege takes over the programme. I'm going to Gabon to meet Peter and find out what elephants are saying to each other that we cannot hear.

Libreville is a laid-back African capital city. No one approaches me or even looks twice at me. I get a taxi from my budget beach hotel to the centre of town to finalise my national filming permit. The driver is a Nigerian. We have a futile argument about which is better, soccer or rugby. We are at loggerheads, as he thinks rugby is boring and pointless, and that is my opinion about soccer. You could say we agree to disagree. I get the document I need from my communications ministry contact in a car park along a long avenue of impressive government buildings. But these large modern buildings are the only sign I see of the country's oil wealth during my three weeks in Gabon. Some say this and other oil-rich nations in the region didn't cut themselves the best deals with the oil companies. Simon Mann is an ex-SAS soldier and businessman who partook in the ill-fated attempted Equatorial Guinea coup in 2004. Having dealt with president Bongo of Gabon personally, Mann describes in his book, *Cry Havoc*, that Bongo should have been getting ten dollars a barrel of oil, but was selling the black gold at a flat rate of one dollar a barrel. Or as Martin Meredith writes in *The Fortunes Of Africa*, Bongo used, "his access to the country's oil and mineral revenues to make himself one of the richest men in the world."

My next step is to see about national parks access. At the National Parks Agency, I take a seat. Who should step out of the office while I am there, but Lee White. White is a Brit who came to Gabon in the late 1980s to carry out PhD research. He stayed and became head of the Wildlife Conservation Society, an NGO. Quoted in Reuters White says, "I had a choice: do I keep studying the demise of Africa's rainforest and the disappearance of chimps and gorillas and elephants, or do I go into conservation and politics?" Well, White chose politics. In 2002 he was made advisor to the president. Overnight Gabon got 13 National Parks by presidential decree, covering nearly 11% of the country. When I visit in 2011, Lee is the director of the National Parks Agency, and in 2019, as a naturalised Gabonese citizen, he becomes Minister of Water, Forests, the Sea and the Environment. Not bad going. I stand up to greet Lee, telling him why I am in Gabon. I am about to ask him about the rationale for the overnight gazetting of 13 national parks in Gabon back in 2002 when his phone rings. "Yes, immediately," he responds, saying to me, "Sorry I have to go, it's the president's office." Creating an eco-tourism sector makes sense in light of the finite nature of oil as a source of revenue. Park infrastructure is another matter and these are wilderness experiences rather than South Africa-style tarmac roads and steak restaurants within national parks.

I meet with Peter Wrege of the Elephant Listening Project. Peter is working on deciphering the infrasonic communication between forest elephants. Together we take the train from Libreville to the CEB Forestry Concession. The locomotive pulls a smorgasbord of carriages of different hues and eras. They are all grubby. I am surprised by some of the scenery. I assumed Gabon would be all rainforest, yet we pass open savanna, rolling green hills and even most surprisingly, dunes.

In the rainforest of the CEB Forestry Concession, I walk with Peter and Modeste Doukaga as they go about changing the batteries and SD cards of the ARUs or Autonomous Recording Units. Once Peter slows down these audio recordings of elephants, he can hear the infrasonic sounds and gradually work out what these sounds mean. It is a slow process though to figure out the "elephant language."

We get to a wooden viewing platform. Later in the day when I see the first of the forest elephants drink from the water, I notice immediately that they look different to the savanna elephants I am accustomed to. Like many species that evolve in forests, this separate species of elephant is smaller. Logically, they'd be smaller, as they live in a more constrained environment. The shape of the heads appears a bit different. Also, forest elephant tusks are straight and their ears are more oval-shaped.

The fact that they live in dense forests means little is known about them. But just as with savanna elephants, we know that this is an intelligent species with complex social systems and behaviour. I'm told that the forest elephants meet at these clearings not only to drink water rich in minerals but also to interact socially. They may find a mate here, or females may assess males, or they may hold greeting ceremonies.

Working on the platform high above the clearing, Peter has set up a real-time spectrogram. We can see the infrasonic rumbles on his laptop screen that we cannot hear. This he pairs with observation. Peter explains that one of the clearest sounds is the musth rumble. This pulsating sound is made by male elephants when they are sexually hyperactive. When females come into oestrous, meaning they are ovulating and thus ready to mate, they too send out a distinctive infrasonic rumble. This kind of communication can be heard up to ten kilometres away, making it ideal for the enclosed rainforest environment. Because females travel in herds, and males tend to be solitary, a lot of communication tends to be between the female members: mothers and calves. For example, they each have their own unique infrasonic greeting rumble. Other typical rumbles are those of "reassurance," "let's go," "calling for Mom," or "go to your mother, you're in the wrong family." But as Peter points out, the science of human communication is not complete, so we are in "kindergarten" in terms of learning how elephants communicate.

From the CEB Concession, we continue south to the border of the Bateke Plateau National Park, on the Congo-Brazzaville border. Following a rainforest hike, we spend a couple of days sitting on a wooden platform built overlooking the Mpassa river. We are waiting for the elephants to make their appearance. When this eventually happens, we all spring into action. Peter with his binoculars, and me with my video camera. The problem is, I am shooting with a small Sony video camera and I do not have a long lens. That means the elephants are just too far away to fill the frame nicely.

"Peter, could I go down and walk a bit closer to get a better shot."
"Yeah, alright."

Strictly speaking, I should not leave the platform. Nor should I creep closer and closer to the elephants, as I am. I am finally getting some good shots of the elephants wading in the middle of the river. I continue to slowly make my way along the river bank, getting ever closer. Suddenly, one of the elephants trumpets in anger. It is a mother protecting her young one. She starts charging me. I turn and run. Fast. I am running through the thick rainforest. My camera is still rolling. I don't look back. I run until I get to the platform and climb back up to safety.

Peter is sanguine. He points out that one of the risks of this kind of research is coming across an elephant on these forest paths. The vegetation is so dense, you only know about it when the behemoth stands right before you. And on our way back we are indeed told to halt by the guide. "Elephant," he whispers pointing ahead. We retreat. We wait a while. Finally, the guide says, "Okay, let's go."

At our camp that evening, we discuss my storyline and how it is proceeding. I explain that I am working around a basic story framework. But I try to stay open as I go along. I try to be organic. Peter tells me about a documentary filmmaker he had collaborated with in Kenya many years previously. He'd come with a precise shot list and he was there to get each planned shot no matter what. That is not how I work. This is real life after all.

My Gabon trip has come to an end. In terms of building up an "elephant dictionary," Peter and his team are still at a basic level. But his work is crucial to figure out the social structure of the elusive and poorly understood forest elephants. And to be honest, the race is on. As usual, the statistics of the conservation status of this species are numbing, shocking and abstract all at the same time. According to the IUCN, the forest elephant, which is classified as critically endangered, experienced a loss of 86% in the 31 years leading to 2021. That makes the 60% loss in 50 years of savanna elephants seem comparatively piffling. Poaching for ivory and loss of habitat is what is causing this precipitous drop in numbers that can surely only end in extinction. And soon. Even more challenging is how to keep the public informed about the global environmental catastrophe without "conservation compassion fatigue" setting in. I don't have the answer.

But given humankind's over-population of the planet, over-exploitation of resources, and destructive behaviour, we need to urgently start living within the earth's carrying capacity. For example, what my neighbour said to me makes sense: the best thing we can do at this stage is to not have any children.

CHAPTER SIXTEEN
Saint Helena island

I am spending more and more time in Cape Town. Even nomads need a base. I'm done with the crummy short-term lease apartments in the Bo Kaap. And so I rent an apartment with a long-term lease in Tamboerskloof, my first home in four years. It is a bit pricey but as long as I keep getting Carte Blanche commissions, all will be well. As it happens, the next few pitches I send to Carte Blanche hit a brick wall. As my savings are rapidly dwindling, I get some AP work that will take me to a remote mid-Atlantic island. In January 2012, on a hot mid-summer day, I set off from Cape Town harbour on the RMS St Helena, one of the last working royal mail ships globally, and the only regular link between Saint Helena island and the outside world. Joining me again is Nicole Mccreedy who will be writing various articles while I work on four Associated Press news features.

Once upon a time, royal mail ships plied the world's oceans, most infamously the RMS Titanic. But times change, and specifically, aeroplanes revolutionised transport. A vestige of that previous era, the RMS Saint Helena travels between Cape Town and the British territory of Saint Helena island bringing mail, supplies and passengers in and out of one of the world's most remote islands. Saint Helena Island is a speck in the mid-Atlantic ocean and has no airport.

Although a modern ship, traditions are kept alive on this RMS. Every evening dinner is a suit-and-tie formal affair, and day and night there is a roster of events and activities. For example, a drag cabaret show one evening, or quoits on deck in the afternoon. Quoits is a game where participants throw a disc as close to the centre. Pub quizzes and shuffleboard. Cricket and afternoon tea. It does all smack of nostalgia somewhat, but perhaps that is because I'm not British.

The ship's captain is Andrew Greentree, who is from Saint Helena island. He tells me that with email and fax, they transport a fraction of the mail that they used to. Nonetheless, the ship remains a lifeline, as Second Officer Mia Henry tells me. "This ship is very important to Saint Helena. It brings in everything. Without the ship, supplies wouldn't get through." And there have been incidents over the years where the ship has been delayed. For an island 100% dependent on one ship for even the most basic of food supplies, that is a precarious arrangement.

The British took possession of Saint Helena in 1659, initially as part of the East India Trading company. The island remains a British territory, a remnant of the British Empire. There was no indigenous population to fight for independence. The island was uninhabited when the Brits arrived. The local population today numbers around 4500, and they are known as Saints. They're a creole people, who are of British and African slave blood.

Finally, after five days at sea, the dramatic volcanic island of Saint Helena appears. It seems insurmountable until we get close, and see the capital, Jamestown, which is located near the water's edge, with a steep V-shaped valley running behind it up to the jagged peaks. There is no harbour, so we get to the island in smaller boats. Jamestown is a historic British outpost, an eighteenth-century English time capsule of a town, with the jarring fluorescent decal contradiction of contemporary British police officers in modern police vehicles. The handful of British administrators and civil servants are derisively referred to as "white ants" by the Saints.

I am told that 80% of the Saints are employed by the UK government. It is truly an island of civil servants, and the motivation to create a local economy, therefore, does not exist. The Saints are British citizens and would like to stay that way, for the benefits accrued. Even if that makes them technically, "dependent." But the British government doesn't want to keep propping up an unsustainable territory. Therein lies the conflict. The solution? The UK government has put in motion plans to build the island's first-ever airport and is pinning its hopes on increased tourism as a source of revenue. That will render the RMS St Helena ship redundant, and radically improve access to the island.

Is building an airport the only solution to making this territory more self-sustainable? Certainly not. How about developing a local agricultural sector so that basic food doesn't have to be imported? Local fisherman Kenneth Williams speaking in the distinctive Saint Helena patois, tells me, "They run the place like the seventeenth century in the twenty-first century." Williams gives me some examples of entrepreneurship that has been blocked instead of nurtured by the government. A beer company, a printing press and a coffee shop, all owned by expats, have all been, "made to shut down." The South African who owned the coffee shop departed under an exclusion order, which is to say he was deported. "You don't rock the boat here," says Williams. When it comes to developing Saint Helena, perhaps the issue is not a lack of resources, but a lack of imagination by the UK government.

The most famous person associated with Saint Helena island is Napoleon Bonaparte. Following the defeat at the Battle of Waterloo in 1815, the British shipped him off to Saint Helena island, where he lived out the last years of his life at Longwood House. Interestingly Longwood House and garden, which is now a museum, is French territory. And a piece of French territory, however small, needs a French representative. I meet Michel Dancoisne-Martineau who fills the role of Honorary French Consul, and curator of the museum.

When I meet Dancoisne-Martineau, he is huffing and puffing about a great injustice.

"You are invited to the governor's house for lunch?"
"Yes."
"This is not right. It is an Anglo thing. We have a French photographer also here visiting the island. Why is he not invited?"

It feels like I have stepped into some kind of minor diplomatic incident, stemming from historic French-Anglo rivalry.

Lunch is at Plantation House, which is the British governor's residence. It is a stately old building dating back to 1791, and all the furniture, paintings and decor take one back to that period, much like a living museum.

Interestingly Governor Mark Capes is a career diplomat rather than a government administrator. As well as many diplomatic postings he also served as deputy governor on two Caribbean islands and tells me, "Islands are becoming my speciality."

I am seated next to Rebecca Cairns-Wicks who recently won an MBE (Member of the Most Excellent Order of the British Empire) for her work on the Millenium Forest of Saint Helena. I'll meet her again soon to find out more about this reforestation programme.

Although a French territory, the Longwood house and gardens where Napoleon Bonaparte was banished, have no immigration entry point. We simply enter the grounds. It is a museum that one can stroll through and glimpse life for the last few years of the exiled leader's life. Emperor Napoleon Bonaparte had already escaped from his first island of exile, Elba, in the Mediterranean. So when the British defeated Napoleon at the Battle of Waterloo in 1815 following the Napoleonic wars, they were determined to ship him so far away that there would be no opportunity for escape again. Napoleon settled into Longwood house, together with a voluntary entourage of 28. According to Decanter wine magazine which reported on handwritten notes sold at a 2015 auction, "They received around 50 bottles of wine a day in total, plus various spirits. They also got a daily food allowance that included 50 pounds (lbs) of beef and veal, 68lbs of bread, 50lbs of mutton and pork, one roasting pig, two turkeys, 12 pigeons and 42 eggs." Napoleon can wander within a seven-kilometre radius of the house. As far as imprisonment goes, this one does not sound too bad.

Just six years later in 1821, Napoleon Bonaparte dies at the age of 51. One of the many legends about Napoleon is that he was killed by arsenic poisoning but there is no evidence to back this up. For the Saints, Napoleon's death probably came as a relief as the island had become such a heavily militarised and fortified zone with 1000 soldiers tasked with keeping an eye on Napoleon.

Keeping the museum functioning has been a challenge due to termites and dampness. Longwood was nearly demolished back in the 1940s due to the chronic damage caused by termites. Fortunately, there has been a great deal of restoration work by French curators.

The island is only about sixteen by eight kilometres in size. That's no more than a rocky outcrop in the middle of nowhere, and I do get exactly that sense here. The feeling of being isolated. The nearest landmass is Africa, and that's 1950 kilometres away. Saint Helena is a dramatic mountainous volcanic island, and the road network entails sharp corners, switchbacks and hairpin bends. At one stage I have to reverse and carry out a three-point turn just to take a corner on one of the public roads. I am told by one of my contacts that drinking is a bit of a problem on the island. And that drinking and driving is an issue. Here lies one of the contradictions of a rule-laden first-world country administration managing a tiny faraway settlement with an indigenous population. Although drivers do get checked for drinking and driving with breathalysers, "the conviction rate is zero because everyone is related to everyone", so for example, it might be that the policeman is your second cousin and prosecution simply does not proceed.

Some parts of the island are as barren as a moonscape, but other areas, peppered with pillar box red British public telephone booths in misty green valleys seem rather like England. Tuning in the car's radio to a local station invariably means listening to country and western music. In the 1980s and 1990s, the Saints lost their full British citizenship and could not live in the UK, so they were very limited in where they could emigrate in search of work. Many went to Ascension island, another isolated British territory 1295 kilometres north of Saint Helena to work at the US military base. Hence the Saints return with a penchant for country and western music. In 2002, the Saints got their full UK citizenship returned. There are many more Saints living and working in the UK and abroad than there are living on Saint Helena island.

The arrival of human settlers on Saint Helena in the seventeenth century was to prove detrimental to the environment. People cut trees for buildings and firewood. Rabbits, cats, goats and other introduced livestock were very harmful to the island's vegetation, as were invasive plant species. Saint Helena went from heavily forested to mostly barren. "This was one of the earliest documented man-made environmental impacts recorded," says Rebecca Cairns-Wicks who is director of the Saint Helena National Trust.

Both the local gumwood and ebony were nearly lost to mankind. The local ebony species was considered to be extinct. That is until two saplings of the ebony were found growing on a cliff in 1980. That rediscovery kickstarted conservation on the island. Saplings started to be grown at the "Scotland" nursery. When I visit they are growing 46 species of endemic plants at the nursery. The Millennium Forest started in 2000 intending to reforest what was once known as the Great Wood. This was once upon a time the largest forest on the island, with a rich biodiversity of flora as well as insects and birds. By 1710 that forest was entirely gone. Between 2000 and 2010 over 10,000 indigenous trees have already been planted here, marking a dramatic change from a dusty barren semi-desert to a young green forest. Will the same biodiversity evolve as was once in the original Great Wood? That seems unlikely, yet it is a big step in the right direction of making amends for past destructive behaviour.

When I visit Saint Helena there is still no cell phone infrastructure. So during my very busy eight days producing AP stories, I arrange meetings and logistics through messages left at my hotel and messages left for me at the Tourism Office. My highlight is while standing in the Millennium Forest, filming with no one in sight, I suddenly get a tap on the shoulder. A Saint has appeared out of nowhere with a note for me, about a meeting. No sooner do I read the note that said Saint has once again disappeared. Life without cell phones is actually feasible!

Saint Helena's first-ever airport opened in 2016 and was built at a cost of about 285 million pounds. The South African construction company that built the airport went bankrupt soon after the project was completed. Upon testing the first flight landings, sudden strong winds (or "wind shear") turned out to be a challenge, and finally, it was decided that only small passenger planes (Brazilian Embraers) can use the airport. The RMS St Helena ended its Cape Town to Saint Helena island route in 2018, although a cargo ship still regularly brings in supplies to the island.

CHAPTER SEVENTEEN
The most expensive Primus beer

On returning to South Africa, I manage to get a Carte Blanche commission. The story is about a run-down, poorly secured nuclear reactor facility in Kinshasa, the Democratic Republic of Congo's capital city. CREN-K was built with the assistance of the USA, just before the Belgian Congo became an independent state in 1960, for medical, biological and industrial research. The reactor is located on a hillside exposed to erosion due to tropical rain. At least two rods of enriched uranium have disappeared over the years, one of which turned up in the hands of the Italian mafia. There is no maintenance to speak of at this, Africa's oldest nuclear installation. The risks are manifold.

I fly up to Kinshasa, and then catch a taxi to the Ave Maria Hotel. My contact is Yulu Kabamba, and we meet in the hotel restaurant. I have already spent a couple of months of phone calls, emails, letters sent, and payments made. I even have a national media accreditation.

"Welcome to Congo," Yulu says, animatedly with a raised fist. "Don't walk around on the streets, and don't film on the streets!"

Yulu is a local fixer who has managed to get hold of the head of the nuclear reactor facility, Professor Luyundulu Ndiku. It seems access to the nuclear facility is assured until Ndiku insists that we first get permission from national intelligence.

My next step is the South African Embassy, where I have a meeting arranged with the First Secretary. A couple of hours later I am ushered into his office.

"It's good that you are meeting us now. Many South Africans come here for business and we only find out about them after they've been arrested."

That's reassuring.

I tell the diplomat what the purpose of my visit is, and that Yulu and I are going to meet the Minister of Intelligence to get his okay for me to film at the nuclear reactor.

"Internal intelligence or external?" he asks pulling out his phone, ready to make a call.
"I'm not sure. I'll phone Yulu to find out."
Turns out Yulu has arranged for me to see the external Minister of Intelligence.

"Ok, wait, there is someone else we should speak to."
The South African official seems quite positive about the country. While we wait he tells me about the nightlife in Kinshasa. "Black and White nightclub is a good one. But be careful of the women. They might start at 30 to 50 dollars. But then the next morning they could push to 100 or more dollars." That's helpful advice from the Embassy but I am not planning on checking it out.

In the meantime, the diplomat's colleague arrives. They phone the minister to let him know I am coming (and that the Embassy knows about me). The three of us take the elevator down. The First Secretary's colleague turns to me and says:

"They might lock you up, but it will only be for 24 hours."
My eyes widen.
"I'm not joking," he adds.
At the Embassy entrance, I am stopped from strolling out.
"Phone the driver and wait until he comes to the front."
As I leave he adds, "you can phone me any time, I'm available 24 hours."
"Thanks very much."

My way of preparing for possible arrest is to eat a really big lunch and drink plenty of water at the hotel.

A little later I find myself in an airconditioned waiting room with red carpets, some faux Louis the Sun King furniture, a wall clock made of copper and a flat-screen tv playing local television. I am with Yulu and Professor Luyundulu Ndiku from the nuclear reactor who is kindly traipsing along. Ndiku wants to cover himself by having an okay from the ministerial level. The professor and I speak for a little while, and then our small talk gradually dies out, the last gasp being a comparison between the weather in our two countries.

Two hours later, I am called into the minister's office. It is an enormous room, also with red carpets, and at the far end, barely visible surrounded by piles of files, the minister. Standing in the middle of the room, and stretching my French to the maximum I introduce myself and my mission.

The minister listens quietly for a while. Or perhaps his mind is somewhere else. Having had many visits to the headmaster at school, this isn't an entirely unfamiliar experience. But then the atmosphere changes.

"You're a what?!" he barks. "Did you say, journalist?!"
"Yes."
"Don't you know what the security situation is in this country?! Impossible."

Given my interaction at the South African Embassy, I am not about to push this guy, and instead, thank him for his time.

Yulu and I leave, and in the car, he suggests we give a "gift" to the intelligence and the science ministers. It seems too little too late. But I let Yulu try to see what he can do.

The following day it becomes clear Yulu is just throwing good money after bad. And as much as it is a remarkable experience to draw crisp 100 US dollar notes from ATMs in a Central African city, it is not something I want to keep doing. I haven't given up though. I pitch Carte Blanche a plan B story—the Lola Ya Bonobo Sanctuary on the outskirts of Kinshasa. This is the only sanctuary for bonobos in the world. Bonobos are apes that are said to be our closest relatives. Unfortunately, there is no interest in this from Carte Blanche.

Then I try the Kinshasa zoo. It is the weekend so I won't get a reply from Carte Blanche. I go ahead and shoot this zoo, an extreme example of why caging animals is just a bad idea. These are some of the most forlorn-looking creatures trapped in disgusting small cages. But there's not enough here for a Carte Blanche story. I can't afford to stay on in Kinshasa, so with a very heavy heart, I depart, having at least enjoyed one Primus beer.

After passing through the organised chaos that is Kinshasa International airport, I find myself sitting on the flight and experiencing an awful empty feeling. I am returning without having gotten the footage of the assignment I came for. It's the only time this happens to me, but it couldn't come at a worse time. And is it me, or is it ironic that the only time I've worked with a fixer is the only time I am unsuccessful in my shoot? Is there something to be said for taking an organic approach and just feeling your way, alone?

***

Back in Cape Town, I am in financial dire straits. I put quite a bit of my money into the Kinshasa trip, and that is gone. I am pitching more stories to Carte Blanche but getting no interest. And there's silence from Associated Press. At this stage, I am probably drinking a bit too much red wine, and despondency has taken over. I can't afford my monthly apartment rental. There's a lot to be said for a friend giving a kick up your ass at the right moment. "Toughen up!" Nicole says. And, just as with Andrew back in 1999 after my first documentary footage was stolen from a Nangurukuru hotel, I kick back into action.

I realise that I have nothing to lose. And that from the position I am now in I can only go up. I ask myself what do I want to do? Well, I have always dreamt of making documentaries for the United Nations. Being a transnational person, and because I believe in multilateralism, the United Nations, flawed as it may be, is humanity's hope for the future. So I phone every UN agency in South Africa, and each time I am told to email my CV. I don't think more of it until I get contacted by UNAIDS asking me to be a videographer on a shoot in Kwazulu Natal. In the meantime, I have had to give up the Tamboerskloof apartment. But I am back in business.

The UNAIDS shoot documents the government's ARV rollout for HIV-positive South Africans. It's a big deal because the previous President, Thabo Mbeki, was (and remains) an AIDS denialist and so for many years the medical treatment did not get to those who needed it. Two studies, one at Harvard University, estimate that between 340,000 and 365,000 lives would have been saved had Mbeki acted to introduce ARVs. Now, with ARV medication finally being rolled out in the post-Mbeki era, HIV-positive South Africans can live normal healthy lives for many years instead of facing illness and early death.

Soon after shooting the footage for UNAIDS, I get contacted by UNICEF South Africa. Am I available to join a UNICEF videographer to go to Angola? Yes!

I fly up to Angola with Suzanne Beukes from UNICEF, a no-nonsense kind of girl engaged to be married. Luanda seems like the Portuguese developed it less than Maputo, but many shiny new buildings are going up. It is said to be one of the most expensive cities in the world because so much is imported and the oil industry inflates prices. Despite the oil wealth, there is a great deal of poverty in Angola. Two and a half decades of war only ended in 2002, and let's just say that corruption by the handful of the elite has been rampant. In Luanda, there is a strange combination of lovely but run-down Portuguese buildings, potholed roads, shanty towns, roadside vendors, ugly concrete buildings, new skyscrapers, and Porsche and Jaguar dealerships.

We meet and interview Koen the Dutch UNICEF Country Director who looks stressed and rushed off his feet. The subject of the first video I will make with Suzanne is Angola overcoming polio. As we finish up he says:

"Don't go out at night."

Needless to say, once we have booked into our hotel, we indeed take a walk on Luanda's streets looking for a restaurant.

We eat fish and potatoes at a local restaurant, and I make the mistake of having a beer. Just one drink the night before can negatively affect my shooting the next day. And walking back to our hotel, wary in a new city, I say:

"Let's not dilly dally, let's walk with some haste."

Back at the hotel, Suzanne says, "Good night young man." I point out that at 39 years old, I am eight years older than her.

We have a four am wake up call but because I haven't reset my phone and am still on South African time, my alarm goes off at three am and I sit around in the lobby waiting until I click why I am sitting there alone when I look up at a clock.

We drive to the north-east town of Uige in a white UNICEF Nissan Patrol. The landscape is savanna, forests and baobabs all the way, with little sign of human habitation for hours. We get stopped several times by traffic cops. This surprises Patricia, also with UNICEF. Patricia comes from Honduras but has spent many years in Angola.

"I guess it is because elections are coming up soon and things are a bit tense. But I've never been stopped before in Angola in a UNICEF vehicle."

One soldier who stops us is wearing a brand-new uniform. He is very particular about checking our passports, looking at the photos and matching them to our faces. This soldier insists that when we get to Uige we must register, another first for Patricia.

Uige is a small fairly well-preserved Portuguese colonial-era town, and more attractive than Luanda with its chaos, dirt and concrete. Upon arrival, we first get photocopies made of our passports in a little shop. These photocopies are barely legible as there is way too much ink. They overcharge Patricia saying that each page counts as two pages because although it is just one photocopy page it has two passport pages on it! Patricia shrugs her shoulders and pays. Then we go to immigration. They seem to know what to do. There is a book where foreigners' details are lodged.

"You must each pay 2000 Kwanza (20 dollars)."
And no, there is "no receipt available."
"What?!" asks Patricia.
The immigration official's Kafkaesque response is to try and sell the whole receipt book to Patricia for 15,000 Kwanza!
"That's enough!" says Patricia, and calls the UNICEF office in Luanda. She then passes the phone to the immigration guy. But he is not interested in talking.
What can we do, but pay the 20 dollars each, sans receipt.
"A scandal," says Patricia. "Everything is complicated in Angola."
I ask Patricia, "everything is challenging in Angola?"
"No, challenging means there's hope."

So off we head to our next Angolan challenge, or perhaps I should say our next Angolan complication. Before coming to Uige, Suzanne had arranged for us to meet and interview a polio victim. So off we go to Papa Joao who meets us at his home sitting in a wheelchair. We set up an interview in his backyard. In the distance we see the town spread out on the hills behind us. The framing is wonderful. It is now late afternoon, and the light is beautiful. Let's commence the interview.

Suzanne asks Papa Joao when he contracted polio.

"Polio?"

It turns out Papa Joao has never had polio. The UNICEF team all look at each other in disbelief. We're on a tight schedule and the major component of the story has just fallen through the floor. Now what?

Back in the vehicle, I suggest we pavement crawl in the Nissan and look for someone who may have had polio. So that is what we do. We cruise along the town streets, slowly, looking for someone in a wheelchair. It doesn't take long to find a potential subject: a young man in a red tricycle wheelchair. The hand-controlled pedals are in front of him, and this is linked to a chain that drives the front wheel.

As diplomatically as she can (but how do you ask this without being direct?) Patricia asks the young man if his disability is a result of polio.

"Yes," and Ricardo Monteiro also happens to be an open and friendly young man of 26 years of age, who agrees to be the subject of our short video. I jump out and start shooting immediately as he rolls along the roadside in his red tricycle wheelchair.

Ricardo faced rejection in his home village due to his disability and finally came to the town of Uige. Here he found employment in a welding shop, making doors and windows out of steel. In 2012 during this visit to Angola, the country is finally free of polio, thanks to the government and the development sector rolling out a vaccine programme. I film Ricardo at work welding, and we conduct an interview. Later back in Luanda we also film sequences of community-led polio vaccination campaigns, and then Suzanne and I co-edit the piece.

From Luanda, we fly down to Ondjiva in Kunene province where I shoot schools with up to 60 students per classroom. The story has to do with a new school wing that will be built.

After more long days rushing about trying to make a plan to get what is needed to be filmed, we head back to Luanda.

"I find it interesting that the conservatives and right-wingers and the very liberals and revolutionaries agree on one thing: that Africa should stand on its own feet, without aid," I say to Suzanne.
"That is just patronising," says Suzanne.

To be fair she is in the aid sector herself, and I am hired to work in said sector. Perhaps I could have added that humanitarian assistance is something separate and who can deny the developing world help with having a meal, a roof over one's head, refugee assistance, and a vaccine? Back in Luanda, we crawl through the terrible traffic to get to a meeting. I set about filming people sitting at a table holding a meeting that goes on for a long time.

Back at Johannesburg airport, Suzanne says, "Goodbye young man," and we go our separate ways.

***

Also in 2012, I am asked to go back up to Angola again for UNICEF. It is a one-day shoot and I get to stay in a Luanda five-star hotel. But sadly, as with the other very rare occasions that this happens, I only get to enjoy the room for a few brief hours of sleep.

Driving to a school in the UNICEF Landcruiser full of people, we get to talking about the United Nations. I say:

"I believe in the ideals of the UN."

Later, the Spanish photographer on the trip teases me about this. But that is what I believe: in multilateralism. It is not rocket science. If the whole world cooperates then we'd have fewer or even no wars.

We get to the school where UNICEF is involved, and I start filming.

But I soon realise there is something fishy going on here. This is not making a video (or as a cameraman only in this case) about those United Nations ideals. This is a commercial. One of UNICEF's sponsors is Starwood Hotels. That is not my issue, after all, the UN gets funding from various sources. It is how Starwood raises its donations for UNICEF that gets my goat. Guests at their hotels are "encouraged" to donate to UNICEF. So Starwood is purely a business, yet is here taking credit for its hotel guests contributing to UNICEF.

It's like when you've paid a lot of money to take a flight and as you settle into your seat, an advert comes on imploring you to contribute to a charity. Why don't you as the airline donate? I've just spent my precious money to be able to fly. Not only that but the said business will then claim corporate responsibility brownie points without having spent a cent.

Back to the present, I am standing with my camera in a Luanda suburb school, looking like an actor who has forgotten his lines, as I think about this injustice. This sham.

The Kunene region lies in the far north of Namibia. It is a mountainous, dry and sparsely populated wilderness. The people who inhabit this tough terrain of extremes are the Himba. The women rub a paste of butter, fat and red ochre onto their hair and skin. Just the ticket for Westerners seeking the "exotic tribes" of Africa. But I am not here with Westerners. After a seven-hour drive from the capital city Windhoek, I check into a hotel in the town of Opuwa with a team from UNICEF Namibia, and three journalists: Namibians and a Zimbabwean. The following morning we head into the Kunene wilderness.

After many hours of driving, we meet Vemupomambo Tjivida at a rendevous point. Vemupomambo is one of the first batches of health extension workers who are bringing basic health services to hard-to-reach communities. 26-year-old Vemupomambo recently completed a six-month training course and now walks long distances every day through this arid terrain, in search of the nomadic Himba. It is arduous work and one needs to be very fit. But he's happy to have the employment, the new skills, and to be able to serve his community.

Following Vemupomambo, we find a group of Himba at a well. In this dry land, the sources of water are crucial to survival. The Himba are pulling out water in buckets to feed their cattle at a trough. Vemupomambo's work is with under-five-year-olds. Being far from health services, these youngsters are vulnerable to malaria, diarrhoea and malnutrition. Vemupomambo checks the temperature and breathing of these infants and asks the mothers many questions. He can dispense medicine where needed. A mother explains to me that they don't own cars, so if there is a medical issue, they have a problem. Health extension workers like Vemupomambo are a positive step for under-five health and mortality in this region.

In the total of five days working on this shoot, only two to three hours are spent shooting the actual story of Vemupomambo and his outreach health work. The rest of the time is travelling and shooting government and UNICEF interviews. On the long drive back along the dusty back roads of the Kunene region, we start telling stories to each other. One of the journalists along for the trip is Moses Magadza, originally from Zimbabwe but now based in Windhoek. As a child, he had taken a bus in Zimbabwe, and when the vehicle came to a halt, a man called out that his bag had been stolen. A traditional healer was on the bus, and he said, "I will find the thief." Everyone was standing around on the side of the road next to the bus. The traditional healer held a ceremony. This ceremony involved pumping up a bicycle tyre tube. And as he pumped the bicycle tube, a passenger's stomach started growing and growing. Thus, the thief was identified and the stolen items were retrieved. Then I told my story of Praia de Zalala in Mozambique, the theft of my sunglasses, and the tyre tube pumping ceremony on the beach. I wonder what happened to the sunglasses thief of Zalala.

***

Traffic in Namibia's neat capital city, Windhoek, pulls off the road as our cavalcade of vehicles drives quickly across town. Blue lights are flashing and sirens are blaring. These are the warnings for all other road users to get out of the way, and fast. To say that I'm not a fan of "blue light brigades" is to make an understatement. To me, it fits into the "abuse of power" category. Yet here I am—in one!

Just before this dash across Windhoek, I had been filming a meeting at the UNICEF offices. Amongst other attendees was Graca Machel, who is the VIP in the car in front of me in the "blue light brigade." Graca was not only married to Mozambican president Samora Machel but also to Nelson Mandela, who needs no introduction. That makes her the first woman in the world to have been First Lady in two countries, according to the Guinness World Records. Her first husband, Samora Machel, died under mysterious circumstances in a plane crash in 1986, which many attribute to the apartheid South African government.

But Graca Machel is a force to be reckoned with in her own right. She served as Mozambique's Minister of Education and Culture from 1975 to 1989. She has a string of honorary doctorates, global awards and honours. And she is an advocate for women's and children's rights, education and development.

At the Windhoek UNICEF offices, she talks about issues facing children in Southern Africa because of poverty, but she also talks about some of the core issues still being dealt with in Namibia as a result of apartheid. Issues around dignity are mirrored in South Africa which ruled Namibia for much of the twentieth century.

Some people ask Graca Machel how her husband, the famous Nelson Mandela is.

She measures her words carefully. "He's old now." Madiba as it turns out, only lives for a few more months, dying at the grand old age of 95 in 2013.

The "blue light brigade" comes to a halt at a five-star hotel. Graca Machel, in the car in front, gets out. The entourage follows her inside. I am going to interview her about the upcoming UNICEF story I am about to film, on young people living with HIV AIDS. Finally, I am ushered into her hotel room.

I can see Graca Machel is a strong woman. Nelson Mandela liked strong women because Winnie Mandela was also one. Graca talks about the value of young people living with HIV and AIDS meeting and sharing their experiences.

In finishing, I want to give her my sixpence worth on what she had been talking about at the UNICEF offices.

"Maybe what we need in Namibia, and in South Africa, is a nation-wide psychologist for all of us."

Graca Machel just looks at me blankly. I leave the hotel room.

I am waiting outside her hotel room before we all leave together again. Graca Machel appears at her door. Spotting me, I get a smile.

I join the communications team of UNICEF to shoot the bulk of this story. To meet and start filming with our story's protagonist we go to Katatura township outside Windhoek. I've been in and out of townships in South Africa many times. Katatura with its corrugated iron structures serving as homes for those coming to the city in search of jobs seems at first glance similar to South Africa's townships. But when I go inside one or two of these shacks I am shocked by how sparse some of them are inside. Practically empty. No belongings and barely any furniture.

In one of these shacks, lives Sunday Ekandjo, a 17-year-old girl who is HIV positive. Her mother passed on the virus to Sunday during pregnancy. I film Sunday with her siblings and go to the shops. Then we go to the Katatura hospital, where Sunday is a member of the teen club. This group of teenagers living with HIV AIDS meet regularly. Being part of a group facing the same challenges helps them deal with the stigma around HIV, and to find acceptance. It helps them attain dignity and keep dreaming. The group also learns about the medication, antiretroviral therapy pills, that is the key to their living many more healthy years. Sunday's dream? To find a cure for HIV AIDS.

***

As a result of fossil fuel emissions, the planet is facing more extreme weather conditions. As a water-scarce, hot, dry country, Namibia needs to find ways to adapt to climate change. The Namib Desert Environmental Education Trust (Nadeet) aims to do just that. It's an education centre located on the edge of the Namib desert that teaches Namibian communities how to live more sustainably. I am visiting to produce a video news feature for Associated Press.

The Nadeet Centre takes its cues from the nature it is surrounded by. The desert is a place of extremes: over 40 degrees in the day and below zero degrees at night. Yet a surprisingly high amount of life is found here. And lessons can be learnt by how nature has adapted to this environment. I go for a walk into the desert with a Nadeet guide and a Namibian community group from the town of Klein Aub here to learn about living more sustainably.

Because the leaves of the camel thorn tree are small they lose little water in the desert heat, and the tree's white thorns reflect the sun's rays. The excrement of the oryx (antelope) is particularly dry and its urine is concentrated, thus saving water. The tok tokkie beetle has adapted to the extreme environment by being able to change its colour from black when it is cool or cold, to white when it is hot. Black absorbs heat, while white reflects the sunlight. Meanwhile, the dung beetle, a great recycler, feeds on faeces.

Taking its cue from how nature has evolved in the environment around it, the Nadeet centre uses water-less toilets (and the human waste is used as compost), solar power for all energy and cooking needs, and nothing goes to waste. About 80% of the waste generated over the four days that the Klein Aub community visited is organic food waste which can be turned into compost. Glass, tin, plastic and metal all serve new purposes.

If the dry parts of the world are getting drier, then how the camel thorn tree, the oryx, the tok tokkie and the dung beetle have adapted to a very dry extreme climate offers lessons for the whole planet. The Namib desert is an estimated 80 million years old. Nature has had much time to adapt. The last century of human history in Namibia has been rather more dramatic.

As the host to the Berlin Conference of 1884, where most of Africa was carved up by European powers, Germany was of course going to get its piece of the cake too. Namibia was a German colony from 1884 until the First World War when Germany lost its colonies because it lost the war. And a brutal genocidal occupation it was. The German colonialists ethnically cleansed the territory of Namibia to make way for German settlers. Over 50% of the Nama and Herero were annihilated. Adolf Hitler, and his European holocaust are often regarded as a freak of nature, whereas Hitler was influenced by and built on the genocidal policies in the colonies. Even the medical experiments carried out on Namibians were to be repeated by the Nazis. Inferior races, racial purity: these concepts came from colonial practice. The Swedish writer Sven Lindqvist wrote about these connections.

When Germany lost the First World War, Namibia was given to South Africa as a "mandate territory" by the League of Nations. South Africa clung onto this de facto "fifth province of South Africa," until finally, Namibia gained independence in 1990. Aside from being the only other country in the world where Afrikaans is spoken, the country shares some more of South Africa's dynamics.

One of the Namibian participants at Nadeet is *Oom* Frans Strauss. He tells me, "The crime rate keeps going up. I was robbed after I came out of a bank in Windhoek [the capital city]. We as Coloured Namibians, and the White Namibians are so few and are not connected. This is now a Black-dominated government and country. To start a new business anyone who is not Black needs a Black business partner."

I've enjoyed my time in The Namib Desert. The hot, sunny days with big blue skies. The open, stark, beautiful landscape. The silence. But most of all the people. It's people that make a place. And in this case, it has been a group of *die bruin mense* (the brown people). I am continuously thankful it has not been a group of German tourists, but rather this warm, light group of Namibians, who manage to find a reason to laugh so often. I enjoy so much being around them. When it comes time to say goodbye, I make a point of standing in front of them, thanking them for the week, and that I've enjoyed their company.

Ida Boois says to me, "We'll miss you."
"Me too," I reply.

And I know we both mean it, and it's a beautiful moment. They don't bugger about with false platitudes. They are real. And I know we are all still a bit haunted by the old colonial relationships. As a friend once said to me, we are all products of Empire. But any barrier can be broken when respect and friendliness come from the heart.

***

With a steady stream of work, life is looking up once more. After the winter spent in a luxury lodge in Hout Bay offering cheap monthly rates in their off-season, I rent, long term, a Vredehoek apartment with views over Cape Town's city bowl. It's a great neighbourhood, and my regular hikes up

Table Mountain start literally at my front door.

I produce several video news features for Associated Press in and around Cape Town, including one on sharks. The story is about the use of "shark spotters" who keep a beady eye on the ocean from vantage points, warning beach users when it is unsafe to enter the water. In my research, I discover that there were just six shark attack fatalities globally in 2010, and more recently, 13 deaths in 2020—meaning there is more chance of being killed by a falling coconut than being killed by a shark. But people's obsession with shark attacks, helped by the 1975 blockbuster Jaws, remains strong.

JP Andrew is a teenager who nearly became one of these rare statistics when he went surfing at Muizenberg. In one bite, he lost his leg and half his surfboard to a Great White Shark. He remembers thinking that this is the end, and indeed he was technically dead for many minutes. In the ambulance, he became conscious and heard a news report about a young surfer who had just been killed by a shark at Muizenberg. That is to say, him. His life was saved at a hospital, but with his brain wiped clean of information, he had to relearn everything, from reading and writing to walking on one leg. He still struggles with mathematics, indicating some brain damage. JP Andrew is philosophical and says the sea is the shark's domain, and indeed, when I meet him at Muizenberg beach, he is putting on his wet suit... to go surfing.

CHAPTER TWENTY
The youth and democracy across Africa

Rewind a few months and I am staying in the Hout Bay Lodge when I get an unexpected phone call. A lady, without introducing herself, starts talking about sending me a contract. I try to think what contract this could be. Then when she mentions the UNDP it starts to become clearer. She's from the United Nations Development Programme in Johannesburg. A few months before this, in the winter, I had spent two weeks of my downtime responding to two consultancy requests for proposals that I had found online. I had spent a full week writing up a proposal for each request and then forgotten about it. It seems I have been successful in one of these. And the budget I put in was, let us say, decent.

The documentary they have asked me to make for them is on the role of youth in changing the course of democracy and development in Africa. I get to choose the case studies and the countries. Considering the Arab Spring is in full swing in North Africa and the Middle East, I want to include this. And, I also definitely must have at least one or more women as case studies.

***

"Are you sure you want to leave Cape Town on such a beautiful day?"

The friendly check-in counter guy makes a dent in my not-great mood.

I am en route to Uganda, the first of five countries I am visiting to produce this documentary. I am travelling alone, shooting, and producing by myself. Would it be easier to have hired someone else? Maybe, but why if I *can* do it myself, and I will work quicker alone? Searching on the net I come across an article in a Ugandan newspaper about a dynamic young Ugandan called Davis Akampurira. Davis is a youth leader, canvassing for the rights of young people. I get hold of Davis' contacts from the journalist who wrote the article and write to Davis, who agrees to be filmed by me while he carries out his youth leadership activities.

It is a six am departure from Cape Town, and it takes until 3 am the following morning to check into my basic but pleasant Kampala hostel. I'm up at 8 am because I have much to do. Firstly and most importantly, I need to go into the media office and get my media permit. This turns out to be easier said than done.

I arrive at the government media building and tell them who I am. After all, I have been in regular contact with them for the last couple of weeks, they have already been sent all the documents they need, and when I phoned them I was told, "It will take an hour to process when you arrive."

The lady looks at my letter of introduction from the UNDP. She shakes her head.

"We can't issue you a film permit, because the UNDP is not a media house."
"But I've been in regular contact for the last few weeks and was told everything is okay."
With her haughty demeanour, she then adds, "…and you'll need a work permit."
Now it's getting hard to keep my cool.
"But I am a media house. Have a look at my website."
"That's nothing. Anyone can make a website."
Now she has gone beyond haughty, to stony.
Anyone can make a website? Are you suggesting I have a fake website?
That is what I am thinking to myself. My blood is boiling now.

It's day one and my shoot is hanging by a thread. I have set up a schedule of travelling in different countries over several weeks, so if this doesn't work, my entire production collapses like a house of cards. Considering these inefficiencies, I am struggling, at this moment, to understand why I like travelling in Africa.

I call Davis, my Uganda protagonist. He wants to do things "by the book." I.e. that I am working legally in Uganda. Yet "by the book" too is open to interpretation—fortunately. Davis, as it turns out, has a university friend who works in the department of immigration. I meet Davis, a confident young man in a snappy suit, and we pay said friend a visit. As it happens, his contact can provide me with an "official work permit" for an unofficial 100 US dollars.

A few hours later, I have my passport back in my hands. Next to my Ugandan tourist visa is an immigration stamp and written out by hand is a three-month work permit with the National Youth Council, Davis' organisation. Davis is more or less satisfied with the legality of my being here. It is not a film permit meaning I need to constantly be aware of where I am filming and should keep a low profile. But if Davis is satisfied, then so am I.

The countries in the world with the youngest populations are mostly African. Uganda is no exception. According to the World Bank, Uganda, with 47.41% under the age of 15, has the world's third youngest population.

This is no accolade. Especially in a developing country with few opportunities. When I visit in 2012, 62% of the youth are unemployed.

There is a state Youth Fund providing capital for young people to start up a business. However, with many difficult criteria such as the need for collateral, it had been hard to access. The youth responded by taking to the streets and facing the police head-on.

Davis successfully campaigned for the government to make accessing this money significantly easier. By the time I visit, over 4000 young entrepreneurs have benefited from the fund.

I drive with Davis to meet several young Ugandans who started businesses thanks to the Youth Fund. Conrad Musingwzi owns a jewellery shop with both locally hand-made items and imported products. "Before it wouldn't be easy, because I never had access to funds. With this youth loan, it will be easy for us to access money with low-interest rates." Conrad has dreams of expanding, getting employees and importing products himself.

In the evening, Davis takes me out for beers with his friends. I have so much on my plate. The days are full of shooting, and in the evenings I am busy with all the logistics of planning the next countries I will visit. So I don't touch alcohol now. Davis noticing is impressed.

"Usually when foreigners come here, and I host them, they drink so much. But not you. That is good!"

On our way through the city later that evening, Davis points out some houses.

"Those are for military staff. They were built by Idi Amin. So you see, not everything he did was bad."

Indeed, that is an argument one can make in many countries and regimes. (I think I might be hard-pressed to look for the positive in North Korea). Idi Amin easily falls prey to the Western portrayal of the African despot. I like to try to look at everyone (even despots) in a three-dimensional way, without affixing stereotypes.

Idi Amin ruled Uganda in the 1970s, and indeed it was a brutal period with approximately 300,000 people killed. In the West, the ruthless Amin was known as the butcher of Uganda.

Interestingly, some Ugandans look back fondly on Amin's rule. It is for the same reason that some Zimbabweans, and Africans, will also always look back favourably on Zimbabwe's Robert Mugabe, who the West also perceives negatively as a tin pot dictator. Like Mugabe, Idi Amin showed the middle finger to the West and kicked out a foreign class who ran the economy. In both cases, they were newly independent states but were only politically independent. The backbone of Zimbabwe's economy was commercial agriculture and Mugabe evicted the white farmers who ran the sector (even if many were second or third-generation Zimbabweans). In Uganda most large shops, businesses and factories were owned by Asians (some brought in as labourers by the British colonialists), and Amin gave them 90 days to leave the country (even if some had been born there). In both cases the effects on the country's economy were negative but the effect on indigenous people's dignity was positive.

Perhaps an analogy is needed for a European perspective. If the Greeks who had fought long and hard for freedom from Ottoman occupation and rule in the nineteenth century, found themselves to be a sovereign state, finally, yet the Turks still ran all the businesses, how would that have been sustainable? It wouldn't. (In the end the mass population exchange of 1923 sorted out that issue).

The road to decolonisation is a bumpy one. South Africa has been touted as exceptional, but the notion of national exceptionalism is simply arrogant. And as the largest settler colony in Africa, what will the nature of South Africa's decolonisation be? We got a taste of that with the July 2021 violent mass looting. Frankly, the decolonisation process is not complete until economic power lies in the hands of the indigenous majority. Nothing less is acceptable. Or realistic. It is simply logical.

Coming back to Uganda, Idi Amin overstretched himself when he invaded neighbouring Tanzania in 1979. Tanzanian forces, with Ugandan exiles, ousted Amin from power, and Amin went into exile in Saudi Arabia until he died in 2003.

After Idi Amin, came Milton Obote, and then in 1986, Yoweri Museveni came to power. And stayed in power.

Since Museveni, Uganda has at least experienced stability.

"We have a free press, and a multi-party system," says Davis. Yet there is much room for improvement.
"I was born in 1987 so I have only ever known one president," Davis laments. "Africa needs strong institutions, not strong leaders."
Indeed.
"One of the African leaders who impress me is Nelson Mandela. His selfless rule. He looked at the broader picture, not just at himself. And he didn't overstay in power," says Davis. Yes, Mandela stepped down after one term in office.

Davis' leadership started when he was head boy of his primary school and he has occupied many leadership roles since then including as president of the Uganda National Student's Association, and Secretary of International Affairs at the National Youth Council. Maybe one day he could be a truly democratic leader of Uganda who steps down after two terms in office. But the so-called "youth bulge" (a young population) needs to be tackled. Building strong institutions is the way to go but with a concomitant population explosion, it's going to be a massive challenge to create a prosperous country.

***

From Kampala, I fly with a stopover at Addis Ababa airport, west to Accra, Ghana. Country number two.

After Kampala, Accra feels flat and spread out. My first port of call is media accreditation. This government office is in what I would call the tropical architecture style. There is airflow through the building thanks to louvres designed into each wall, which also keep out the sun. That is a great concept in a hot and humid country like this. It is a pity that the more modern buildings in Accra are conventional square blocks that depend on air conditioning for cooling. A young beautiful personal assistant leads me to the media accreditation Mama. I hand over my passport and other documents that I had already been in touch with them for my accreditation. The Mama is friendly, yet while I wait on the sofa I notice a disconcerting sign on the wall.

"The government has noted with grave concern negative documentaries being made by foreign media. And so from henceforth, all film crews are to be accompanied by an official who will ensure that you stick to an agreed storyline, and the documentary has to be okayed by authorities before being broadcast."

A critical media? Shock and horror!

A free media? I don't think so. Perhaps the central tenet of journalism is independence. Journalists should be allowed to operate without interference from anyone and that includes any kind of oversight. No one has the right to run through what you are writing before it is published, because that is editorial control. A free press is exactly that: free.

According to The Economist, Ghana is one of only a handful of African countries that fall into the "democracy" category, albeit as a "flawed democracy." It is a flawed democracy if the press is not free or is quasi-free.

At the media accreditation office, nothing is said to me about a minder coming along, and I certainly do not say anything. So, 45 minutes later I leave the building with my Ghanaian media accreditation. I am ready to start shooting.

My online research led me to a Ghanaian NGO in Accra called Youth Empowerment Synergy. Here I meet with Emmanuel Edudzie who tells me about the Youth Manifesto that they are busy putting together. The ultimate goal is that this manifesto is a cogent voice for the needs of Ghana's youth that can be implemented into national policy.

I am introduced to Amos Katsekpor, a student and youth leader who is helping to gather the information for the Youth Manifesto. With Amos, I travel to the Jamestown area of Accra. In a building next to the landmark Jamestown lighthouse, Amos meets with a group of young people who will give their input to the Youth Manifesto.

Amos introduces the Youth Manifesto and asks for feedback. Some points are raised: we talk about 15 to 35-year-olds as being the youth yet teenagers are ignored, the need to focus on illiteracy, how the disabled can be better integrated into society, and the lowering of the voting age.

Amos and I take a series of buses across town to a radio station. Here he is interviewed and takes more feedback from young people.

Back at the NGO Youth Empowerment Synergy, the Youth Manifesto has taken shape. Some of the key areas youth have highlighted include youth-friendly health services, whether the education policy should provide for free education or whether quality should come first, and that the youth want to be more involved in decision-making.

I am in Ghana at the time of the elections, and I trail along as Amos and his team meet presidential candidates to get their support for the Youth Manifesto. I have remarkable access to an election rally for Nana Akufo-Addo who does not win this election but will go on to win the next election. Making my way through the throngs, I am allowed all the way through and onto the stage next to the forerunner for the upcoming elections.

A Youth Manifesto is the kind of document that any democracy should have. Considering that as with Uganda, and all of sub-Saharan Africa, the "youth bulge" is a huge issue, a strategic document with the views, aspirations and perspectives of the Ghanaian youth is doubly important here.

***

From Ghana, I fly back to South Africa, but again via Addis Ababa on Ethiopian Airways. Arriving at 10 pm at the airport and stopping at the transfer desk, I am told I get free hotel accommodation due to the length of time until my connecting flight. That sounds good in principle but when the bureaucratic process takes three hours that eats into any sleeping time one might have.

I lived in the Bole area where the airport is located from 1997-1998 but I don't recognise anything on the short two-kilometre ride in the minibus to the hotel. There has been so much development. After I drop my bags in my room, I go downstairs to eat dinner. I notice a man looking at me. Every time I glance up from writing in my notebook I see him staring assiduously at me. At some point he makes a scene pretending not to speak Amharic, asking a waiter for a lighter. At the hotel entrance, a woman enters and promptly sits at the seat right next to the front door. After I finish eating, I walk away to the lift, turning one last time. The waiter is gesticulating to "lighter man" that I am going up. In my hotel room, all the pieces fall into place. They, the government I assume, are keeping an eye on transit passengers (who have no visa). Then I struggle to sleep, remembering how I was harassed and intimidated at Bole airport back in 1998.

At that time I was working on a local Addis Ababa newspaper. On one of my flights out of Addis Ababa, at the old small airport, as I am about to board the flight I hear my name being called. A man, with several armed soldiers, tells me to follow him. We walk through a labyrinthine set of corridors. Finally, we enter a room where my luggage is on the ground next to a giant X-Ray machine. Standing in a circle around the luggage are about fifteen armed soldiers clutching their weapons.

"Is this your suitcase?"
"Yes."
"Open it."
Crouching on the ground, I open the bag. Inside are bras and other women's clothes. Looking up at the barrels of the guns, I explain that my sister is on the same flight, that we have the same suitcase, and that this is hers.
"What is this device?" one of the men shouts at me.
In my sister's suitcase, amongst her ladies' items, is a plastic bendable ruler which she uses for jewellery design.
The soldiers are all tense. I take out the ruler and explain what it is. Something innocuous.

"No. Plastic explosive." they bark at me.

They start cutting it up. Soon they are satisfied that it is no more than a flexible ruler.

Other items are checked in her suitcase. Finally, I am led onto the tarmac and onto the plane, which has been delayed by an hour. Why the show of force? I presume intimidation, seeing as I was working as a journalist.

Back to the present in my transit hotel. I finally manage to fall asleep but have a terrifying dream that I am about to be killed by these agents. The alarm goes off after about one hour of sleep. I get dressed, and head back to the airport in the arranged minibus, out of Ethiopia and another Bole airport experience.

***

Country number three is Tunisia, and I arrive in the capital Tunis on a flight via Cairo. It has been less than two years since the Arab Spring was ignited here in Tunisia. It happened because of corruption, a dictatorship, and lack of opportunities, and it spread fast across the region. I want to meet young Tunisians who were central to that uprising. Back in South Africa, I had gotten in touch with the Afro-Middle East Centre in Johannesburg which put me in contact with a Khamis Ennouri in Tunisia, who in turn gives me a contact of a certain Mohammed, based in Tunis, who he assures me will be able to assist. It's all rather tenuous.

Having gathered various documents, I received my media accreditation from the Tunisian Embassy before arrival, so I hit the ground running. As soon as I have a local sim card at Tunis airport I call Mohammed. We arrange to meet.

"Yes, I can introduce you to a youth who was part of the revolution."

To get some gender balance for the documentary, I ask if a woman is available. Yes. But that does not materialise.

The next day, travelling with Mohammed in a taxi we head to one of the poorer suburbs of Tunis.

As we drive, Mohammed turns to me and says:

"Don't worry, I am not secret police."
"Okay."
"I work in a factory. I make jerseys."
"I see."

I don't know this guy from a bar of soap. And I just don't have a feel for this country.

Despite George Bush's referring to Africa as a "country" it is made of many diverse cultures, and the Arab North as compared to sub-Saharan Africa is perhaps the biggest divide.

Mohammed leads me to a nondescript white building. We enter and walk up a flight of stairs.

Through a corridor is a room. Mohammed opens up for us to enter.

In the room is a group of students. I am introduced to them all, and we communicate in French. Specifically, Khalil Banaoumin is identified as someone I can interview, as a leader. Although this is a preliminary meeting, I ask if I can start filming.

"Okay."

I pull out my camera and for the next three hours interview them all on their experiences of life before and during the revolution.

Khalil explains that before the revolution there was much fear—of the regime and particularly President Ben Ali's secret police. There was no freedom of speech, and meetings and assemblies were prohibited.

Khalil and this group of students used to meet secretly in the room I am filming. As one of the students points out, walls had ears, and this was the only safe place to gather. Here they spoke about the kind of country they wanted to have. They wanted dignity and freedom.

Another student says, "To be honest we didn't expect the day would come when we would get rid of Ben Ali."

Following the self-immolation of a street vendor, Mohamed Bouazizi, in December 2010, vast crowds took to the streets calling for the downfall of President Zine El Abidine Ben Ali, coordinating the uprising using Facebook.

A month later Ben Ali fled into exile in Saudi Arabia.

I want to know if these students who participated in the revolution feel that it was successful.

At this first critical question about the revolution, I notice in the corner of my eye, my interlocuter Mohammed stiffen.

According to Mohammed, the revolution was a great success and there is nothing else to say.

Mohammed keeps telling me he has other business to attend to, yet he doesn't seem to be able to pull himself away.

The students tell me that they have gained the right to assemble, to create any organisation, they now have freedom of speech, a free press, the freedom to be filmed by me... but that their revolution is an ongoing work. People must protect the gains made even if it means another revolution.

Having got footage of the students singing their revolutionary songs, having conducted interviews, and getting a couple of shots of Khalil walking on the street, I know I have made a good start. Not bad for day one. Khalil leads us out to the street and an event taking place around the corner. Khalil's father runs a children's charity helping kids in the neighbourhood. I am asked to go on the stage and say a few words. I didn't expect this. I walk up to a sea of children's eyes, and in the best French I can muster, say, "I am here from South Africa, in solidarity with the people of Tunisia." I get a few nods from my student friends.

It's the day that I get to be a politician for a few minutes. And it's also the day I get some nice footage of a group of youth who recently were on the streets and brought down a government. I would like to meet Khalil again to shoot some more sequences.

"No problem," he tells me.
In words that will soon haunt me, one of his compatriots says to me, "Khalil is a very honourable and responsible man."

We all part ways, and I go back to my hotel in the city.

Two days later is my birthday, and I have an arrangement to meet with Khalil at 10 am. Khalil does not arrive nor does he answer his phone. I call Mohammed, who helpfully suggests that maybe Khalil is in a meeting. A part of me can't help fearing the worst. All afternoon and evening I try Khalil's number, as well as the two people who know him, Mohammed and a translator, Ayman. To no avail. Khalil has disappeared. I shoot some other scenes with another youth organisation in the meantime.

The next day, having gone through the footage and interviews I have, I am starting to wonder if I can make the story work with what I shot on that first day. Maybe it is possible. Especially with sourced footage of the revolution added.

I check my emails, and my father has written to inform me that my uncle has just died. He took his own life. Yesterday, on my birthday. I am about to go out to the ancient site of Carthage, and I decide to go anyway. It is overcast and cold. I feel shocked by the news. For some reason at Carthage I arrange for a guide to take me around, something I never do. She is telling me about being a Mediterranean person, and what a mix that is. She is telling me about ancient Carthage and what an important trading hub it was in the classical world. But I just can't focus.

"Please can we stop this early?"
She takes it as an affront.
"I got some bad news today," I tell her.
She takes a step back. "From your family?" she asks.
"Yes from my family." How did she know? She is understanding, and I wander about the old ruins by myself, just trying to make sense of something that does not make sense.

The next day, running through my footage with another translator, I decide that I probably have sufficient video. I don't stop trying to phone Khalil but it is to no avail. He has pulled a runner. Is it me or would a short text message saying he is no longer available be the decent thing to do? Or perhaps the shifty Mohammed was involved in the mystery of the disappearing protagonist.

The Arab Spring spread across the Middle East region to Egypt, Libya, Yemen, Syria and Bahrain and elsewhere. Tunisia is considered to have been the only real success story as the revolution resulted in constitutional democratic governance. In reality, a decade later, many of the old issues such as unemployment and corruption are still very much at the forefront of discontent in Tunisia.

***

It's a short hop from Tunis across to Cairo, Egypt. Country number four. There are specific and expensive customs procedures I have to go through, to temporarily import my camera equipment into the country. Then I settle into the City View Hotel, located next to Tahrir Square, the epicentre of the recent—and incomplete—revolution.

Also thanks to the Afro-Middle East Centre in Johannesburg, I have a youth leader contact. I have emailed Mohamed and he is expecting me. I fetch my media accreditation and this time there really will be a government minder. But only for a part of my shoot.

I head out to meet my contact Mohamed in a historic cafe in the Cairo city centre, with its beautiful but grubby nineteenth-century buildings. I wait. And wait. Unfortunately, Mohamed does not appear.

I start looking for alternatives right away, getting in touch with an Egyptian producer, Wael Omar who says he can probably find someone for me. Meanwhile, the following day Mohamed reappears, and we have coffee. He is an option as a protagonist. That is until I meet the contact person Wael had suggested.

I meet Seif Khirfan at Sufi Cafe and Bookstore in the Zamalek area, Cairo's version of Manhattan island. It's a characterful and historic cafe. Seif is a generous spirit, an articulate and patient medical doctor turned activist turned journalist. And he was in the heat of the revolution.

When Seif appears, and after we have introduced ourselves, he drops a reference to homosexuality. I say:
"I don't understand the issue. They've always been a part of society everywhere."
Soon I realise that is the comment that means I pass the test. Now Seif will work with me.
Seif tells me about the South Africans he had met on holiday in the Sinai peninsula.
"I didn't know that some White South Africans were actively working against the apartheid government."
"Yes, but a minority."

While Seif goes out of the room for a few minutes, a young Egyptian woman sitting at the next table gets talking to me. Her name is Mai and we swap emails. Seif has a wry smile when he reappears to see Mai and me talking. It might seem quite innocuous and banal that the conversation between Mai and I took place. Yet in the Arab world, this is probably irregular.

Seif and I make arrangements to meet soon and start shooting. Seif is my protagonist.

In my downtime, as with every country on this shoot, I walk the streets of Cairo with my little Sony palmcorder video camera, surreptitiously getting shots of people and city street scenes. I sit in coffee shops and local restaurants, walking the city up and down, all the while getting visuals.

I find myself at Tahrir Square, the site of the recent revolution. At one end is the giant modernist Mogamma government building, at the other end the rose-coloured Egyptian museum, and on the other side the typically grubby nineteenth-century Cairo city centre apartment buildings. The year before, I had watched the revolution on international news channels, wishing I was here. And now I am.

Today Tahrir square is full of tents. I will soon "officially" (with a government minder) go to Tahrir and interview some of these people to find out why they are camping out on the square. Thinking that perhaps I can already get a couple of shots with my little camera, I approach the crowds at Tahrir. My camera is in my pocket, ready to pull out. Then in the corner of my eye, I notice a man in a beige coat, collars turned up, wearing Ray Ban aviator sunglasses. He is keeping an eye on me. I click immediately. Could it be more obvious that he's a government agent? I keep my camera in my pocket and walk on.

Seif and I spend a full day together, with me interviewing him, and getting some visuals of him in the city. He has also provided me with some photos I can use of the period of the revolution.

Like Tunisia, Egyptians had been living with corruption, a lack of human rights, and police brutality under President Hosni Mubarak's regime. Add unemployment to the toxic mix and it seems almost inevitable the 30-year regime could not be sustainable—in hindsight at least. Western journalist Robert Fisk describes the situation, "The filth and the slums, the open sewers and the corruption of every government official, the bulging prisons, the laughable elections, the whole vast sclerotic edifice of power has, at last, brought Egyptians on to the streets."

Seif explains to me that in the two years before the revolution, human rights violations and torture were being uploaded online and onto social media. Then, on January 25 2011, Facebook posts encouraged people to demonstrate against police brutality. Ironic considering that is the National Police Day.

Seif joined in the throngs making their way to Tahrir Square. For his trouble, he was shot with 23 pellets. As the uprising continued Seif worked as a medical doctor, but he saw how the Egyptian media portrayed the uprising negatively, casting the revolutionaries as traitors. There was no coverage of the live ammunition, the injuries, or the deaths. So with compatriots, Seif started a satellite TV channel presented and produced by the youth. They were telling the true stories from the streets for 18 months until being forced to shut it down due to a lack of advertising revenue. But Seif's transformation from doctor to journalist was complete.

The Egyptian revolution lasted less than a month. By 11 February Hosni Mubarak resigned. Stating that he was born in Egypt and would die in Egypt, Mubarak, unlike Ben Ali of Tunisia did not pull a runner. For his trouble, he was sentenced to prison but then released in 2017.

I go to Sufi Cafe and Bookstore and buy a copy of Wael Ghonim's book, Revolution 2.0. Ghonim's Facebook page played a significant role in instigating the Egyptian revolution by bringing Egyptians onto the streets. He paid for that with eleven awful days in the hands of the security forces.

Even though Mubarak has been deposed, the revolution is not over. This is clear by the tents on Tahrir square housing unsatisfied young Egyptians. I return to Tahrir with Seif, and a pudgy and nervous government minder, Eslam. We find a protester camped on the square willing to be interviewed by Seif. For Said Salah, living in a tent here on Tahrir, the only thing that has changed post-revolution is the removal of Hosni Mubarak.

At one point during the interview, my government minder, Eslam, huffing and puffing as he tries to keep up with us, turns to me and says, "This is not a good image of Egypt here." Yeah well, this is reality. But he doesn't stop us from interviewing the revolutionaries.

Taking me aside again, Eslam says to me, "Usually I would only go to Tahrir Square with a journalist if I was accompanied by five bodyguards. But this has been short notice. If I say, "Let's go," you need to pack your gear immediately and move out."
Eslam looks around anxiously, and frequently asks me, "Finished?"
"Not yet."

Finally, we are, and we move off.

In the evening, I shoot Seif and fellow journalist Ahmed Elassy in conversation about the people camping out at Tahrir Square. This will work as an introduction to the Tahrir Square shoot. They insist that I film the conversation in a bar while they drink beer. It is a nondescript building in Central Cairo. A hole-in-the-wall bar without a name. Ahmed points out that there are a variety of people on the square, with different motivations for being there, and that Egypt is not monolithic. It is not only Arabic, not only Islamic.

Later I also join Seif at another bar where he is playing the percussion. He explains the phenomenon of more people going out at night than usual during this tense period of the revolution, and compares it to Beirut's lively nightlife during the civil war in Lebanon, what I refer to as, "the Beirut Factor."

The demands of the Egyptian revolutionaries are bread, freedom, justice and dignity. Despite the overthrow of Mubarak the aims will not be attained. By 2013 the democratically elected Muslim Brotherhood is deposed by the military. Despite all their talk of democracy, the West of course will quietly support the illegal military takeover and removal of the Muslim Brotherhood, because of its Islamophobia. Al-Sisi swaps his military uniform for a suit and the regime reverts to something akin to the Mubarak era, except that Al-Sisi is the bland version of Mubarak. Mubarak without a personality. What of the future? As the oft-quoted Syrian playwright, Saadallah Wannous said, "We are condemned to hope."

Egypt has been interesting, and it has been a successful shoot. The City View Hotel organises a taxi for the airport. In front of the hotel's entrance are four lanes of traffic, two lanes in each direction. And it is gridlock traffic. Bumper to bumper, immobile cars. With incessant hooting. The fact that we need to be going in the opposite direction does not deter the taxi driver. He manages to edge himself 180 degrees around into the other side of the road, inch by inch, with the generous use of the hooter. A remarkable piece of driving.

At Cairo airport, I get stamped out of the country and install myself at the airport bar to enjoy a much-deserved beer. A fellow passenger notices my accent and as it turns out he is also South African. Vernon works in the oil sector in Saudi Arabia. He is going home to see his family.

"I make US$ 17,000 a month."
It's hard to believe but maybe it's true.
"I was in Colombia before. The women are beautiful."
"So I've heard."
"Yes, I met one and I ended my marriage back in South Africa. But finally, I went home to my wife and kids. She hasn't forgiven me yet. We're still patching things up."
Vernon tells me more about his halcyon days in Colombia. Certainly a world away from Saudi Arabia where he now works.
"If you could go back in time would you do things differently?"
Vernon only pauses for a second. Smiling he says, "No."
I've just started my fourth World War Two POW survival book which I tell Vernon.
He says "you never know when you might need survival skills."
"True."
I say to Vernon: "It's not just Germans and Japanese capable of doing these things. The dark side is present in all, or most people."
Vernon doesn't say anything, he just gives me a look. Some time later I click. Vernon is Coloured, and the look he gave me probably has to do with race relations and history in South Africa.

Later we walk together, beers in hand, to catch our flight to South Africa.

***

My fifth and final country for the production of this documentary on youth and democracy is Mozambique, and I drive, over two days from Cape Town to Maputo. Old habits die hard, and I stay at Fatima's backpackers. In the morning I awaken to a thud. I immediately get up, knowing that my car is hemmed in by other cars in the small parking space. I make my way downstairs, and true enough, a young Dutchman working in the renewable energy sector (aren't they all?), in a white double cab Toyota pick up is trying to do the impossible—squeeze through a gap that his vehicle cannot. The thud I heard was his 4X4 bashing the front of my car.

"How the hell did you think you could get your car past mine?" I shout at him.

He doesn't have much to say for himself except that his insurance will pay for the damage.

I have a lot of memories of Fatima's, having stayed here regularly since 1996. But pretty much all the staff are new except for one of the cleaning ladies—the one with the disfigured face. I rise to greet her and I get a kiss on each cheek. The staff used to know me as the one who was en route "to the north." But now, aside from this one lady and one of the guards, it's just the walls that can talk.

In my quest for a protagonist I had been in touch with the Youth Parliament of Mozambique, and they had referred me to Suzete Sangula, a proactive member of the Youth Parliament, and currently Chairman of the Assembly of the Mozambican Secondary Students Association.

Suzete has agreed by email to participate in the documentary, and she meets me at Fatima's. Everything seems promising considering she is actively involved in informing young women of their rights at schools. The documentary badly needs a female perspective. Suzete and I agree to meet again soon to start filming.

My next stop is to get my media accreditation. I go across to the *Gabinete de Informacao*, to whom I had emailed my film permit application a week before. Within five minutes I have my accreditation. No fee and no questions asked. It has been by far the easiest film permit of the five countries I have been producing the documentary in. And that is how it has been for me working in Mozambique for the last several years over many trips. Five years later, in 2018, everything will change. From being free, the government announces that foreign media will have to pay US$2500 per trip for media accreditation. Local media also get hit by crippling fee hikes.

Fortunately, these exorbitant price hikes have yet to be implemented, not least because of a constitutional court decision.

Mozambique is still a new country. It only got independence in 1975. Since then the same political party has been in power. State institutions are weak at best. Insecure governments can't handle criticism, and there is much to criticise in Mozambique, from chronic corruption to an Islamic militant war in the north. Putting a lid on media coverage is a logical if ham-fisted means to deal with negative perceptions of the country. But it further degrades the limited democracy the country has because a free press equals freedom of speech. And freedom of speech is fundamental to democracy. Of course, there are caveats. Hate speech and incitement to violence are not acceptable. Radio station broadcasts played a significant role in the 1994 Rwandan genocide, for example. And the quality of journalism indeed varies—but it is your responsibility to source news from outlets with the highest acknowledged journalistic standards, and to source news from a variety of sources. Don't count on social media messages for your information—seek out the most reputable news outlets.

I always enjoy being in Mozambique. At an internet cafe, I buy a sim card, so I am connected. Interacting with the Mozambicans, I am reminded of why I like this place. Mozambique is *a terra da boa gente*—the land of the good people.

Suzete became an activist when a teacher at her school impregnated a fellow student. The pregnant girl had to drop out of school, and the teacher was not punished. For Suzete the status quo was unacceptable, and she set out to improve the situation for the rights of women and girls in Mozambique. It is simply barbaric that parents in Mozambique and many other countries, will sell off their 13-year-old daughter to a strange man, often quite a lot older, for cash. Any dreams, hopes, and aspirations that girl may have had will be dashed permanently. Her education will be terminated. Instead, her lot will be pregnancy, raising children, cleaning and cooking.

In a summer tropical downpour, I drive over to a university to meet Suzete. I'm surprised my little car doesn't simply float on down the main road, the inundation is so heavy. I meet Suzete at a meeting with her and the Assembly of the Mozambican Secondary Students Association. Suzete explains that one of the key messages for female scholars is to work hard and get good marks. That lessens the chance of a male teacher offering to pass the scholar in exchange for sex.

Suzete and I arrange for me to film her running a workshop at a secondary school. We drive there together, only to discover that they know nothing about it. So for something to shoot, we go to the home of one of the scholars who has already attended one of Suzete's workshops.

I film Carolina Namburete in her garden telling Suzete all that she gained from one of Suzete's workshops. Despite being the daughter of "traditional parents" Carolina found the confidence to tell her parents that it is up to her if she wants to marry, and who she wants to marry. Suzete also asks Carolina's brother, Egas, how Carolina changed after the women's rights workshop. Her brother explains that he understands that Carolina has the right to follow her path in life and that he is now doing much more at home such as cleaning and cooking.

There is no disputing Suzete as a modernising force for change. At the time of my visit, she has already held 30 workshops at schools, impacting the lives of many teenagers. It is strange then that she should keep asking me, "Why are you not married? Why don't you have a family?"—rather traditional questions, if you ask me.

The next time we go to the secondary school they are expecting us, and interspersed with music and dancing to keep up the energy levels, Suzete asks some students about women's rights. Early forced marriage is recognised as a problem in society, and as Suzete says these are "not early marriages—they are forced unions."

***

Having worked on the edit with Dan Clayton of Fixer Films, it is time to screen it for the UNDP. I fly up to Johannesburg and enter the Fort Knox of a UNDP building. Following the screening, attended by various staff, none of which work in communications or media, I get feedback.

"We appreciated that it was at street level."
"Thanks."
"And we love Suzete, she's such a dynamic young woman. Can you put her at the beginning of the documentary?"
"Yes, I can."
"And, because this is the year of the woman, we'd like to see more women in the documentary, such as in the Arab Spring sections."
A pause from me as I digest this.
"With all due respect, I just returned from North Africa, without having shot any woman because I wasn't asked to."
Another pause from me.
"But I'll see what I can do."

That is the difference between being asked to produce video content by a broadcast professional (who one can even learn from) and someone who doesn't understand what it takes to produce video. If you want women in Egypt doesn't it make sense to ask me beforehand, rather than whimsically asking me to add it at the end of the production? Anyway, I got a couple of "looks" when the staff left the viewing! I then went on a mission to track down footage of women in the Egyptian revolution. And of course, I could find it. And of course, considering how well I was being paid, it should not have been an issue. Jump? Yes sir, how high would you like me to jump? That is my mea culpa, folks. And that is the nature of producing NGO-type videos—the story parameters are theirs for you to fulfil.

CHAPTER TWENTY-ONE
"If It Works"

During 2013 I produce several Associated Press features in Cape Town and other parts of South Africa. A story that stands out is how a group of housewives in Cape Town's southern suburbs are saving the Western Leopard Toad from extinction. This toad, with chocolate brown spots against a yellow background, is only found in a few specific locations in the south-west corner of the Western Cape province. Rampant urbanisation has resulted in the toads facing almost certain death as they migrate across busy roads to their breeding ponds. They are known to travel up to eight kilometres. About 70 volunteers, most of them housewives from these suburbs, have been helping the toads safely across the roads. These volunteers either physically pick up and move the toads across the road, or collect the toads that fall into buckets placed in the ground along the roadside, and then take the toads across the road. I spend an evening with volunteer Suzie J'Kul in her Toyota Prius as she saves these endangered toads. Her comment to me about why she does this has stayed with me. "These days on TV we see so many problems and crises all over the world. But we can't really do anything about those. That's why I decided to focus on doing something here in my neighbourhood."

What I have also thought back to many times is the comment I got back from the Carte Blanche Managing Editor when I produced an insert for them on the Sixth Extinction. In the history of our planet, we've experienced five mass extinction events, the most recent being believed to have been caused by climate change when a meteor hit the planet and resulted in the extinction of dinosaurs. Today, human impact through pollution, deforestation, over-fishing and agriculture are all contributing to a loss of species so rapid scientists are referring to it as the sixth extinction. Scientist and sixth extinction activist Dr John Anderson reckons that we as a species only have about 100 years left unless we do something drastic to live sustainably. As case studies, I look at the protea odorata, a near extinct flower, and the critically endangered riverine rabbit. It's a story close to my heart. The cameraman on that shoot has an interesting idea: to utilise a TV monitor behind the interview subject for video and graphic visuals. I ask the Managing Editor whether I can use this technique. After all, Carte Blanche is a formula TV show. She says, "if it works." It seems an abrupt comment at the time, yet actually, it's a profound comment for any creative pursuit. It did work.

I also shoot three UNICEF videos in Namibia. In Cape Town, I purchase a run-down Lower Woodstock house. I am a property owner once more. Things are looking up compared to just two years back when I was broke and had to give up a rented apartment.

CHAPTER TWENTY-TWO
Smashing xenophobia through theatre

A lot of Africans forced to flee their homes because of conflict end up in a refugee camp in another African country. Just as in the West, these migrants are not always welcomed by locals. I've been asked by the United Nations High Commissioner for Refugees to produce a documentary on a theatre production in a refugee camp in Malawi. The purpose of staging the play is to bring together refugees and Malawians in the production of this performance, thus creating ties between these two communities.

My week in Malawi will encompass the last days of rehearsals and the staging of the play. I land at Lilongwe airport, and just as my father did when we left the country in 1985, I take a lungful of air. Those bush aromas say "home" to me.

I am driven directly to a rehearsal in the Crossroads suburb of Lilongwe, and immediately start shooting. I intend to find two protagonists: a Malawian and a refugee who are participating in the play, which is a fantasy soccer world cup final story. I haven't identified them yet, so I make sure I shoot everyone at this rehearsal.

The next morning, a Monday, I walk across to the UNHCR offices to have a meeting and work out my shoot strategy. En route, I pass an old man on the side of the road. He is begging. I walk past, thinking I'd like to give him something, but not money. Suddenly I remember I have a packet of peanuts in my pocket from the flight to Malawi. I turn back and give it to him. A newspaper vendor, who is walking past, says to me loudly, "May God bless you."

After my meeting at the UNHCR, I have lunch at my usual spot, under the trees in the quiet city centre area. Rice, beans and spinach. Cheap. Simple and decent. But I'll admit it gets monotonous after a few days. A young man is shouting, proselytizing to the patrons. Everyone ignores him. When I leave I pass another man on a street corner shouting his fire and brimstone-sounding message from the bible.

Just 40 kilometres north of Lilongwe, Malawi's capital city, is the nation's only refugee camp. Dzaleka has a dark history. Before democratisation in 1994, this was the site of a political prison. Today it is easy to find Malawians or long-term expats speaking in positive terms about former president Hastings Banda who ruled from independence in 1964 until 1994. Banda, the "benevolent dictator" who managed the country relatively efficiently. But there is no getting around the thousands of people killed, detained and tortured during his rule.

Before 1994 Dzaleka prison was the site of some of these human rights abuses. Then in 1994 when Malawi became a multi-party democracy, Dzaleka was reconfigured as a camp for people fleeing conflict, primarily the Great Lakes region states such as the Democratic Republic of Congo.

I am surprised by how the camp looks. There is a sense of permanence here. It does not consist of the archetypal rows of white tents. Instead, it looks practically like a typical Malawian village. Brick and mud houses, markets, communal well points, restaurants and butchers with their meat hung outside. When I visit there are around 20,000 people there. Just seven years later that has shot up to 50,000 people who must stay within the camp and somehow eke out an existence, with insufficient food aid provided. And that sense of permanence is all too real for the camp inhabitants, who as in so many other refugee camps globally, see the following generations born and raised—in limbo.

Faraja Musangwa is a 19-year-old Congolese from the troubled eastern region of his country. He will be my refugee protagonist.

"I was in a theatre group there—that's why I fled. [The theatre group] was against there being children in the military. In my village, people were forced into the military including children. Mai Mai rebels came looking for me, to kill me. They came to my house and took me by force. They raped me."

Faraja was taken up to a mountain and interrogated about his involvement in the theatre group. They decided to kill Faraja, and two men came. They had knives. First, he was raped again. Then the men got into an argument. Faraja grabbed the opportunity to make a run for it. He travelled through the bush east to Lake Tanganyika, and then the long trek down to Malawi. Meanwhile, his parents were killed by the Mai Mai rebels. Returning for Faraja would mean death by the Mai Mai.

Faraja has taken on the role of parent to three younger family members. That is quite a job for someone who is not yet an adult himself. He does this by selling second-hand clothes or hunting for the occasional jackal. He lives with his sister and two other extended family members in a tiny mud hut that is practically bare inside. The only possessions I spot are a small wood-fired cooking stove and two pots. I interview Faraja and get some shots of him in the camp. Then I travel with him to Lilongwe for the next rehearsals.

Jeremy Avis and Rebecca Askew, two wholesome but wild-eyed Brits, are the directors behind the theatre production of a famous footballer who is tempted by the promise of money to fix a soccer match. Upon meeting

Rebecca, she practically presses herself against me. I am nonchalant. I can see she and Jeremy are a couple. They are clearly "in sync" and on the same wavelength. They are amusing in the British way.

The cast consists of 280 Malawians and refugees, so Jeremy and Rebecca have their work cut out for them. Faraja plays the lead role of the footballer who is tempted by money to throw the game. Primary School teacher Prisca Goma is a Malawian who is rehearsing with Faraja and the other actors. I see her and Faraja interact and decide to make her my second main protagonist. It is a good choice as there is chemistry between them.

I travel with Malawian David who is the all-round production manager to the old town market in a minibus. The minibus is loaded with passengers and it is even more of a squeeze with my big camera bag. At the market, I implement my "shoot first ask questions later" methodology. David is perusing items to buy. I get shouted at again and again for filming people. If I was to ask everyone at a market for permission before filming I'd be there all day. But being shouted at gets tiring. David finds me a lift back to the city centre with a friend called Rasta who hoots and shouts to all and sundry on the way there. So much posturing as only a 20-year-old male could exhibit.

In the evening I go out with some of the UNHCR people, Jeremy and Rebecca, and Rheena the attractive British Council Director. Rheena's handbag is ripped off her arm outside the restaurant. Girls, handbags are a liability in Africa.

In the restaurant, the conversation turns to Robert Mugabe, Zimbabwe's long-term president, then still in power (and still alive). Rheena, who is of south Asian origin, says, "He makes me embarrassed to be Black."
"It's nothing to do with that," I say. "Power corrupts and absolute power corrupts absolutely." Jeremy nods in agreement.

Meanwhile, the week-long shoot is jam-packed. I travel with Prisca, my Malawian protagonist, to her aunt's house where she lives. Here ensues an authentic conversation as Prisca tries to argue against her aunt's xenophobic views. I keep quiet and film.

"These refugees bring problems. They bring diseases. A certain refugee was a robber. They don't feel mercy. Killing is not a problem. Why don't you encourage them to return home?" says Prisca's aunt.
"How can they go home if there is war?" asks Prisca.

Prisca tries to explain that the refugees who are working in Malawi are taxpayers. She says that if only her aunt could spend some time with the refugees, she'd change her views. After all, that is what has happened to

Prisca. Before getting involved in the theatre production, Prisca didn't like refugees. But weeks of rehearsals together with the refugees have changed her perception. She sees them as people now, who fled a war with the clothes on their backs.

And even better for me is the spark between her and Faraja. During a break in rehearsals, I film Faraja and Prisca as they drink coke together. They talk about their family members, and how much they enjoy working together. It is emblematic of the crux of the storyline, and it works.

The final shoot day is the performance at Dzaleka Refugee Camp. The team scrambles to make the final arrangements, such as finding reliable electricity for the speakers. Camp members stream in and the play begins. Faraja's character in the play does not give in to the temptation of a bribe, and he goes on to score the winning goal. The closing scenes of the documentary are of Faraja and Prisca hugging and celebrating.

My intensive week of shooting is over, and on the drive to the airport, Askal from UNHCR says to me she knows about a refugee story with a happy ending. "Oh yes?" I say.

"Tresor, from DR Congo, had to flee because the lyrics of his music were critical of the regime. He has now put together a band and is performing in the camp. They have all sorts of plans."

I take Tresor's phone number from Askal. Little do I know I'll soon not only be back to make another documentary at Dzaleka, but this time I'll experience living in the camp. The best way to find these stories is on the ground, rather than through online research. First though, a return to Mozambique.

After a visit to Rwanda to produce a short documentary on child malnutrition for UNICEF, I land a big fish.

I have been sending in ideas to Al Jazeera for their Witness strand for six years, without success. More recently I meet the then Commissioning Editor Dominique Young, twice in person, when she is in South Africa. For the first meeting, I fly up from Cape Town to Johannesburg to have a cup of coffee with her and pitch some ideas, but she is not interested in any of them. On the second meeting at Cape Town's V and A Waterfront, I run through a few ideas with her. Suzete, the women's rights activist in Mozambique, who I filmed for the UNDP documentary, catches Dominique's attention. Having already not only met Suzete but spent several days shooting her and the work she does, I am familiar with the ins and outs of the storyline. The story gets commissioned.

This time instead of a two-day drive, I take a two-hour flight from Cape Town to Maputo. Al Jazeera has specific video camera requirements, and mine is not sufficiently good. I have decided to hire a Sony EX1 in Maputo. First I get settled into a room above Mundo's bar on Avenida Julius Nyerere. Staying in the room next to me is a White Zimbabwean whose skin looks battered by the sun. We are standing next to the railing looking down at the street scene below.

"I was working further north, out on a boat every day, shirtless. Turns out I now have skin cancer. I'm getting treatment for it." Skin cancer. Who knew?

He asks me what I am doing in Maputo. I tell him I am making a documentary about women's rights. He gives me a "huh?" look. This guy is all macho energy.

The next morning I go to Pipas Forjas to rent a Sony EX1.

When I meet Pipas I say, "I met and interviewed your father, Jose, a few years ago about Ilha da Mozambique's architecture."

No response. Is it a case of the son in the father's shadow (and literally, as they share the same property)?

As I know from experience, back in Madagascar when I temporarily used almost the same camera, shooting with an unfamiliar camera is risky. I run some tests in my hotel room. The first issue I pick up is my fault—the camera doesn't shoot at a sufficiently high bit rate for the Al Jazeera specifications. Following a flurry of emails to various technical experts, I decide we can work around this. I run more tests with Gizela, my local sound woman, who does not have the right cables with her. Then I spot a couple of specks of dirt inside the lens. I return the camera to Pipas, and Gizela introduces me to another contact who may have an EX1 for me to rent. Truly, life is like cinema—a series of obstacles to overcome! I track down a small production company in Maputo and rent their EX3 after negotiations with a tough-nut businessman called Perreira.

Meanwhile, I meet up with Suzete, Rosa the translator, and Carolina, a further character in my documentary about women's rights activist Suzete. As we part, Suzete turns to me and says:

"You should marry Rosa."
Jokingly I say, "I want to marry you!" to Suzete, who replies:
"I'll never get married. My heart is broken."
"Since when," I ask.
"2011"
"Suzete, that's three years ago."
"It's yesterday," she says.

Being a women's rights documentary, and as I am not a woman, I decided to employ as many women as possible. That includes Gizela the sound lady, Rosa the translator, and the video editor back in Cape Town. One of the advantages of having a local crew is that they have a rapport with my subjects. And that is good. You want your subjects to be at ease.

At a school, Suzete talks to a crowd of scholars at a high school. As I discovered on my previous trip, achieving women's rights in Mozambique, as in most African countries, has a long way to go. Despite being prohibited by law, early marriages are widespread in rural areas. It's not rare for girls as young as 12 to be married off. That is a major cause of the under-enrolment of girls at schools. Those who do make it to school face the risk of sexual abuse by teachers. Domestic violence is widespread. Some shocking archaic traditional activities live on: "purification" is when a newly widowed woman is obligated to have unprotected sex with a member of the deceased husband's family.

Talking confidently in front of a class, Suzete personalises the issues by explaining why she became an activist. It is the same explanation she gave when I filmed her for the first time for the UNDP documentary. When one of her school friends became pregnant by a teacher, the outcome was being kicked out of school, kicked out of her house, and the teacher went unpunished. This injustice would not stand for Suzete.

In the evening I return to my room above Mundo's. As I open my door, the

White Zimbabwean's door next to mine opens, and a very young Mozambican woman silently slips out and into the night. Inside my room, I review the footage. I am starting to actively hate this heavy, cumbersome and unfamiliar video camera. The autofocus is terrible, and I will need to use manual focus a lot more consistently. It means I have to ask my main protagonists to wear the same clothes at next week's school event and get some in-focus wide shots to cover myself.

Suzete lives with her parents where I film the whole family working in the garden. Her mother says, "Suzete will never get married because she talks too much!" Unfortunately, Suzete's father has decided he doesn't want me and the crew shooting at the house anymore. It is understandable as it is intrusive. But it's a pity as I would have liked to get more interactions. I discuss this setback with Dominique, the Al Jazeera Witness Commissioning Editor, and she asks me who else Suzete could interact with who may be critical of what she is trying to do. I ask Suzete and she suggests her friends who are diplomats-in-training. It soon becomes clear that Suzete is very disappointed that she was not selected for this course. She has not figured out that an activist and a diplomat are polar opposites. And her role is activist—she's a warrior. Anyway, we meet up with her student diplomat friends, and I film a scene outside their campus in which they are only too happy to argue against the whole concept of women's rights. One of Suzete's male friends, a particularly slick soon-to-be-diplomat, says the reason domestic violence has increased in Mozambique is that women want to be like men, and are not fulfilling even their most basic roles, such as serving a meal in the evening. The girls respond by saying they don't wish to usurp men, but simply to be respected.

Carolina is a case study of a girl who has been to Suzete's workshops and as a result, there have been changes in her household. Following the information Carolina received, her brother now helps around the house including cooking and cleaning. Carolina also got involved with a neighbour, a woman who was regularly beaten by her husband. Carolina brought this woman to one of Suzete's workshops, and this neighbour returned home, empowered, and reported her husband to the police. Things have changed for the better in that household too.

As the 14-day shoot progresses, Suzete is getting harder to work with. She alternates between flirting outrageously ("what beautiful blue eyes you have," "why don't you have a girlfriend?") to barely acknowledging me. When I ask her *Mas uma vez* (one more time) when she enters a building or leaves a room, I am met with grumbling. Her passion and energy are transmogrifying into sulkiness. To be reasonable 14 days of this must be exhausting. And yes, when so many documentaries necessitate directing real people to act (walk in, sit down, leave the room) how authentic are documentaries? We assume documentaries are truthful yet the best we can hope for is that they stay close to the spirit of the truth. They are actually just the filmmaker's version of the truth. Meanwhile, Suzete's changing attitude towards the production is perfect timing for the shoot's next crisis.

It's day eight and I arrive at her house with my entourage. Suzete appears at the front door… with a radically different hairstyle. Clearly, she has spent the "production funds" I gave her on a haircut. It's not a haircut, but braids. With red colour worked into it. Why is that a problem? I am shooting 14 days of footage but it will not be chronologically edited! The scenes are shot randomly as and when participants and events happen or are available. How can she appear in some shots with her old hairstyle and other shots with her braids? That would jar. I have to think on my feet now. "Suzete, where did you get your braids done?" It's a place nearby. "Let's go," I say. I film her there just so that I can try and find a way to work in the hair change and hopefully make the scenes with the old haircut work in the storyline before those shots with the braids.

At the next school workshop, a further technical crisis: the audio cable was plugged into the camera yet was not switched on at the camera. I don't have audio. Not only that, but the same thing that happened to me in Madagascar with the same camera, has occurred again. The EX3's monitor settings were accidentally touched and so everything I shot is over-exposed. It is not possible to re-shoot these scenes. I can only hope that these shots can be salvaged. On my last evening, I walk downstairs and finally enjoy the bar I have been living above these last two weeks, where the White Zimbabwean with skin cancer is holding forth.

Back in Cape Town, the second expert I meet, a colourist, saves my over exposed shots. Talk about a design fault on the EX3, yet to happen twice to me, only I can take the blame!

By the time I take in my footage to be edited back in Cape Town, I have a "paper edit" ready, and we mainly assemble the cut. I manage to tell the story of Suzete and her old hairstyle in the first half, and her new hairstyle in the second half. Dominique is impressed by how mature some of the Mozambican scholars appear. How insightful some of them are. Very true.

For all the second and third takes Suzete had to endure, she does also get something back. In the following years, I get contacted several times by viewers who want to help Suzete. She gets several cash donations for her NGO, a computer and other assistance. It is most of all gratifying to me because it's rare that one feels that one is making a difference. One of her beneficiaries is the Canadian Ambassador's wife in Maputo. I get an email from this lady saying she is sitting at a cafe waiting for a very late Suzete. I immediately phone up the Canadian Ambassador's wife and apologise on behalf of Suzete. Then I phone Suzete, who is sitting in a minibus, and who seems nonchalant about keeping the Ambassador's wife waiting. And we're talking about a potential donor for her NGO.

***

As well as this Al Jazeera project, in 2014 I produce two UNICEF videos, one in Namibia and one in Rwanda where for the only time ever I have the strange experience of a government minder along for the entire shoot which is about overcoming child malnutrition. On my day off I visit the Kigali Genocide Memorial. Walking through the rooms filled with photographs of victims is one thing, but the piles of shoes of the genocide victims are a bit hard to bear.

Meanwhile, I keep producing my bread and butter Associated Press news features such as one about the world's biggest Meccano model, made inside and filling up Graham Shepherd's lounge and dining room in Grahamstown. It weighs 1.3 tonnes and is 12.5 by 4.9 metres, which is diminutive compared to the 96-metre-high Bagger 288 Coal Extractor it is based on—a coal digger that was the world's biggest land-based vehicle when it was introduced in 1978.

CHAPTER TWENTY-FOUR
Refugee camp musician

Tresor Mpauni was an up-and-coming musician in the Democratic Republic of Congo, when his lyrics, critical of the state, caught the attention of officials. Tresor was forced to flee and ended up in a refugee camp in Malawi. Having only just gotten back on his feet, Tresor has brought together some other talented musicians in the camp to not only play music together but to record an album.

I have discussed a documentary about Tresor with Al Jazeera and they are interested. The story I plan to tell is the journey taken to record that album: the hurdles and challenges he faces to get it done. What's the catch? Al Jazeera has not committed to the story, and Tresor has informed me that he plans to get the album recorded in the capital city, Lilongwe, very soon.

So, taking a gamble, I use my own money to fly up to Malawi and start shooting the story. Arriving at the airport I fill my lungs with the air and its distinctive aromas. Is it wood fire? Or insects? I'm not sure but it hits me hard, taking me back to my childhood.

My contacts at UNHCR from my recent trip there, have offered me a lift to Dzaleka refugee camp and it does me no harm to arrive under their auspices. Tresor bears a strong resemblance to Patrice Lumumba, independent Congo's first leader who was assassinated by the CIA and Belgian state because they feared he was leaning a bit towards the Soviet block. Once they made Lumumba disappear in a vat of acid, they put in his place their kleptocratic henchman, Mobutu Sese Seko, and the rest is a sorry history.

Tresor, as a performing musician in the southern Democratic Republic of Congo, had simply stated that since independence every president in the Congo has been brought in from the outside. Soon after that Tresor's neighbour's told him plain clothes police were snooping around looking for him. These characters are the last ones you are likely to be seen alive with. So, Tresor packed a small bag and crossed into Zambia that night and has not been back to his home country since then.

I spend the night in the camp with Tresor, who lives in a brick building which would have been part of the original political prison. It is strange to think that I spent four idyllic years of my childhood 45 kilometres away from a prison where at the same time much torture and death took place. In my sleeping bag on a concrete floor is by no means a luxury night. It's a rough night with little sleep. There is much snoring from the various souls in the building, a muezzin call to prayers, and a national anthem being played on loudspeakers at some point in the night. In the morning I find I have been bitten by unknown insects. I have large welts all over me. I ask to use the toilet, a communal brick affair beyond an open rubbish dump. I peer inside the building and decide that no way I am entering. I'll walk a long way to find a bush to urinate behind instead.

Tresor and I eat at a local hole-in-the-wall restaurant within the camp.

"Refugees are not allowed to work in Malawi, and they can't leave the camp freely."

It is life in limbo here, and for Tresor what a fall it must have been from being a university student living a life of relative privilege in Lubumbashi, to existing in the unhygienic and constrained circumstances of Dzaleka. At first, he fell into a depression. But he picked himself up. Making music again was his mission.

Tresor introduces me to some of the musicians he plays with, and I start shooting their rehearsals. Tresor works hard, spending full days with me, being interviewed, and showing me many of the typical camp activities. He never complains.

It's my third morning awakening in Dzaleka Refugee camp. I must admit staying here is partly for reasons of economy—it's free and I am on a tight budget. This story has not been commissioned after all. I write to Soraya from Al Jazeera at the camp internet cafe, hoping for an update, but receive no reply. But of course, living in the camp is great for shooting too. I think a typical crew would travel in and out every day from Lilongwe, but I am with Tresor 24 hours a day, and that allows me to get shots and sequences that I wouldn't otherwise. This morning, at dawn, Tresor rises and washes his clothes and shoes outside the run-down building he calls home. I film it and it's a nice sequence. But I have even more welts on my body and face following another night on the concrete floor of the old prison camp building. Could it be a spider? A cockroach? The snoring issue is ongoing. This is roughing it like I haven't done in a long time.

When I ask Tresor if I can film him while he queues for food, as all the refugees in the camp do, he suggests I get permission for that. I enquire via my UNHCR contacts. Then the Malawian national commissioner for refugees finds out that I am in the camp filming not for UNHCR, but Al Jazeera. Horrors! A real documentary! I am told to meet him in Lilongwe. Askal, my UNHCR contact informs me that the government will want to limit what I film, to ensure the camp is not made to look bad and to view the documentary before it is aired. Hell will freeze over before that happens. No journalist allows anyone else to have editorial oversight.

Tresor and I get a lift to Lilongwe in a UNHCR Toyota Corolla. It's only when we sit and close the doors that I realise how much both of us reek. What an aroma! The first stop for me is a budget hotel, where I can clean up properly before my meeting.

Stress is building up, as there is so much to organise, and so much at stake. I go for a run and then do some yoga. The stretches, organised in sets of positions, together make up a whole. Maybe that is why yoga works. Maybe that is why filmmaking is also satisfying—one organises many different shots in such a way that it makes sense, and forms a whole. It is not hard to see the appeal when you consider just how messy life is.

I wait for Askal from UNHCR to travel together to the national commissioner of refugees.

At a restaurant, I ask:
"Can I have a coke?"
"We have cokes and fantas."
"I'll take a coke."
"You want a coke?"
"Yes, a coke."

I am a bag of nerves by the time I get to the national commissioner of refugees with Askal. He seems aggressive.

"We have been monitoring this guy, Tresor. He is a poet?! These refugees are here as visitors. And he goes on stage talking about rights?! We are not comfortable with that."

Then changing tack, "We will want someone from the government to liaise with you, to work with you."

"I'm an impartial journalist. An independent journalist. I need the freedom to express myself freely. I can't have the government censoring me."

"We want someone to work with you."

Just then I remember my national media council letter. I have got as far as getting national filming permission, all that remains is to go and pay the 100 US dollars. This I have not done because I do not have the money for it! But I have a letter saying I have been granted permission to film. I pull out the letter, and Askal's eyes widen. It turns out to be a bit of a rabbit being pulled out of a hat.

"Oh," the national commissioner says, "Then it's okay. Because if there is a problem it won't be my head on the chopping board. You can proceed."

What a relief. Everything had felt like it was on a knife edge, and now all is alright once more.

I stay in Lilongwe as Tresor will be performing at a poetry evening. The venue is The Living Room, and all evening long Tresor's friends congratulate him on the fact that Al Jazeera is making a documentary about him. And when Tresor goes on stage he goes out of his way to thank me: "Neil from Al Jazeera!" It leaves me squirming because of course the documentary has not been commissioned—yet. I have told Tresor it is not 100% sure, but this seems not to have registered. This leaves me even more determined to get the documentary made and sold even if it is not with Al Jazeera.

The next evening I take a taxi to see Tresor perform at a club. I remember as a child hyenas could be seen on occasion in the outskirts of this small city.

"Are there still hyenas around in Lilongwe?" I ask Andrew, my regular taxi driver.
"One night, late, I was driving to the airport, and we stopped at the turn-off. Then we were encircled by seven hyenas."
"What would have happened to you if you had been outside the vehicle?"
No reply. That bad.
"How many capital cities in the world does one come across hyenas on the way to the airport?"
"Indeed!"

We get to the nightclub where Tresor is performing. I am wondering to myself, why is it I don't live here? Just then my nostalgia is tempered.

A nightclub guard, armed with an AK47, approaches me.
"Where do you come from?"
"South Africa."
Antagonistically he says, "Oh you are a Dutch, like P W Botha." (South Africa's second last apartheid-era president)
"No I am not Dutch," I say, walking into the nightclub.
"Yes you are," he calls after me.

It's a good performance and I meet a Malawian policeman who tells me his perceptions of refugees have changed 180 degrees since hearing Tresor's music.

The following day I shoot some scenes with Tresor taking minibus taxis to meet with Malawian musicians that he is collaborating with. As usual, I shoot first and ask questions later. In so doing I am shouted at, again.

"You people just come here and take, and then you go away."

Back at Dzaleka camp, I join Tresor when he goes to eat with friends, who he refers to as his family. I am filming and hoping for an interesting and authentic conversation. That is to say as authentic as possible with a video camera present. Unfortunately, the dialogue is all too stilted. That night it's back to a concrete floor and all night snoring.

In the morning I phone Soraya at Al Jazeera. I call ostensibly to give her an "update" but what I want to know is when are you going to commission this documentary?! She remains non-committal. I realise while talking to her my mood is low. A strange sort of depression has set in, as it did the last time I was staying in the camp. Is the general camp malaise weighing on me?

While walking through the village, who should Tresor and I bump into but Faraja, who was my protagonist the year before in the UNHCR documentary I made. Faraja, bearded appears to be a young man. But when he sees me, he runs up to me and gives me a big hug. Tresor looks on in surprise. Faraja is but a child and a traumatised one at that. Part of me wants to take him back to Cape Town, to help him.

In the evening we eat with Tresor's "family" again. This time there is a nice exchange where Tresor is asked, "Isn't it a bit pointless to make an album by refugee musicians? Who'll listen?" Tresor insists there is a large global audience out there. My spirits lift significantly after shooting this scene.

By now Tresor has achieved his online crowd-funding target, and after some more rehearsals, it's time to head back to Lilongwe to record the album. The best scene in the documentary is the band walking into the camp office to ask for permission to leave—while playing and singing! This was Tresor's idea, and that's the advantage of working with fellow creatives!

In Lilongwe, I film the album being recorded, Tresor and the refugees collaborating with Malawian musicians. The producer works from his small bedroom with some basic equipment and is self-taught, "Thanks to Mr Google." Visually this is not great as I had envisioned a recording studio! It's okay though—emblematic of basic conditions. I know magic is going to happen when the two charismatic Malawian musicians arrived at the bedroom recording studio, and that is certainly what happens. The positive conversations between the Malawians and Congolese musicians, and the music that they make together is excellent for the story.

I take my last taxi ride to the airport with my regular driver, Andrew, and use the last of my money on a cup of coffee. In addition, I am R18,000 in the red on my credit card! I believe I have the footage for a decent documentary, despite wearing all the hats as usual: cameraman, soundman, producer, and director... but I have no commitment from Al Jazeera yet.

After checking in for my flight, the electricity goes off. It has been off about 50% of the time over my last two weeks in Malawi. Passengers are instructed to identify their baggage. Some White South Africans have some cans taken out by an official, and are told, "Flammable substances cannot be taken on board."

"But this isn't hand luggage, it's for the hold," the South Africans reply testily.
Upstairs the White South African turns to me and says, "You give them a bit of power and they think they rule the world."
A bit of power? I think to myself. But they rule the country. They have all the power!

Soon we are ushered out of what turns out to be an unmarked business-class lounge, that we had mistakenly sat in.

As we all move to the economy zone, the South African says loudly, "$50 to sit in that shithole?"

Ah yes, golden moments at Kamuzu International Airport.

Back in Cape Town, and broke, I set about rustling up some Associated Press work as soon as possible. Two months later, while commuting from Cape Town airport to my house on my motorbike in the evening after returning from a shoot in Durban, I have a rock lobbed at me. Thank God it does not strike me, lodging instead into the chassis where the front light had been. I only realise what has happened at the moment of impact, and I see a tall male Xhosa youth in a blue shirt and a black hoodie, his arm outstretched. Is he about to throw another rock at me? Then I realise his arm is in the air from the rebound of lobbing the rock that struck my motorbike. I have no front light, but I keep riding, all the way home. On the way, I realise that I was nearly killed. Had I fallen over, he would have robbed me, maybe stuck a knife into me. This is what happens on the N2 highway. There are so many shacks with desperate unemployed people living along this highway. And the whole country was built on violence—it's in the DNA and it's the foundation of the nation. Back in Woodstock, feeling a bit traumatised, I tell my neighbours what happened. "Oh, that's a dangerous area!" says the one neighbour. But Mr Ching next door is more realistic about just how close I had come to being killed. I realise there and then that this incident has been epochal for me. I don't want to live in a country with this level of violence. I want to leave. But where to? To emigrate is a big step.

Three and a half months later I get a wonderful email from Soraya at Al Jazeera. They're commissioning the documentary! I feel like a million dollars. The gamble paid off. After editing, I head over to Europe and North America for some travels. Included on my itinerary is Greece, as there is a Leonard Cohen Forum meet-up at Hydra island, where Cohen lived in the 1960s. At Pefkaki restaurant, the waiter appears to take my order. It seems the ghost of Leonard lives here at Pefkaki. The waiter looks just like him. Whether he's the illegitimate son, or simply the lingering ghost, the point is here is Leonard, still on Hydra, still weaving his magic. That evening I spot a Greek Cohenite with a beautiful smile. And with that, my fate is sealed.

My Morocco travel documentary that I made (12 year earlier) in 2002 opens with a quote about Plato returning to Athens at age 40, after 12 years of travel. I did not know at the time, nor when I arrived in Athens at age 40, how prophetic those words would turn out to be.

After my travels in the US and Canada, and before the first of many return trips to Greece, I head over to Ghana to produce a short documentary for UNICEF about preventing ebola and cholera. In the course of my travels with UNICEF we stay one night at the Aguetuoso Ecotourism Hotel, 700 metres above sea level, providing much respite from the general humidity of Ghana. There is much grumbling from the UNICEF driver because he won't be able to pocket quite as much of the generous daily UNICEF per diem staying here as he would at one of the usual stopovers. Here at this tranquil mountain respite, the local chief asks me to film him eating and informs me that everything here is grown organically. Then he asks us what our mission is, and where we come from.

"We are with UNICEF, and I am from South Africa."

That seems to satisfy him (or so I register later). He then asks my French colleague:

"Where is your home?"
"A village in France."
"And what are you doing to uplift *your* village?"

No reply.

CHAPTER TWENTY-SIX
What could possibly go wrong?

When I set off on one of my work travel projects, I usually take a taxi from my house in Lower Woodstock to the airport. If the taxi driver is a so-called Coloured, he will be chatting the whole way through, probably telling me all kinds of stories. If the taxi driver is Black (Xhosa), he'll be silent the whole journey. If the taxi driver is White, he'll be justifying why he is a taxi driver. Today it is the latter. "I lost my job because of affirmative action."

I produce two Associated Press news features in Namibia. The first is on Mary-Anne Bartlett's Art Safaris. This is a wildlife safari with a twist that will appeal to those of an artistic bent. Instead of just viewing the wildlife from a vehicle, participants sketch and draw the animals, under the guidance and tutelage of Mary-Anne.

I meet the entirely British and over-60 group at a hotel in Windhoek, Namibia's capital city. We're in the run-up the British referendum on exiting the European Union. The group goes out of its way to explain why they are voting leave.

"We've been a sovereign nation with our own government for 1000 years. Yet we have a group of bureaucrats in Brussels, a country not 150 years old, dictating to us many, many petty rules and regulations. That is not what we signed up for when we joined the European Economic Commission in the 1970s." And indeed, as well all know, the leave vote wins and the UK crashes out of the European Union, and not Greece as was expected a year or two earlier. A bumpy ride will ensue for the UK.

The first stop is the Na an Kuse Game Reserve where our group sets themselves up in chairs under some thorn trees. Then, a cheetah appears, and walks languidly amongst the artists, purring loudly, then slumping on the ground at their feet. What a beauty! What amazing visuals I am getting! Cheetahs are known informally as the dogs of the cat family because they become tame so easily. They're the world's fastest land animal, and the least dangerous big cat.

Cheetahs have already vanished from around 90% of their historic range in Africa. This is simply because wilderness areas make way for human habitation. Cheetahs are often killed by farmers who consider them to be livestock predators. The cheetahs here at Na an Kuse have been taken away from situations where they were in conflict with livestock farmers. It's a safe haven.

The group also go to Okapuka, a little north of Windhoek, where they sketch rhino, ostriches, giraffe and other wildlife from a game drive vehicle. Instead of just snapping a picture with a camera, they sit for 20 minutes, half an hour or more, really getting a chance to get a deeper sense of the animals and the environment.

The other news feature I produce is in Swakopmund on extreme sports. The highlight is skydiving. As I peer over the edge of a tiny plane flying high above the clouds, every molecule in my body screams at me, "don't!" How could I be expected to step into nothingness? But I do—I jump out and feel the deafening rush of wind. And then the floating silence as the parachute opens. Then the descent back down to planet earth. That has been the biggest thrill of my life.

From Windhoek, I take the 20-hour Intercape bus to Livingstone, Zambia. I experience a truly spellbinding moment as we travel along the long straight highway through the Caprivi strip. At sunset, the bus slows down to a crawl and then stops. I look up and see dead ahead two separate herds of elephants crossing the highway. One by one the elephants make their way across and into the thick dense bush. Pure magic! And across a major highway, not "on safari."

At the Namibia-Zambia border, the immigration procedure is a bit slow. I take a look inside, and then muse outwardly, "They only have one staff on duty." The European travellers with me harrumph and shake their heads patronisingly. That is not at all what I meant.

On the bus from Livingstone to Zambia's capital city, Lusaka, the passengers begin the journey by being given a sermon by a preacher walking up and down the aisle. I don't understand but it sounds like fire and brimstone. He continues when we set off, then when he does stop his preaching, he walks up to the front. Standing next to the driver he says loudly, "I like this bus." Just then the bus comes to a halt on the side of the road. The driver makes a phone call, and then stands up to make an announcement.

"The air conditioning doesn't work, so a replacement bus is being sent."

I presume not from heaven but the bus depot.

We all stand around outside in the sun waiting, finally continuing our journey to Lusaka on another bus.

After a night at Sue and Kelvin's place, I get a lift to the bus station.

"I am not voting in the upcoming elections. I have never voted. They are all corrupt. All in it to line their pockets," says Kelvin to me on the drive there, wending his way around the massive potholes.

On the bus heading to Northern Zambia, loud distorted gospel music is blasting through the loudspeakers. Out of sheer frustration, I hold my soft hat up against the speaker which is just centimetres from my head. Then I try taping my hat against the loudspeaker. The passengers behind me are tittering by now. One of the bus employees has been watching and kindly offers to swap with me. I move from the front left seat to the front right where the speaker doesn't work. It is slightly less noisy but ahead of me lies ten hours yet of monotonous high volume gospel music. But sitting here gives me a chance to speak to Joe, one of the two bus drivers who alternate on this long route. Joe tells me about his schedule. Non-stop driving between Lusaka and Mpulungu in the far north of Zambia, with five hours at home every third day.

It is dark when he slows down to manoeuvre around an overturned truck in the middle of the highway. One needs one's wits about one to drive these roads in the darkness. After midnight we stop at the side of the road for a break. I get out, stretch my legs and relieve myself, all the time grumbling under my breath about the blasting gospel music and the fellow next to me taking up too much space when I look up and see the most incredible display of stars and milky way. Magic!

At Mpika, Joe the friendly and warm bus driver gets out and finds me a taxi driver, Trevor. I am dropped off at a decent little hotel, and Trevor returns in the morning for the last leg of this trip.

Just after sunrise, I am sitting in his taxi, the ubiquitous grey (literally and figuratively as these are unofficial Japanese imports) Toyota Corolla. Trevor says of me while chuckling:

"Joe said to me 'take very good care of him.'"

This is Zambia's Great North Road linking Lusaka with Dar es Salaam in Tanzania. In this particular area though there is little traffic and the road surface is in bad condition. Trevor slows down. At first, I think it is to avoid another pothole. But about 800 metres ahead of us I spot the pervasive African police roadblock. Trevor has come to a complete halt by now. He turns to me:

"Do you have a driver's licence?"
"Don't you have one?!"
"I forgot it!"

So we swap seats and I drive up to the traffic cops who stop us and ask me for my driver's licence. After a cursory look at the baggage in the back, we are waved through. A little later I stop and Trevor, who I assume has no licence at all, takes the helm once more.

Then we turn off the Great North Road and drive along a dirt road until reaching a rather unusual sight. Shiwa Ngandu is an ivy-covered brick mansion that seems a slightly incongruous sight in rural Central Africa. The 100-year-old home with nine bedrooms was the brainchild of British aristocrat Sir Stewart Gore-Browne. The third generation of the family lives here and the home is now open to guests.

Charlie Harvey is Sir Stewart Gore-Browne's grandson. He's gruff and short, yet gets chatty later as he shows me around. They've had all kinds of people here at the home which is on a 23,000-acre estate. "We had an Arab sheikh and his henchmen fly into our airstrip. He made me an offer to buy it all, which had some conditions including cutting down all the wattle trees. I had a Chinese guy come here offering to buy my dog. That was to eat, of course. I told him to fuck off. We had Spanish royalty here for hunting. But every day it took them so long to get ready that it was always too late to set off! But they were wonderful people." Charlie also told me that since getting meningitis he cannot tolerate coffee, tea or alcohol.

I do not have the budget to sleep at Shiwa Ngandu, so I stay at the nearby Kapeyshe Springs. The campsite is run by a sibling of Charlie. One can loll about or even wash in the hot springs that are surrounded by greenery and palm trees. It's a beautiful spot.

At the camping site, there's a coterie of 60-something European retirees in 4x4 campers, and the usual South African entourage of multiple 4X4s, fully self-sufficient, and set up in laager formation. There's a German couple who have travelled through South Africa and Namibia.

"Now you're in the real Africa!" I say to them.
Apropos nothing in particular, he says, "But Europeans never really belong here."
"But Europe is not my home, so what about me?"

No answer to that one.

I meet Felix, a German voluntourist who is working as a mechanic here. He tells me, "I lived with the Masaais in Tanzania, and went to their school. If the children ask "why" they are punished, because the teachers don't have the answers. Therefore African children are taught not to be questioning." I am wary of making such broad statements.

In the morning, as I am packing my bag at my little tent and wondering how I'll get back to Shiwa Ngandu without paying $35 for a lift from the Hot

Springs people, I notice a couple getting ready to leave in their 4X4 Landrover. I walk up to them and ask if I can get dropped off at Shiwa. It's only about five kilometres away but you'd think that I was asking the world of them. But I won't take no for an answer and the 60-something Australian couple relent.

In the vehicle, the small talk turns to my other travels and I mention that my girlfriend is Greek.

"When we were sailing around the Greek islands we saw all these lazy Greeks sitting around drinking coffee. In the middle of the day!"

Of course no Australian goes out for a coffee in the middle of the day, I think to myself.

"My girlfriend's family work 9 am to 7 pm Monday to Saturday running a family business in Athens," I reply. "They're the most hard-working people I know."

Now they'll need to backtrack a little. "After my heart attack, my cardiologist in Australia was a Greek-Australian. He was very good."

Stereotyping is a worldwide problem.

I am dropped off at Shiwa and the Australians go off in their travel bubble. As I approach the brick mansion, I am reminded of the Chinese guy who offered to buy Charlie Harvey's dog to eat it. This happens because as I approach the house said dog comes running out, barking and then takes a nip at me. The bloody dog bit me! I shout out loudly, "Call off your dog!" Charlie appears and takes the dog away. I then have to try and be polite as I continue the research for my news feature on Shiwa N'gandu.

It is with Trevor the taxi driver who has no driver's licence, that I retrace my steps to Mpika. There are no police roadblocks to pass through. I then take the 2 pm bus back south to Lusaka which arrives at 1 am. Fortuitously there is a 2 am connecting bus east to Chipata. Unfortunately, it is fully booked. But when I am told that at the ticket office, Golden, a fellow traveller in the queue with me says under his breath, "Wait." Finally, when the jolly bus driver arrives, a stool is organised for me and placed at the back of the bus in the aisle.

"Are you sure you are okay with it?" the driver asks me.
"Yes."
"You are a peaceful passenger?"
"Yes!"

In fact, when I set off from Mpika 12 hours earlier I had set myself a goal to not complain throughout the two-bus 20-hour marathon journey. So maybe it's that simple. Just decide on what attitude to have. We arrive at Chipata a couple of hours after sunrise. As is often the case, a friendly fellow passenger makes sure I get into a taxi to a nearby hotel. The following morning I make my way the 20 kilometres to the Malawi border by minibus taxi.

This is one of my favourite corners of Africa. In 1995, I travelled from Pretoria to Nairobi and back in a VW Kombi with a group of fellow students. Liesel de Lange's father had not only lent us his 2.1i VW Kombi but also had the engine overhauled just before the trip. Unfortunately, when the mechanics put the engine back together they put the old water pump back on. The motor was overheating throughout the long haul, and so we were coaxing and nursing the vehicle to the equator and back without figuring out what the issue was until the car got back to Pretoria.

Liesel's father let us use the vehicle but on one condition. "Whatever you do, don't cross any border with drugs." That sounds sensible. It's not like we were a bunch of druggies, but like many other backpackers who spend time relaxing at Lake Malawi, we had gotten hold of a cob of "Malawi Gold," the famous local marijuana. The day before our departure out of Malawi and over the border to Zambia, I donated the Malawi Gold to a South African honeymoon couple in a series 2 Land Rover at Cape Maclear.

On the approach to the Malawi-Zambia border at Chipata, we spot a guy in a SADF trenchcoat, hitchhiking. The SADF was the old apartheid-era South African national military—until very recently there had been national conscription for all White males, and a war to head off to in Angola. We stop to give him a lift. He turns out to be a wild-eyed ex-soldier who had travelled from South Africa to Nairobi for a job as a driver and was then told, "no thanks" and given 50 pounds sterling for his trouble. Thus began his 4000-kilometre odyssey back to Johannesburg with practically no cash. At the border, we all exit the vehicle and go through the border formalities together. Stamp out of Malawi and then stamp into Zambia. Getting back into the Kombi on the Zambia side, our long-haired ex-SADF hitchhiker pulls a Malawi cob out of his military jacket and starts rolling himself a big joint. We all look around at each other, eyes wide.

That wintry night we camped in Chipata. I remember the icy cold shower, beers at the bar, and spending the night outside in my sleeping bag next to the fire. Oh yes, those were the days.

Back to the present, I have crossed into Malawi at Chipata and made my way by minibus taxi to Lilongwe. I am feeling a bit weird. Not quite myself.

In my wisdom I am not taking malaria prophylaxis, so the first thing I do is go to a pharmacy and get tested for malaria. Negative. I am not convinced, but I head out to produce a story on permaculture.

Before independence in 1964, Malawians ate a fairly diverse range of vegetables, known as "bush food." This would include indigenous crops such as millet, yam and sorghum. Then-president Kamuzu Banda, to modernise the country, introduced large-scale maize as a mono-crop. And that is the contemporary situation. Heavy dependence on maize. The problem is maize doesn't offer enough nutrition and worse than that, maize is not an indigenous crop (it comes from Latin America). That means it is not resilient to droughts, as an indigenous crop would be. So when a drought occurs in a maize-dependent situation, there is hunger or even famine.

The solution is to return to growing a diverse array of indigenous crops—so far more of a dream than a reality. Permaculture encompasses this and it is also so much more. Permaculture is a complete system of sustainable living. It's a design approach encompassing living and growing vegetables, where multiple crops are grown in harmony and provide year-round crops. Yes, it's complex.

My first stopover on my permaculture research is Kristof Nordin who came to Malawi as a peace corps volunteer... and stayed. He offers permaculture training in Malawi. His family chose to live rurally and simply and to send their kids to a local school. But when he visited the school, and he saw the other children sitting there, heads lolling from acute hunger, he chose to pull his kids out of the local school. According to the World Food Programme, 47% of Malawian children under five years old have stunted growth due to malnutrition. It's a shocking statistic. Child stunting causes often irreversible growth and cognitive under-development.

At his home, Kristof has created a food forest consisting of 200 different crops. Nutritionally varied food is available year-round. Rainwater is stored for use during the dry season. Mulching creates a protective cover over the soil to minimise evaporation. I also visit a school project where thanks to a permaculture project, 1200 learners are enjoying food security.

In the evening, I am feeling weak. I have aches and pains, and diarrhoea. These are classic malaria symptoms. I head back to the pharmacy in the City Centre area. The malaria test comes back negative. Back at my hotel, I am feeling worse and worse. I am convinced it is malaria, so a few hours later I call a taxi and go back to the pharmacy for a third test. Positive. I get the requisite medicine, and I ask the nurse:

"What kind of malaria is this? Could it be cerebral?" Cerebral malaria can

kill within three days.
"If it was cerebral you'd be confused."
I head back to my hotel. The diagnosis seems unscientific. I bury my head in the pillow, groaning: "I don't want to die."

This has been an eventful trip. So far I have survived 3000 kilometres of African buses, I've been bitten by a dog, and now I have malaria. That is a real spanner in the works because malaria is a serious illness leaving one very weak. In the morning I head out to another permaculture project to complete my story. This I manage by shooting in a minimalist manner and walking very little. I am floored when I get back to my hotel and decide to treat myself to three nights at the four-star Capital Hotel, right around the corner from my cheap hotel. I am used to roughing it when travelling as a freelancer but considering I am ill and the hotel has a weekend special, this seems the right thing to do. I can barely walk ten metres I am so weak. So room service is ideal at this time.

In summer when the winds are right, parts of Greece experience fine African dust that blows over the Mediterranean. I write in my diary: this murderous continent blows its red dust across an ocean onto a Kallithea balcony where a heart gently and patiently beats for me.

Lying in the lap of relative luxury and watching TV, my blood boils. The first six minutes of the (state) news is taken up by President Mutharika's trip to Addis Ababa by private jet, to receive an honorary doctorate. His excellency is quoted as saying, "It is an honour for me, but it is also an honour for all Malawians." He repeats this, really driving the point home that yes this an expense Malawi cannot afford, but it's justifiable because it's for all Malawians. The following morning I read in a private newspaper a more critical appraisal setting out the costs of hiring the Embraer aeroplane—US$5250 per day. "His excellency is on nothing more than an ego trip when you consider that Malawi is one of the world's most impoverished nations, technically bankrupt, and about to face a famine following a drought and a serious lack of maize. Meaning the government has to go out with a begging bowl to the donors to ask for maize donations. Under the circumstances wouldn't it have been more appropriate for his excellency to make an announcement saying he is honoured to receive the honorary doctorate and that his Ambassador in Addis Ababa will receive it on his behalf?" Not a chance.

I am weak, with aches and pains. But I am in a fairly luxurious hotel, so with every complaint I have, I simply phone reception.

"Hello, when will the wedding banquet end?"
"This evening."

In the middle of the night I call reception again.

"Hello, are your beds heated?"
"No, they are not."

Later I realise it is a fever and I am sweating profusely.

I phone the hotel pharmacy.

"Hello, what drugs have you got?"
"Ibuprofen. First, it makes you high and then it makes you sleepy."

Walking to the pharmacy, which is downstairs, takes ages. I stop twice to rest.

She's right, these drugs do make you high.

I change my return flight to South Africa, which involves a taxi to the airline office. Just walking to the hotel entrance is utterly enervating. Four days later, still feeling the sickness down to my bones, I head to the airport and like an old man make my way to South Africa.

***

En route to what are becoming my regular visits to Greece, I stopover in Kenya and Tanzania, to produce Associated Press features. At Dar es Salaam airport, I start quietly fretting that my baggage won't be transferred to Nairobi with the different airline I am connecting to. I enquire but as I am in transit I cannot physically go to the transfer desk. But I manage to get to a lady in an office who gives me the world's most withering look when I express my concern about my baggage transfer to another airline. Well maybe I am just being neurotic, so I relax and eat a buffet lunch. When I arrive at Nairobi airport I am peering over the immigration officer's shoulder while telling him I am there for "tourism purposes" (as the media accreditation looks too complex and expensive). I can see the baggage from our flight going round and round on the carousel. The immigration officer is slowly looking through my passport. I don't see my orange backpack on the carousel. I finally get stamped in and go and wait at the carousel. Gradually the passengers disappear with their bags until I am the only one left next to an empty carousel. I am approached by someone at Swissport and sure enough, it turns out that my bag did not make it onto the flight. I was right.

"We'll send it here on the next flight."

With that, I set off carrying only my camera bag but no clothes. A taxi takes me to the Velvet Lodge not far from the airport. I hardly sleep. Yes, I have my camera gear but not my tripod which is packed with my clothes in the missing orange bag. I am back at the airport at 6 am. The Swissport office is just opening. There haven't been any flights in yet so there is no sign of my orange backpack. Thinking the worst, I imagine that my bag has by now disappeared into a small back office in Colombo, Sri Lanka. I have a connecting flight to Malindi where I'll start my first work project. With Swissport's phone contacts in my hand, I fly down to the coast and straight to the Kipepeo Butterfly Project where I am warmly welcomed by project manager Hussein Aden.

"Feel at home. You are safe here. You are welcome."

The Kipepeo Butterfly Project is located at the Arabuko Sokoke Forest Reserve, which consists of about 400 square kilometres of coastal forest. Rich in biodiversity, including about 800 different species of plants, the reserve has also been at the brunt of illegal logging. The project provides alternative livelihoods to illegal loggers and unemployed Kenyans. Around 300 butterfly farmers earn money seasonally by collecting butterflies and harvesting their pupae—instead of logging. The pupae are sold to live butterfly exhibits in Europe and North America.

I shoot the whole story without a tripod by precariously placing my video camera on top of two stools, which are balanced on top of each other. I can't do pans or tilts so the shots are fairly static, but I also shoot some handheld shots for dynamic visuals.

That afternoon I manage to procure a Tusker Beer t-shirt and a Kenya tourist hat, and head to a nearby simple hotel to wash up. I phone Swissport Nairobi.

"Yes, we have located the bag. It is here in Nairobi."
What a relief.
"We'll put it on tomorrow morning's Fly540 flight to Malindi."
Hallelujah.

I arrive at Malindi airport the following day at 1 pm after finishing my shoot at the Kipepeo Project. I wait for some time in the Swissport office. *What is taking so long*, I wonder. The flight with my bag was expected three hours ago. It takes more phone calls before finally I am given a news update.

"Your bag was sent to Zanzibar."
"Zanzibar?! How does that help me?!"
Once I have calmed down sufficiently, I explain to them that my next stop

is Mombasa, in Southern Kenya.

"No problem. We'll have the bag sent to the Mombasa airport."

I have lost my faith in anything Swissport tells me. I am fuming when I leave by taxi to get a *matatu* bus down to Mombasa. The whole way down I am on my phone sending out emails to various Swissport and airline offices (though not Sri Lanka—yet) trying to be as proactive as possible in this wild goose chase. Unless I micromanage this I won't see my bag.

I arrive at Mombasa airport in the late afternoon. I have to hand in my passport to access the customs area. The customs officer sees my Tusker beer t-shirt, and says, "We are blood brothers!" I am not a religious person but when I then see my orange backpack being offloaded from its Zanzibar holiday, I raise both my arms in the air and say *thank you*, partly to my blood brother but partly to the Gods of Baggage. Upon being given back my passport the security guy smiles and says, "Welcome to hospitable Kenya." He's right, it is, and I tell him so.

I take a taxi to a *matatu* bus that has space for one more and is about to leave. We head south over the border into Tanzania, arriving at Tanga at midnight. I stay at my usual cheap but decent hotel across the road from the bus station, with its warm and friendly staff.

From Tanga, it's a short flight over to Pemba island where I'll shoot a story on an underwater glass hotel. The trouble with expensive resorts such as Manta Lodge with its underwater glass hotel room is that because they charge so much money they feel they have to put in commensurately extra effort into guest relations. Meaning it's fake. The only authentic experiences are when you travel with locals and stay at the places locals stay. It is just as well well I can't afford these expensive joints!

From Pemba, it's a short hop to Dar es Salaam where I connect to Athens, Greece.

CHAPTER TWENTY-SEVEN
The forgotten Western Sahara

Most of the productions I have made have been for broadcasters, so I haven't put much effort into sending my documentaries to film festivals. The documentary has been sold, the broadcaster owns it, and I move on to the hustle of trying to create the next project. However, I do send out Tresor And The Camp Musicians, my Al Jazeera Witness documentary about the Congolese migrant musician, to the FiSahara Film Festival, and it is accepted. This film festival takes place in a remote refugee camp in Southern Algeria, aiming to highlight the plight of Western Sahara. Western Sahara? This was one of Spain's two African colonies and when they finally relinquished control in 1975, northern neighbour Morocco moved into and violently took control of the territory. So what? Well, according to the Organisation of African Unity (now the African Union), the former European colonial boundaries are to be respected as contemporary sovereign nations. So Western Sahara deserves to be a country just as with any other African state. But it is a territory under annexation, and many of its people who fled in the 1970s, languish in Algerian camps. I decide that the opportunity to visit sounds like an adventure not to be missed, and I so attend. Thinking that a week living with the Saharawi refugees in their camp will proffer up a documentary, I take my camera and start shooting on the charter Boeing 737 from Spain to Tindouf, Southern Algeria.

From Tindouf military airport visitors to the film festival are transported in a cavalcade of Toyota Landcruisers through territory that the French Foreign Office advise against all travel. We arrive late at night at the camp where the festival will take place, and wait for our baggage to appear. We are then finally sent to the *haima* (home) that we have been assigned. I am with an eclectic group that I never quite gel with. This includes a Palestinian musician living in France, a Palestinian filmmaker living in Palestine and an Ecuadorian. The Palestinian filmmaker is Reham Gazali, and with her permission, I will document her experiences in the camp. It's well after midnight and we are offered tea by our host at the *haima*. Upon hearing I am South African, the father of the household says, "Nelson Mandela!" smiles, then adds, "Apartheid" and smiles. Yes, that is what we like to be defined by.

Reham is running a documentary filmmaking workshop for the Saharawi women of the camp. She opens the class by saying, "Western Sahara and Palestine are both under occupation. I hope that next time I see you, you'll be in your homeland and have achieved independence." The class discuss potential documentary projects they can make together, until eventually deciding on a short documentary on henna hand art. I am filming the activities.

I interview Maglaha, one of the documentary class members at her *haima*, where I meet her father, Selik, and drink tea. Finally, I experience the hospitality of the Saharawi that everyone talks about. There is a weird air at the *haima* where I am living for the week. It is dirty and the family seem miserable. At night, the Palestinian musician in our group asks me to hide his bottle of whiskey in my bag. As someone Western-looking he presumes I won't have a problem if caught with alcohol in this conservative Muslim country. I give the financial tip we are supposed to give to our host family instead to Maglaha and her father.

Meanwhile, because I am tracking Reham throughout the festival, I miss all the FiSahara events including the film screenings. The festival director is pretty surprised that I don't even make it to my documentary screening. On the last evening, I attend the closing event. It's a strange phenomenon when tourists choose to holiday in a refugee camp. "Activist tourism," one might call it. I meet Camille, a French journalist with Le Monde. She had tried to cover the Saharawi issue by visiting the Western Sahara region of Morocco herself. For her trouble, she was arrested at gunpoint in her hotel room by Moroccan soldiers on her first evening and escorted back to the airport. "And my Gmail account and phone were hacked."

Back in Cape Town, I track down a translator, who works on the mammoth task of providing me with English transcriptions for all my raw footage. I don't know what much of the dialogue is, as a lot of it is in Hassaniya Arabic. Then I slowly work on an edit. The final draft is a 15 minuter which comes out quite nicely. I send it out to many broadcasters but I don't get any interest. Finally, Journeyman Pictures, a well-known operation, agrees to distribute the documentary for me. There have been no sales to date. I am not embarking on another self-funded documentary again. Of course, it doesn't have to be all or nothing. Many filmmakers start by shooting a small amount and use this as a way to figure out the story and raise funding or broadcaster interest for the project.

CHAPTER TWENTY-EIGHT
Ghana by Uber

It's my third visit to one of my favourite countries. I arrive at Accra's brand new airport and then negotiate a ride to my Airbnb studio, owned by an Israeli called Gidi. From there I head over to the Ministry of Information for media accreditation. Once again I appreciate the architectural design of these older government buildings that take into account the hot and humid climate. High ceilings, passageways with louvres that allow a flow of air into the building, yet keep out the sun.

The process is pretty quick. In less than an hour, I have my media accreditation. But as with the previous visit, there is just one curve ball. I am given a letter as I leave which reads: "He is also directed to ensure that copies of the video clips are made available to the information services department for a conformity reality check before the video is aired publicly as directed by the national security council secretariat." The chances of that happening are zero. Editorial independence is one of the basic tenets of journalism. I'd lose any credibility if I had to get my story checked before publication. What is surprising is that Ghana is ranked in the top three for free press in Africa. Yet I haven't had this request made in any other African country.

The following day I set off to begin shooting the first of four Associated Press news features. To get around Accra and beyond I use uber. Uber is cheaper than regular taxis and there's no need to carry cash. This is a great concept both hypothetically and in the developed world. In Ghana, putting uber into practice has some flaws, probably a reflection of some of the dysfunctionalities here. Even though uber works with GPS and location data, the uber drivers here invariably start by sending a message, "Where are you?" This is a reflection of the complicated urban geography—landmarks play a bigger role than addresses.

After much messaging with this morning's uber driver, it is agreed that we will meet at the Deloitte building, near my Airbnb. I stand here, on the pavement, staring at my phone. And I watch how his vehicle is getting further and further away, despite his messages to me saying, "I am nearly there." Eventually, I give up and cancel the ride. I restart my search. At first, the search function seems stuck. Eventually, I locate a new uber driver, who naturally asks me, "Where are you?" After much messaging, we agree to meet at Villagio. I cross the busy four-lane highway, no mean feat at rush hour, and finally, get to the new uber driver. Thank goodness I set off early this morning.

I meet up with Joelle Eyeson and Kwame de Heer of Hive Earth. Joelle is

British-Ghanaian, and her husband and business partner Kwame is Ghanaian. Joelle's parents are Ghanaian and she grew up in the UK. A few years earlier, with a group of friends who were all British but of African parentage, Joelle came to Ghana intending to start a business. The realities of making it in a different culture, in a developing country with several challenges to operate in, resulted in the group returning to the UK. Except for Joelle. She stayed. With her business and life partner, Kwame, their business is rammed earth buildings. Locally-sourced sand, silt, clay, and stones are poured into a temporary wall structure and then pounded, or rammed, into a hard man-made stone, mimicking sedimentary rock. This is a construction method that has been around for millennia. Most famously the Great Wall of China was built using rammed earth. In West Africa, using mud to build houses and large buildings has been around for a long time, and some of these have survived for centuries. Rammed earth takes this to the next level, creating more solid yet eco-friendly buildings— without the need of utilising expensive imported cement.

I travel with Joelle and Kwame to a rammed-earth construction site a short distance outside Accra. I ask them whether there's scope to roll out low-cost rammed earth housing to the government. Yes, they reply. At the rammed earth construction site, I see the process of adding the mixture of local raw materials and how it is rammed by hand into a hard substance. And at another near-completed rammed earth construction site back in Accra, I see the unique wall patterns with the wavy layers of different substances distinctly visible.

Getting near the end of the shoot Joelle concedes that going large-scale is tough.

"If you try to get the government on board you need to pay before you've even seen anyone! They all want a cut! Everyone wants a cut! No one puts their country first."
"We need more Thomas Sankaras," I say, referring to the Burkinabe social revolutionary.
"Also," adds Kwame, "we came fifth in a start-up presidential competition. The prize was 30,000 Cedis. But then we discovered it was a loan! The worst part was there was a multi-million dollar budget for the initiative. So where did all the money go? Five-star hotels and conference facilities for government delegates! And the government has its conference facilities!"

The following morning I assume the standard uber waiting position: standing on the pavement in the tropical sun, staring at my phone. The driver arrives and informs me that his GPS is not working. "No problem," I say, "I'll give you directions using my phone." This young man is particularly friendly and relaxed as Ghanaians are. And curious too.
"So you're American?"

"No, South African."

"Oh, so you're an African?" he asks looking at me with a smile through the rearview mirror.

"Indeed."

We talk about the work projects I am busy with. Then as we approach our destination, he asks:

"So how is that apartheid thing?"

"Well, it ended 25 years ago. It's history."

He smiles and says, "but there's still some remaining?"

"Well yes. It takes time to change people's mentality."

"We hope for the best in South Africa," says the driver as he drops me off.

"Us too."

After a visit to a rammed earth brick production company, I take another complicated uber back to my Airbnb where I chat with the owner Gidi, an Israeli businessman who has been operating in West Africa for a long time ("Nigeria is my favourite"). He asks me how things are in South Africa with the Whites. Feeling pessimistic I say:

"In Zimbabwe, they took the White farmers' land, collapsed the economy, the Whites left the country, and problem solved."

"When the South Africans first came here (after 1994 and democracy) they had an attitude of we-know-better," says Gidi.

In the late 1980s, just before South Africa became a democracy, a South African writer called Ted Botha travelled north into Africa and wrote a book called Apartheid In My Backpack. Sometimes I feel like that. Not sometimes. Again and again and again.

I am now juggling all four AP productions, which means dashing around trying to organise interviews, shoots, and logistics and staying abreast of four different stories. I have three weeks in Ghana and ideally, I'd stay longer to have less pressure, but the cost of accommodation would eat into my profit too much if I did.

Today's uber is a terrible driver. When I ask him to pull over in the city centre, he swings sharply without looking. I see there is a car right next to us and I shout, "Stop!" he stops with an inch to spare. I get out and walk. Within seconds I am dripping with sweat in the tropical humidity.

One of the stories I am covering is coastal erosion. I am navigating my way through the University of Ghana campus looking for Professor Kwasi Appeaning Addo. I find his air-conditioned office and am ushered in. The Professor explains to me that Ghana is losing its coastline for several reasons starting with the reduction of sediment from the Volta river as a result of dam construction. Illegal sand mining on beaches for construction has a further impact, and finally the sexy reason for media: climate change. "Sea levels are rising about 3mm a year…and expected to increase." A hard engineering solution has been groynes which are concrete structures perpendicular to the coast that trap sediment moving east and west thus building up beaches. Kofi Agbogah runs an NGO called Hen Mpoana. Through Kofi, I'll learn about alternative solutions to the coastal erosion issue. Kofi arrives at the Professor's office. He begins a long informal chat with the Professor. The Professor tries to draw me in from time to time, but Kofi won't have that. Finally, about an hour later, Kofi turns to me and says:

"Welcome, Neil. That's how things are here."

Kofi will travel with me soon to some of the coastal areas. First, I need to get across town. And that means uber. It takes some time and many messages before the driver arrives at another part of the campus. "Where to?" he asks. I give him the address that I had put into the app, and the driver says, "Oh that is quite far. I have a problem with my wheel." I get out and cancel the ride. I start searching for a new ride. Wheel guy is chosen as my replacement. *No!!*

I eventually pull into the Hydro government offices. I am here to get a government interview for my coastal erosion story. After a long chat with Ernest, an official there, he explains that I would need to interview the director, "Who is coming soon." It is another long wait but Ernest is happy to chat. He can't talk about the coastal erosion issue, but we talk about politics. I explain the "Gupta state capture" phenomenon under President Zuma in South Africa—large-scale corruption. Finally, the director arrives.

I say to him, "We've been discussing politics."

The director says, "When I was 36 and I completed my master's degree, my father asked me, do you want to enter politics? I decided no, I joined the ministry and became a technocrat."

"What if governments were run by technocrats—wouldn't that be better? With party politics, the priority is winning elections, and the second is the best interest of the country. Whereas technocrats put the best interests of the state first."

"Yes," replies the director, "but people love power."

Finally, someone has come up with a good reply to my technocracy thesis. It's an illuminating discussion, however, there are various protocols that I need to follow—permissions from higher up—before I can interview the director. I say goodbye. Even these high-ranking officials give me the cool

Ghana handshake. You shake and then click your fingers on release.

An uber adventure gets me to another government building where I begin the process of permission to interview the director.
"How can we be of service?" asks the civil servant to me.
Wow, that is a professional and friendly government.

Afterwards, I buy water from a lady across the road, and as I pass her the two Cedi note, I see she has a 50 pesewa coin change seemingly ready. "Ah, you knew I'd pay with Two Cedi. You had the change ready!" She gives me a big smile. I know where I belong. It's less how they are, but more how I am with them—comfortable. But Ghanaians *are* laid back and friendly. I ask a Dutch lady about this. Poen has lived most of her life in Ghana and I have met her to chat about chocolate production in Ghana, one of my stories.

I tell her how much I like Ghana, "Peaceful, friendly people."
"Yes, that's West Africa. But especially Ghana. Just go up to Burkina Faso and it changes a lot."
"The French influence?"
"Maybe. But I don't think so. Take the Swiss. They're so difficult and it relates to the difficulties, historically, of living in a cold mountainous country. North of Ghana you enter Sahel and Sahara territory which is a much tougher life. Here you just throw some seeds on the ground and they grow."

I take her point completely. Here there is so much sunshine, rain and good soil. Therefore, content people.

I assume the uber position and stand on the hot pavement staring at my phone. I wait a long time watching the taxi's movements. It is going further away from me when a message appears, "Your ride has started. You are on your way." *No! I'm not! I'm standing on the pavement. Cancel!* I start the process all over again. Eventually, I am in an uber.

Stopping at a set of traffic lights, I ask a lady selling peanuts if I can take a picture of her from the car window.

"No. Not unless you buy peanuts."
Then she asks me, "Are you married?"
I say, "Yes" not least to avoid being propositioned.
In her language, the peanut seller tells the uber driver, "I will organise him a wife," and the driver translates for me. The light changes to green and we set off. Just another day in Ghana.

Travelling in a vehicle I have rented for the day, I head out of the city with

Kofi Agbogah from the NGO Hen Mpoana. Kofi is promoting the sustainable use of mangroves because healthy mangrove forests play a key role in preventing coastal soil erosion.

"Worldwide, mangroves have been recognised as good systems for coastal protection. During the 2004 [Indian Ocean] tsunami, towns that were located on the other sides of the mangroves were protected as if nothing had happened. Here in Ghana mangroves are very well protected by law, but in some areas, mangroves are planted and cut by people on an unsustainable basis."

In addition to preventing coastal erosion, the mangroves are home to biodiversity including plants and fish. Kofi works with communities to try and ensure sustainable harvesting of mangroves for timber. Travelling along Ghana's coast with Kofi I also get some shots of the groynes the government has built—long concrete structures built out to sea that regulate the flow of ocean currents, thus limiting coastal erosion. These are the "hard engineering" solutions to coastal erosion.

We also visit the ruins of settlements that are the remnants of villages that have been swept away by the sea. The empty concrete structures of Fuveme village are one such washed-away town. Most villagers, who were fishermen, have moved inland from Fuveme village and taken up pig and goat rearing. According to Professor Kwasi Addo Appeaning, the shoreline here has moved between several metres to over 100 metres inland, with a 42 % loss of houses. Nationwide Appeaning says about two metres are being lost every year to coastal erosion.

Back in Accra, I set about visiting Agbogbloshie, where e-waste is recycled. Agbogbloshie is a sprawling site that encompasses the recycling of car and computer parts, the making of new items such as pots from scrap metal, and a constant black smoke from a vast landfill site. During my research phase, I came across the Agbogbloshie Marketspace Forum ("an alternative architecture for making") and had a zoom meeting with the founders. Following a half-hour discussion, I felt more in the dark than before, so I watched their 20-minute TED Talk video. It is in English but so jargon-heavy that it is hard to make sense of. Nonetheless, I arrange to visit their project at Agbogbloshie, only to discover... there is nothing there. My fallback is a guy called Joseph who also has an Agbogbloshie project. I head into town, via another uber adventure, and meet him at Cafe Kwai. My white t-shirt, after the Agbogbloshie visit, is not so white anymore. Two Frenchmen in the Cafe look me up and down, pause and stare in distate. Joseph, noticing my scruffy t-shirt, does not stop smiling. Joseph got Ford Foundation funding for his "exposé of specific stakeholders and entities that benefit and contribute to the dystopia that is Agbogbloshie." Jargon such as "ideated" are further red flags. What I get out of the half-hour discussion is that he makes contemporary African Art and he is currently carrying out research that he "might self-publish."

I take a normal taxi back to Agbogbloshie. I notice the engine warning light is on. I have noticed this also in uber taxis. My theory is that if there is no engine warning light there is a problem.

At Agbogbloshie, I go to the Green Advocacy Ghana office. Finally a project a journalist can sink his teeth into. Generally, e-waste recyclers burn electrical cables to get to the precious mineral within, such as copper. The toxic gases released are hazardous to the environment and people's health. Hence the pall of black smoke that hangs over Agbogbloshie. Here at Green Advocacy Ghana, wire-stripping machines are provided for the safe access of the precious copper for informal e-waste recyclers. The value of this copper is up to three times higher as it has not been damaged by burning. I feel cynical after the long and round about route I had to take to reach an NGO actually doing something useful, and it seems a searing exposé is called for. The other exposé is on the media itself. Agbogbloshie gets a huge amount of media coverage for its dystopian e-waste recycling of Western junk, yet this phenomenon exists in many other places globally including China, often on a larger scale. It seems it is a case of "churnalism" rather than journalism, where the same story gets told on repeat by journalists too lazy to do the legwork of researching the issues in depth and finding fresh case studies.

As part of a story I am producing on cocoa, I set off at 3 am to visit a cocoa farm out of Accra. We hurtle along at high speed in the darkness, finally arriving at sunrise in rural Ghana where I will see for the first time where chocolate comes from.

Ghana and neighbouring Cote d'Ivoire are the two major global cocoa producers. Unfortunately, as with other raw materials that Africa is rich in, the raw material gets exported to be processed into chocolate and other products elsewhere in the world. However, in the last few years at least ten boutique and cottage industry chocolate producers have sprung up in Ghana. That is the angle of my story. Ghana is producing its chocolate, and I visit several of these producers in Accra. But I need to include visuals of cocoa production.

According to the Ghana Cocoa Board, there are 900,000 cocoa farming families each with an average 2.5-hectare cocoa farm. I walk with one of these farmers, Nicholas Narwortey, in the dawn light and shoot him as he cuts down cocoa pods, that resemble papaya fruit. Inside these are cocoa beans which after being fermented, are dried out in the sun. I also visit the local Cocoa Board offices and try for an interview but they seem reluctant and pass me on to a higher-up contact. Back to Accra, I go.

It is early morning and I standing outside my Airbnb waiting for an uber I have arranged. I stare at my phone. He is not moving. Then finally I get a message, "Cash only. Please change to cash." I try to change the settings but of course, you can't after the fact! He arrives. I explain that I can't change the settings now. He leaves. I call for another uber taxi. Take two. Eventually, I get moving.

It's my second last day in Ghana and I am visiting the Ghana Cocoa Board for the third time. I have been emailing and phoning for three weeks and even had a Ghanaian try and phone on my behalf! All to arrange a simple interview. I meet the Senior Public Relations Officer who welcomes me into her office. She eyes me slightly suspiciously and asks me:

"Is this an investigative story?"
"No. Simply looking at the growth of home-grown chocolate producers in the world's major cocoa-producing country."
"We want media to be balanced," she says. "If you're doing an investigative piece can you be balanced?"
"No, this is a positive story."

While handing me a free cocoa powder package, the public relations lady admits that the delays in granting me an interview had to do with concerns about how journalists are covering the cocoa sector. Child labour is still prevalent here and in neighbouring Cote d'Ivoire, where a journalist investigating this issue recently got knocked off.

Anyway, I get my cocoa board interview. But despite my best efforts, I do not get a government interview on the coastal erosion issue. I keep trying until my last day. Most recently the director at Hydro was not available due to being ill. Indeed I recall seeing him sniffling away in his freezing air-conditioned office. Now on my last morning, I walk over from my Airbnb. It is only 15 minutes away but I am drenched in sweat in this humid climate. The director's secretary arrives at 8.15 am and in a half whisper tells me the director will be an hour late. This is too tight for my upcoming flight out of Ghana.

"An hour? I've been coming back and forth for two weeks. It's a matter of respect!" I bluster.

I walk out and bump into Ernest, the deputy, who phones the director and confirms he'll be there in one hour. Ernest kindly drives me back to my Airbnb. "It's not that the director doesn't want to meet you." I have a last quick shower and grab a normal taxi. I don't have the time for an uber misadventure. Just then the director's secretary phones. "The director is available." It's too late. I have one last chocolate interview near the airport, and then I need to catch my flight out. I go to Kristy Leissle who's a cocoa expert. I had tried to get her to meet me earlier because I knew the Director interview was tight, but she couldn't because... as it turned out, she had a zumba class. Anyway, I interview her but in my rush to repack my bag I leave my precious notebook at her apartment. I am about to go through passport control when she phones me, and bless her, she takes a taxi to the airport to bring me my notebook. Just in time.

Three years later, I get back in contact with Joelle to find out how her rammed earth business is going. As it turns out she and her husband Kwame have undertaken a new business direction. In trying to build up a rammed earth building sector in Ghana they have faced major hurdles: lack of access to construction sites has resulted in Joelle and Kwame building roads to housing projects to build! Lack of water or electricity at construction sites also makes these projects all the more expensive to undertake. In some cases, they have faced situations where people arrive claiming they are the rightful landowners! Things move slowly in Ghana and being a cash-based society construction can be slowed or halted depending on the client's cash flow. But Joelle and Kwame have not given up on their rammed earth dream. They have moved into the commercial sector, creating their striking and eco-friendly designs in Accra for high-profile clients with a decent budget and in a city environment where construction can be undertaken easier. Best of luck to them.

CHAPTER TWENTY-NINE
Bumpy ride to a prison island

Like the island of Alcatraz near San Francisco, Cape Town's Robben island has a long history as a place of banishment. In the case of Robben island that history goes back even further, to the seventeenth century, and includes being a political prison, and a period as a leper colony.

It's only about 14 kilometres from the city of Cape Town to Robben island, but with the swell on the ocean, today's ride over leaves me green about the gills. Nausea stays with me for the rest of the day. On the ferry I overhear staff saying the sea is too rough for the ferry to be in operation. If they made the wrong call, it shouldn't be too surprising. After South Africa attained democracy in the early 1990s, the former political prison whose most famous prisoner was Nelson Mandela, became a museum. That started well, but devolved into, "gross maladministration, plundered public funds, under-qualified leadership and no real consequences for those responsible for mismanaging this World Heritage site and one of the most important monuments of our history," according to the shadow Minister of Arts and Culture following a 2008 audit. As of 2022, there has not been an improvement.

The reason I am revisiting one of the most important political and cultural sites in South Africa today is that the country's marine protected areas have just increased from 0.4% to 5.4% of territorial waters. This large increase includes the area around Robben Island. I'd like to find out whether the Robben Island Marine Protected Area help protect the heavily poached rock lobster and abalone, the fast disappearing African Penguins, or help fish stocks recover from chronic over-fishing in this area.

The highlight of a visit to Robben Island is being taken on a tour by a former political prisoner. I get to meet and interview Thulani Mabaso. Mabaso is curt, and large-bellied but not unfriendly. While he is recounting how he planted a bomb in one of the apartheid-era defence force buildings that left 57 with minor injuries, "But did not kill anyone," I am thinking to myself, how cool is this guy? He took action against an immoral system. For his trouble, he was sentenced to 18 years in prison, six of which were on Robben Island. "They treated us like the enemy. They wanted to break us down."

Leaving behind the tatty-looking prison museum I take a drive with museum employees to get some more shots of the island. A scientist I had spoken to said the danger of the 20 new marine protected areas is that they become simply "paper parks"—parks in name only. It is unclear whether the adequate funding and staffing needed will be provided. Sabelo

Madlala, Robben Island Museum's Environmental Manager, tells me, "There is a lot of abalone poaching taking place on the island." That sounds ironic considering another scientist I had spoken to, whose name I won't mention, tells me, "People from the Robben Island Museum are involved in abalone poaching."

African Penguin monitor Andile Mdludli tells me that in the last 14 years the African Penguin population on the island has crashed from 6500 to 1100. Later I speak to Dr Katta Ludynia at the South African Foundation for the Conservation of Coastal Birds who tells me much larger marine protected areas are needed if the African Penguins are to survive. They forage over very long distances. And, there would have to be reduced fishing quotas too, or closures of fishing seasons, so there are fish in the ocean for the penguins to eat. It seems the marine protected areas are a step in the right direction but much more needs to be done if we care about our marine life and resources.

During the drive around the five square kilometre island, another former political prisoner is sitting with us, rigid, unsmiling, thin, arms folded. When I am dropped off at the harbour, I turn to wave good bye to him. He turns his head and looks the other way.

CHAPTER THIRTY
Back to the childhood haunts

It's the early hours of the morning in Cape Town, and my taxi to the airport has just arrived. I ask the driver to stop at an ATM so that I have the cash to pay him. I get my cash, jump in and we set off.

"This is not necessarily the safest place to withdraw money—3 am in Salt River!" I say to the driver.

"Yes, and they'll rob you whether you live in the area or not. My friend lives here and he got mugged in broad daylight recently."

I tell the driver I haven't been mugged, but I did have a rock thrown at me while riding my motorbike on the highway.

"I know of at least three similar cases. In one case the driver was killed, and in another, a woman was paralysed. They dropped rocks from highway bridges. And those guys don't get caught. Meanwhile, they're clamping down on traffic fines. I know a guy who had to get bailed out of jail for R20,000 of traffic fines."
"I read we have one of the biggest police force to population ratios in the world."
"Untrue," says the taxi driver, "for every 20 crimes committed there is one policeman."
"So, they're just overwhelmed?"
"Yes."

I am en route to producing a series of Associated Press video news features in Malawi. First though, a stop over at Secunda, about 130 kilometres east of Johannesburg, and set amidst the coalfields of Mpumulanga province.

That evening I find myself on the most surreal game drive I have ever been on. I'm in a Landcruiser with scientists, searching for serval cats in the shadow of the Sasol coal-to-liquid industrial plant. To my left is the massive industrial complex—and the world's single biggest emitter of carbon dioxide—and to my right an 85 square kilometre natural buffer wilderness zone where serval cats are flourishing.

Serval cats are classified as "near threatened" and one of the reasons the species is under threat is the trade in animal furs for religious purposes in South Africa and the region. But within the Sasol Secunda secondary zone, the servals have no human or predator threats, and as they can slip in and out of this area, they form what is known as a "metapopulation" or source population for the region. On this evening's game drive, with the industrial plant's acrid smell wafting across to us, we spot porcupines, reedbuck and *dikoppie* (the spotted thick-knee wader) but no servals which are both abundant and elusive.

Daan Loock is Sasol Secunda's Land and Biodiversity Manager. "We formalised the serval research here in a scientific paper published in Nature. The key finding in that article was that the density that we have on-site is almost tenfold the density described in other areas like the Kwazulu Natal midlands and Tanzania's Ngorogoro crater. So the key finding was a density here of almost 100 animals per square kilometre." That makes this massive coal liquefaction plant home to the densest known population of this wild cat species.

Daan has been using camera traps as part of his research, so I can use his serval photos for my story. But video is always best and so the game drives continue until late in the evening in the quest for video shots of serval. With us, this evening is Lourens Swanepoel, a carnivore ecologist from the University of Venda who is studying the rodents that the servals feed on.

Lourens says he is one of only a couple of White faces at the University of Venda, and that they are openly discriminated against. "We want this to be a Black-only university," the black staff tell him.

This forms part of a building trend—the "de-Europeanisation" of education in South Africa, the ending of "eurocentric teaching methods." Every action, it seems, has an opposite and equal reaction.

"They don't want to get published anymore," says Lourens of the academics at the University of Venda.
"But isn't that the cornerstone of academia?" I ask.
"What they do write are factually incorrect opinion pieces."
"So, are standards dropping?" I ask.
"Yes, you only need 30% in mathematics in the final school exams to get into university, even to study mathematics."

It's another evening spent cruising around the wilderness without getting shots of servals. We spot them, but they are just too far for me to capture on camera.

The following day I am out with Daan again, and I mention to him that Lourens seems a bit frustrated at the University of Venda.

"He's trying his best to emigrate to Canada—as an ecology statistician. After all, the ecology is completely different there." Daan has similar aspirations. "I've already spent R120,000 in investigating emigrating to Australia. But it's much harder when you're older like we are."

Finally, in the late afternoon, beautifully backlit, a serval crosses the road in front of us, and I get at least one decent serval shot. Video journalism is not geared toward wildlife photography which usually requires a lot of time. But I have Daan's camera trap serval photos, and I have shot other sequences and interviews, so I have what I need.

***

From Johannesburg I fly up to Malawi. I have four AP features lined up here, and as usual, it is going to be an intensive period. The budget is such that I need to get everything done in a relatively short time frame. And that means juggling all the interviews and visuals needed concurrently.

In 2020 there were 627,000 malaria deaths globally, the vast majority of which were in sub-Saharan Africa. Most vulnerable are under five-year-olds. Two-thirds of the global deaths due to malaria are among the under-fives. After 30 years of development, the first-ever malaria vaccine is being rolled out in Malawi, Ghana and Kenya. The vaccine is only 30 to 40% effective, yet even that could drop malaria deaths by 66% in 2026, according to The Lancet.

It is day one in Lilongwe and I am once again smitten. I can't get used to how friendly people are here. *This* is the place I love. I walk up from the city centre to Capital Hill. These are the haunts of my childhood. The streets I used to roam as a boy. Capital Hill is where the government ministries are. Despite the "heightened security because of the upcoming elections," the taxi driver had told me about, all seems calm. In fact, I stroll right into the ministries compound, right past the soldiers at the entrance, carrying my bag and tripod. The ministries are spread over a spacious, green, peaceful area with indigenous forest in places. I start walking. A soldier from the entrance appears at my side.

"Where are you going?"
"Health ministry."
"Footing?"
"Yes, footing."
"Ah, it is too far."

The soldier insists I wait. Soon a car appears and he waves it down. The soldier asks the lady, in her sixties, to give me a lift. The driver gives the soldier a long, hard and sharp stare. It seems to go on for ten seconds. But she fully concedes and I get in. Later, upon reflection, I think to myself it is because the soldier is going out of his way to help a White man that she was annoyed with him. She is irritated at his colonial-era hangup.

"Thanks very much, I appreciate the lift."
"That's alright. I recently retired. I used to work at the Health Ministry."
"How are you enjoying your retirement?"
"Oh, it's nice. I'm planning a holiday. Meeting a friend now."
"I used to live in Lilongwe, and it's so nice to come back. The place of one's childhood."
"Oh, your parents lived here?"
"Yes."
"I also grew up in other countries. Kenya, USA."
"Oh, what did your parents do?"
"My father was a diplomat."
"Me too."

Then her phone rings and she takes a call. As we park at the Health Ministry she ends her call.

"Thanks again," I say as I get out of the car.
"What's your name?"
"Neil."
"That's a nice name."
"And yours?"
"Tapendwa."
"I'll remember that."
"You better!"

I meet and interview Malawi Ministry of Health spokesperson Joshua Malango who also assists in arrangements for me to visit a site where the malaria vaccine is being rolled out.

I take a minibus taxi 25 kilometres south of Lilongwe to Nantenje village the following morning at 8 am. At the clinic, I meet the nurses and start filming the vaccine rollout. At a certain point, I start wondering about the age of the vaccine recipient.

"She looks quite big for a five-month baby," I say to a nurse. She looks more like 18 months old to me.

The nurses murmur amongst each other.

"This is not within the guidelines," I am told. That is, the first dose should be given at five months of age. Finally, a mother arrives with a baby for her vaccine. Once I have filmed the injection being given, shot enough footage and interviews, I arrange to go back to the mother and baby's home to film and interview the mother there, asking a nurse to come with me to translate from Chichewa to English.

Alinafe Bright lives in a red brick hut where the few material possessions hang in sacks from the ceiling. Her five-month-old baby sleeps on the floor under a mosquito net every night and has not had malaria. With this vaccine, her chances of not contracting or dying from malaria have improved significantly.

I travel back to Lilongwe with a lady from the clinic, who notices my eligible bachelor's looks.

"Are you married?"
"No... Yes, but it is like a marriage without a church."
"Oh. Do you have a baby?"
"No I don't. I met my wife when she was 39 so it is too late."
"She didn't already have one?"
"No."
"You must break that contract and look for a 25-year-old."
"That would be difficult."
"You love her too much?" I nod to her.

When I get back to the city centre I realise I didn't take stills—photos. I have just started doubling up—adding text and photo stories also for AP, and they specifically asked for stills. I will go back soon.

Only 11% of Malawi has access to electricity and this drops to 4% in rural areas, according to the Malawi government. The "Solar Mamas" is a group of eight Malawian women who spent six months in India in 2016 training to be solar engineers. They have brought back these skills to help light up their villages. 200 Malawians previously dependent on candle power, now have solar lighting and charging facilities thanks to the "Solar Mamas."

In Chimwala village, not far from Lilongwe, I meet Ethel Chirigona. Because she's a Jehova's Witness, Ethel says she has never been to school and is illiterate. She was trained in India to install and maintain small solar power systems. She uses solar light at home to work at night making beer which she sells in the village. And she has set up small solar systems for villagers. But solar lights and charging are a business. And when I hear that there are monthly payments expected from the communities I think perhaps this is a red flag. Whoever uses the solar systems are supposed to pay the "Solar Mamas" a rental which is also used to maintain the solar systems. "Not everyone pays," says Ethel. That does not surprise me considering the level of poverty in Malawi. "I'm only getting 2000—3000 Kwacha a month when I should be getting 10,000.

Those who are not paying shouldn't benefit anymore."

Back in Lilongwe, I head out for one of my meetings. I hail a tuk tuk taxi. I love the negotiations here.
"How much is it to the city centre?"
"4000"
"Make it 3000."
"Okay."

I meet up with Team Lazarus to produce a story requested by AP. Team Lazarus is an international group of musicians and artists who are helping busker Lazarus Chigwandali. Lazarus was discovered by Swedish music producer Johan Hugo when a clip of Lazarus' music found its way online. As a result, Lazarus has an album coming out soon, and a documentary about him, executive produced by Madonna, has also been made. So why the fuss? Lazarus is an albino, and unfortunately, people with albinism are being targeted and killed in Malawi and several other parts of Africa. These are ritual murders. Some witch doctors use albino body parts: skin, bones, and hair which are believed to have supernatural powers. In Malawi, there have been 26 abductions leading to murders of albinos in the last six years. Others have had limbs hacked off while alive. So, Lazarus has become the poster boy for raising awareness about the scourge of albino killings.

I travel with Spiwe Zulu and other young Malawian members of Team Lazarus in Lilongwe, for me to meet and interview Lazarus. En route, I find it interesting to hear the conversation about Hastings Banda, Malawi's president from independence in 1964 until 1994. Banda is generally considered to have been an autocrat, a dictator. Yet the guys talk about what a tight ship Banda ran, how little corruption there was, and how efficient the state was compared to now. It's the "benevolent dictator" theory.

Lazarus lives in the suburbs of Lilongwe. I meet the musician and his family.

"We face a lot of discrimination on a day-to-day basis. And we live in fear because anything can happen to us at any time."

Spiwe points out that the house is not safe. The plan is to raise enough money to build a house that can be properly secured, so Lazarus and his family can live without worrying about being abducted.

With Team Lazarus I stop for lunch at a restaurant one of their friends own. One of the guy's shoes is broken—the sole is hanging off. Someone from the restaurant is sent out to a cobbler and returns quickly with a beautifully repaired shoe. That is one of the good things about being here. Everything can be repaired or recycled. In Cape Town, the shoe could be repaired but you'll wait a week. In the West, I would guess the shoe will likely be thrown out.

Just one month before my visit to Malawi, Cyclone Idai tore through Southern Africa. According to Nature, the international science journal, this has been the second deadliest cyclone in the southern hemisphere. I am going to visit survivors of the cyclone in the south of Malawi. After a bus down to Blantyre where I catch up with my childhood friend Randy Martins, I find myself on the scenic drive down to Chikwawa in a minibus taxi. It's a short drive but the drop is precipitous—from 1000 metres above sea level down to the hot rift valley at 100 metres above sea level. I check into the very pleasant and good value, Memories Lodge.

One of my contacts is a local journalist. Steve Chirombo helps me during my day of shooting, particularly with translations from Chichewa into English. Travelling in a car I've hired for the day, I start with an interview at the Red Cross office, and then we make our way to a small transitional camp, comprising 100 temporary corrugated iron and canvas homes that the Red Cross has set up. As always one personalises the story with a case study. Ellen Madson is a mother and widow who lost everything when the cyclone swept through here and is now living in this temporary camp. This is one of 173 temporary camps nationwide with 86,000 people now considered to be internally displaced. Over 800,000 people have been affected by the cyclone in Malawi.

Because the Red Cross camp is the end of the story, I film Ellen arriving with her remaining possessions and unpacking. Then we drive the one and a half kilometres to the middle part of the story, Mwalija camp. This is where most of the people from her village of Mwalija are living in makeshift shelters made of thatch and black plastic. Ellen is lucky to have been selected to move up the hill to the Red Cross camp as she is a single mother. Finally, I shoot the first part of the story. The site of devastation at the original Mwalija village near the Shire river. Every one of the brick houses here is either badly damaged or a pile of rubble thanks to flooding from the river.

Surveying the pile of bricks that was once her house, Ellen tells me, "It started at 2 am.... at first the water was at my knees and then it was at my chest...." With some other villagers, Ellen and her children spent the next 21 hours on an elevated concrete structure fending off crocodiles. Then a government boat arrived and saved them. Ellen didn't just lose her possessions and food. "I lost everything including the livestock that was an income earner for me and my children." There appears to be unanimity among experts that these kinds of extreme weather events are a result of climate change and will likely worsen. What is being done to address climate change is too little too late.

Back in Lilongwe, I meet with Team Lazarus once more at Lilongwe City Mall. Just two years earlier, Lazarus nearly became a statistic while busking here. Some people lured Lazarus into a vehicle with the promise of money but planned to murder him. Lazarus was lucky to escape.

Today I get some visuals of Lazarus playing his music outside the shopping centre. Meanwhile, my health has been deteriorating fast. I pop into the nearby pharmacy for a malaria test. Negative. I go back and keep filming. But I barely have the strength to stand up. Team Lazarus kindly drive me to the ABC Hospital, where blood is taken. Negative for malaria, but I'm told I have a bacterial infection and start a course of antibiotics. My guess is the stress of producing these four stories in a short time frame that has caught up with me—again. I struggle along, weak, until the final interviews are filmed, and then fly out.

Upon my return to Cape Town, Steve, my journalist contact in Southern Malawi where I produced the Cyclone Idai story sends me a text message: "We just had an incident. In the wee hours of yesterday, robbers attacked some EU Observers at the Lodge you stayed at when you were here. They went away with some cash and a laptop. The EU Observers are ok and have been evacuated to Blantyre. A very bad and savage attack. It shocked us." I missed getting robbed of my cash and gear by violent AK47-toting gunmen by just six days.

What better way of leaving South Africa to live in Europe than a trans-Africa trip, a consolidation?

On a hot mid-summer day in Cape Town, I lock my house's front door with not a small amount of trepidation. I put my black backpack into the boot of the taxi I had phoned ahead for and settle into the back seat.

"To the train station. I'm travelling from Cape Town to Cairo using trains," I offer up without being asked. Perhaps because I don't believe I am undertaking something of this magnitude I need to say it out loud, to make it real, to make it seem possible.

"Are you travelling alone?" he asks. When I reply in the affirmative he adds, "You should run a tour from Cape to Cairo. People would love that." I'm not sure I see myself as a tour guide, and this is probably more of a once-in-a-lifetime experience. "Maybe," I reply.

A few days before I left Cape Town I consulted a psychic. It's not something I usually do, and she sought me out rather than the other way around. "You are about to go on a long journey," she begins. Psychics never say that. "You are carrying a black backpack. Standing at a train station or an airport someone will slide out the laptop that zips up behind the main bag. You should padlock that zip." Her description of my bag is accurate, so I buy a padlock to secure the laptop. And when I enter my train compartment at Cape Town station I padlock my bag to the luggage rack metal bar using a chain I bring along. It may sound extreme but there are plenty of reports of robberies, including armed robberies on South African trains.

The thought of travelling up Africa using trains together with the crime statistics on South African trains leaves me with more than a faint sense of unease which is only heightened by the overly relaxed 21-year-old Dutch backpacker sharing my compartment who oozes youthful enthusiasm and naivety. I ask him for the time. "I don't have a phone anymore. Last night after we were drinking on Long Street I got mugged walking back to my backpackers. Some guys with knives took everything I had with me." He seems wholly unperturbed, as if this is the expected part of the adventure. Maybe it is. "Don't walk around drunk at 4 am on dark streets that you don't know in any city," I say to him.

The beautiful mountains and vineyards of the Western Cape make way for the wide open spaces of the arid Karoo region as the sun sets. I-don't-have-a-care-in-the-world backpacker is gallivanting with other young travellers elsewhere on the train leaving his few remaining material possessions strewn all over our compartment. It's like being in a teenager's bedroom. But I am pleased to be alone. I have just read a definition of a loner as not someone lonely, but a person who needs time to contemplate. What better place to think than on a train, watching the world go by?

I have spent half my life travelling Africa, for pleasure and work. Going from the bottom to the top of the continent by rail satisfies my love of train travel, but it's also a way of connecting the dots of all the regional trips I have undertaken. And because there is a heart beating gently and patiently for me just across the Mediterranean from Cairo, perhaps this is my swansong Africa trip. But I doubt it.

There is prolific snoring from the bed beneath mine throughout the night. In the morning the dry Karoo makes way for the veld typical of the northern parts of South Africa. I-don't-have-a-care-in-the-world backpacker sitting amongst his last remaining worldly possessions mentions casually that there is an English traveller on the train who travelled down from East Africa by trains and experienced a 48-hour delay on one journey. This breaks my reverie. Another motivation for undertaking this Cape to Cairo journey is to make a documentary. This train traveller sounds like someone I should interview.

I track down Helen, who runs tours for women backpackers, with just minutes to spare before we reach Johannesburg and I ask her about her journey down from East Africa using trains, on camera. "The biggest delay I had was on the TAZARA train. We had a 24-hour delay where we ran out of fuel and food." I'll be taking the TAZARA soon. Maybe I should bring along food supplies. My somewhat organic approach to filmmaking has just received some structure. From now on I will find someone to interview on each train I take, and sometimes between train rides too.

In Johannesburg, I meet up with and interview author Patricia Glyn. I just finished one of her books, *Footing With Sir Richard's Ghost*, about walking from Durban to Victoria Falls in the footsteps of one of her ancestors. I thoroughly enjoyed following her adventures through the beautiful African landscapes. Patricia is an adventurer ("with a small a," she adds) and a journalist. In short a kindred spirit.

"It's really important to trust local knowledge. If the local people say don't go there, don't go there." She adds, "Although the journey has a structure: by railway from here to there, anything can happen. Don't go with pre-conceived ideas." Wise words for life in general. In case you hadn't guessed, Patricia is also a motivational speaker. Her last words, "Courage is about overcoming fear, not the absence of fear," have hardly been uttered when I spill my coffee over my audio equipment thus losing the rest of the interview recording.

At Johannesburg train station a soldier appears out of nowhere while I record a "piece to camera" about my frayed nerves negotiating the streets of this city which is renowned for crime. "Are you lost?" he asks. I guess they have been watching me walk up and down looking for a good spot to talk to my video camera. There's a 75-metre walk between the suburban Gautrain station and the main station. I spot a dubious character who has his eyes on me as I get a shot. I put my video camera into my bag and make a break for it. I walk quickly past him ignoring his offers to help me. Once safely across the road and inside the main train station a litany of dubious characters approach me to ask for money or make fun of my colourful Indian shirt as one unbalanced-looking individual does, shouting "Hari Krishna," at me over and over.

It is not without a small amount of relief that I enter the carriage, and meet Clement a Swiss train driver who takes his holidays… on trains of course. Clement has just spent six months in Stellenbosch studying for one semester at the university there. "I met a girl, a Coloured. But we had to say goodbye. She can't come to Switzerland… unless we marry, and I'm not doing that." He seems in high spirits nonetheless, although the steady stream of text messages would indicate that not all loose strings there have been tied up.

Even though South Africa is my own country I don't trust the security situation, so I am pleased to meet Clement and have a travelling companion. I set up the camera to interview him about his passion for trains. "I've taken trains in Europe, Southeast Asia, Israel Palestine, Latin America…" We eat dinner in the restaurant car and while discussing Africa, Clement says: "Europeans came to Africa to teach Africans how to be civilised." I am dumbfounded. I turn to catch the eye of one of the Black staff who is staring at Clement.

Is it remarkable that in the 21st century a young adult from Western Europe sees Africans as primitive peoples without a history who needed civilising. Maybe it is not remarkable because those are simply ongoing beliefs that have carried through from the time when Europeans needed a justification for their imperial endeavours in Africa. Ironically White South Africans, who still carry that stigma of racists thanks to the colonial-apartheid past, have to confront our history every day. In a new democratic dispensation, as a minority, we White South Africans have had to adjust to non-racism. Meanwhile Europeans, Australians or North Americans have not had to confront that same past, simply because they are in a majority. Hence, presumably, all the fears around immigration in those places—as White people become less dominant demographically, so they may too have to face their prejudices. Multiculturalism is dynamic, exciting, interesting, and it is the future. It is also hard work.

Coming back to the throwaway remark by the Swiss train driver, what is civilisation anyway? Archaeologists say there is a list of criteria a society has to meet such as political hierarchy, distant trade, and handicraft specialisation. If that is the case what about the ancient civilisations of Egypt, Axum, Sudan and Niger? What about the Great Zimbabwe civilisation of the Middle Ages? What about the city-states and kingdoms in existence when Europeans started colonising Africa in the 19th century? What about the checks and balances in place in existing traditional political African systems, now lost in the imported European political systems these countries inherited and are saddled with?

And anyway, what was so civilised about the 400-year European slave trade, not to mention how destructive that was to African societies? Twelve million Africans were enslaved and taken to other continents resulting in a societal breakdown in Africa. What was so civilised about the Belgian genocide in the Congo, where approximately half the 20 million population were exterminated? Or the German genocide in Namibia of Nama and Herero people? An apology was finally forthcoming from the German state in 2021, described as a "step in the right direction" by the Namibian president. The bottom line is, Europe has not reckoned with its past.

Later in the evening, still in the restaurant carriage, the train staff say it is time to leave. Clement says, "Don't worry about that," and insists on staying for the night, sleeping on the carpet. I stay with him, only because I don't trust safety on these trains and in this country. But I don't feel good in the morning when staff reprimand us for staying in the restaurant car. It's not a nice attitude and I don't think it would be tolerated on a Swiss train.

When we disembark at the South Africa-Mozambique border, I "lose" Clement, and go on alone. Getting stamped out of South Africa I tell the immigration officer I am travelling from Cape Town to Cairo by train. "You're doing what?!" he says shocked. He calls a colleague and repeats my mission. She looks at me like I am crazy. I am sent off with a "good luck". Ironically their concern going north of South Africa is safety. Yet, crossing the border into Mozambique all my safety concerns vanish. There is crime north of South Africa but it is a lesser variety.

From the Mozambique border to Maputo it's in third class only, which is ridiculously cheap and a wonderful experience amongst the people. The excitement and adventure keep me buoyant despite practically no sleep the night before.

Navigating the streets of charming Maputo with its Portuguese style is less about crime, though it exists, and more, as usual, about avoiding the corrupt police on the lookout for a bribe. I constantly keep an eye open for the AK47-wielding grey uniformed police. I immediately cross the road if I spot them. I've had too many run-ins with these crooked cops already.

The Maputo to Zimbabwe border train consists of new Chinese-made carriages, and first class is air-conditioned. This is a necessity in Mozambique's searing summers. My travelling companion is Valeriano, a friendly retired underground train driver. Like so many Mozambican men, Valeriano spent the bulk of his adult life working in the mines of South Africa.

"I came home once a year, for a month's holiday, for 45 years."
"And family?"
"They're in Xai Xai"
"That couldn't have been easy?"
"Not easy, not easy at all," he says wistfully.

I'm heading for Zimbabwe whose unemployment rate is estimated to be over 90%. The economy went into a tailspin following the evictions of the white commercial farmers in the early 2000s. The informal sector offers some hope for the masses of unemployed. This includes cross-border traders, small-scale business people who buy and sell in neighbouring countries. Many of these Zimbabweans are women. Walking through the train to the third-class compartments I meet one of these traders, Nyaradzai. "I come to Mozambique by train in order to buy second-hand clothes which I take back to Zimbabwe to sell so that my kids can go to school and so that I can buy food. I bring second-hand car batteries to Mozambique to sell them." Entrepreneurship is alive and well in rural Southern Africa.

At one of the train stations, I disembark and start getting some shots of people getting on. I am approached by two belligerent security guards. "You cannot video here. You must delete this video."

I play innocent saying, "I was just looking, not filming." I show them some other pictures. They insist I was filming and demand I delete the images. I've been through this before and there is no way I am deleting anything. I keep at it, firm yet polite, and finally manage to break away from them and alight. I stay on the train for the rest of the journey.

We arrive at Chicualacuala at dawn and walk over to the Zimbabwe side. I walk with the crowd, following my nose. The Zimbabwe immigration office is very orderly and their toilets are spotless. The Zimbabwe immigration officer asks me, "What is the purpose of your visit?"

"Tourism. Visiting friends."

"Occupation?"

Once again I can't say I am a journalist or documentary filmmaker—without accreditation. And I have already produced critical reports about Zimbabwe in the past, so who knows what list of undesirable journalists I am on in Zimbabwe. So I say, "Sociology Professor".

"You're not going to publish your work here in Zimbabwe?"

I smile, *"No!" Sociology Professor?! Bad choice.* I need to come up with a better profession. Soon.

I wait most of the day at the side of the railway tracks under a huge mango tree with a handful of other passengers and some ladies selling sadza, the staple food in Zimbabwe. It's quite enjoyable doing nothing. The local music blaring at distortion level, the smell of wood fire, soil, and vegetation, and more things that I cannot put my finger on all make me feel at home here. My reverie is broken by a soldier and policeman. They approach to ask where I am going and what I am doing there. It doesn't help that I chose to wear an olive green shirt and trousers today which I only just realised makes me look quite military-like. They visibly relax when they see how relaxed I am. Friendly, confident and polite is the right approach. They leave after a few questions.

A sympathetic off-duty policeman then approaches and suggests I go to his house and make use of his bathroom to shower. Anywhere else in the world and I'd probably be very reluctant, but here in rural Southern Africa amongst people I know and like, I say, "Yes, thanks," and proceed to have a refreshing shower and change my clothes. It's close to 40 degrees centigrade here in mid-summer and although the train to Chicualacuala comprises new Chinese carriages it had no running water.

Finally, in the mid-afternoon, our train to Bulawayo arrives. There's no station here—we climb aboard by pulling ourselves up from ground level. Clement the Swiss train driver has reappeared and is standing close to me in a queue where I overhear his conversation with a CID Officer, the Zimbabwean plainclothes police.

"I am a CID officer on this train."

Clement laughingly says, "Ah like the CIA in America?"

Later on board, I say to Clement, "Don't joke around with those guys."

After 37 years in power, Robert Mugabe has just been ousted as president, but it's the same party, ZANU PF, in power and the repressive nature of the old regime has not changed at all. A fellow passenger sidles up to me and says, "Mugabe has gone but nothing has changed here."

I choose my words carefully, "All I know is what I read in the media." He smiles and walks away.

The train carriages date back to the 1950s. Straps that hold the fold-down beds in place are made of leather, and all the fixtures are solid steel. Images of "Rhodesian scenes" (Zimbabwe's colonial name) are etched into mirrors. An archaic sign says, "Please do not expectorate, loiter in the corridors, lean out the windows." As worn down as the train is, it is a wonderful historic experience.

I walk through a few carriages to get to the restaurant car. There are a few guys drinking beers at the threadbare bar but it is otherwise deserted. A sign says, "Civil servants, don't despair. Loans for school fees, medical expenses." At the bar, I ask for water, but they don't sell any. Considering the heat and my lack of water I am not sure how I'll make it until tomorrow. One of the beer drinkers turns to me and says, "Here, try this," passing me a bottle of Chibuku, the local beer with a porridge-like consistency. I have a sip. It tastes good. I say thanks to the guys. They are drinking but they are not aggressive. I order a Castle beer and sit for a while with the beer drinkers. One of the many plus points of Zimbabwe is that most people speak English, and often quite well. For his faults, Robert Mugabe as a former teacher can be thanked for a literate and well-spoken nation.

I meet a small-scale farmer who has 6 hectares of land. He is about 65 years old and a rural Zimbabwean yet we can easily converse in English. His land was given to him by the state following the eviction of a White commercial farmer during the controversial and chaotic land reform programme. But he's working his land. He agrees to be interviewed. We walk to the back of the train, to the cargo compartment and before he offloads his bags of fertiliser I interview him. After he has told me where his farm is, and what he is farming, he says, "Come with me. You can take half the land."

I guess he is mainly joking, yet if I had said, "Can I visit?" I'm sure he'd have agreed.

"That is a generous offer, but I must continue on my journey" I reply. If I wasn't always in such a hurry I may have had many more interesting experiences in my life. Unfortunately, there is no audio for this interview. I had used a backup cable which appears to be faulty. I am utterly frustrated.

The scenery here in the Lowveld is spectacularly lush in the summer period. It's mile upon mile of seemingly virgin bush. It's the landscape of my childhood.

Of course, it's not virgin. The train makes seemingly random stops.

Looking out the window there are ladies cooking meals in small cast iron pots over fires to sell to passengers. One of these passengers offers me his bottle of water. It's the kindness of strangers, although I am not sure if this water is safe to drink.

In the evening I relax in my compartment, which I have to myself for this train has few passengers. I am rocked to sleep by the train's rhythmic motion, stars visible through the open window, wearing just my t-shirt and shorts.

The sunrise is spectacular. I then discover that the bar serves milky tea at breakfast, so I rehydrate with a few cups. The scenery has changed now. This is the Highveld and it is drier. Shades of brown and few trees.

Fifty hours after leaving Maputo we pull into Bulawayo station and I rest and relax at Ursula's Rose Garden Airbnb, in suburban Bulawayo. But not before visiting Gordon Murray who is the Bulawayo Train Museum manager. Gordon, wearing breeches and using a magnifying glass to read his notes explains that he has recently had an eye operation. Gordon spent his whole career on the Zimbabwe railways and is a fundi on the history of rail here. After I walk around the many historic steam locomotives surrounded by waist-high weeds ("We're going to get a gang to cut down the weeds soon") I ask about the state of the trains in Zimbabwe today.

"I believe they've signed a 400 million deal with South Africa, so I believe they're going to get new passenger coaches, and rail wagons and new engines…" This is great news for future train travel in this wonderful country.

My route has a historic antecedent, and I ask Gordon about the famous Cape to Cairo Railway dream of nineteenth-century arch imperialist Cecil John Rhodes.

"Cecil John Rhodes' dream was to have a railway line from Cape Town to Cairo, for the colonisation of Africa, basically."
"But the dream was not fulfilled?" I ask.
"No, it wasn't because he died in 1902 and the railway line only reached Victoria Falls in 1904."

Beyond Victoria Falls more railway lines north were laid during the colonial and post-colonial eras, and although it's not possible to travel entirely by train from Cape to Cairo, it remains one of the world's classic journeys.

My next train will take me overnight from Bulawayo to Victoria Falls. I enter the "Terminal Lounge" at Bulawayo train station and sit across from a young English couple.

Emma says, "This station is like a time warp from England in the 1950s." It's true, I hadn't noticed but not much has changed here since the colonial times.
"Are you also heading up to Victoria Falls?"
"Yes. We've taken a few days' break from our overland trip to do our own travelling."
"Oh, what is your overland trip?"
"Cairo to Cape Town."
"Oh, I am travelling from Cape Town to Cairo!"

Emma is a young archaeologist from England and I want to interview her for my documentary. She agrees.

Once again the battered train is nearly empty, probably a result of the dire state of the economy. Or buses are more popular. I don't settle in yet, because interviewing Emma is my priority, and as with other interviews I need to do it when the train is stationary so that the noise of the moving train doesn't affect the audio. Emma sits next to me in my compartment for a few minutes before the train leaves and I ask her about her journey from Cairo to Cape Town. She is much more enthusiastic about the first three countries: Egypt, Sudan and Ethiopia because of their wealth of history and culture. "South of Ethiopia is just about seeing wildlife. Egypt was amazing. You've got all the stuff from the Pharaonic period, the temples and so on. But what really surprised me was Sudan. I found the archaeological sites there were fantastic." The pyramids of Sudan are definitely on my list of places to see.

In the morning we pull up next to a Rovos Rail train. This is their five-star three-day Victoria Falls to Pretoria route. I am sure travelling on this regular train I am on is a more rewarding experience, but without a doubt, the luxury Rovos Rail train is a whole lot easier. I know—I took it in 2010. A baboon jumps from the top of the Rovos train onto our train. It sticks its hands into the buffet car window in an attempt to steal some food. The train conductor shouts at it and hits his hand against the side of the train. The baboon jumps back onto the Rovos train roof and stares belligerently at the train conductor.

We pass the coal mines of Hwange and then through Hwange National Park. But sadly there are no sightings of wildlife. At Victoria Falls I visit the falls on the Zimbabwean side. A large sign warns that filming for commercial purposes without a film permit will result in arrest and prosecution. I enter and stroll around getting shots with my little video camera. When I read a "piece to camera" it is nervously, looking left and right in case any guards are patrolling. Victoria Falls is one of the great natural wonders of the world and at the beginning of summer, the rate of water falling over is increasing daily. I say all this to my camera quickly.

The Zimbabwean immigration officer is involved in a conversation and stamps me out seemingly without looking down at my passport. Across the bridge and in Zambia I feel calmer, having left behind a country with wonderful people and landscapes but marred by authoritarianism. At the restaurant overlooking the falls and the historic bridge, I call Greece via skype on their wifi. I turn the camera around so that she can see the iconic view I have.

Entering Zambia I am asked about my profession by the immigration officer. This time I am better prepared. "Computer software engineer." For once this does not elicit further questioning, and is way preferable to "journalist." After a night in Livingstone in a dingy backpackers lodge, I arrive at Livingstone train station a bit early. To be specific about seven hours early. I while away the time by ruminating and staring at the clouds. I notice from the corner of my eye another passenger has arrived. He is a young man who has been inching his way closer to me on the platform's wooden bench while staring hungrily at my bag. I get up and move away. When I look again he is again closer to me, typing furiously on his basic model cell phone and smiling, seemingly to give me the impression of innocence. I get up and move to near a soldier. When I turn to look for the hungry passenger he is gone. One of the things I like about Zimbabwe is that as a White guy I can blend in. That's because it was a settler colony (even if many of those settlers have left). Here in Zambia, I am in for a more raw African experience. From here on I stand out.

After six hours of waiting, I have a what-hell-am-I-doing-undertaking-this-massive-trip moment. But then the train arrives and I can finally get back to the clackety-clack of passing African landscapes.

The scenery is lush and green with the occasional rural village and some fields of maize. After a good night's sleep, in the morning I watch chickens inside large wooden mesh containers being loaded into the cargo hold together with goats and ducks. In the restaurant car, there is a crowd of drunken guys, and it's 8 am. These guys are aggressively drunk. The Zimbabwean train drunks seemed somewhat more articulate and sophisticated than this lot. I stagger my way back to my compartment. But that's not because I joined the Zambian train drunks at propping up the restaurant bar, but rather that the rail tracks are as worn as I remember when I last rode this line 20 years ago. As a result in places the train pitches left and right like a ship in a storm. But the train itself is in good condition.

I am sharing my compartment with Kennedy, a Zambian agriculture student who agrees to be interviewed for my train documentary project.

"It's my first time on a train… it's beautiful."

"Where are you going?"

"I'm going to Kitwe to visit my brother. I haven't seen him in five years."

I am curious to ask Kennedy about agricultural development in Zambia. I like the fact that there is so much wilderness, or "bush" but the potential for agriculture is huge what with all this land, sunshine and water. Showing me pictures on his cell phone of some of the crops he grows at home ("I've got gifted hands") Kennedy says, "My dream is to start producing most of the crops for ourselves rather than importing them." I would love to see Zambia become food self-sufficient but I would also love to see as much wilderness conserved as possible.

Six hours late the train stops at Kapiri Mposhi at 4 am. I alight and the train security guard invites me to wait in their office until daylight as "It is not safe to go anywhere in the dark. Many criminals" The other Zambian passengers wait outside on the platform in the dark. The two railway security guys want to know my opinion on many matters. Family planning ("yes, key to development"), Christianity ("I believe in God but I don't subscribe to a faith"), and being a "White African" they want to know which ethnicity I belonged to, which tribe. I was stumped by this question. Us White Africans are strange animals indeed.

The guards insist that the MA22 Lodge is the best hotel in town ("high quality") and so at 6 am a taxi arrives and takes me there. It is very basic and I take one look at the free breakfast and leave the restaurant. I walk the two kilometres into town to find something to eat. Whereas in Zimbabwe no one notices me, here every person stops to gawk like I'm the first White person they have seen. The interactions also often feel that way. Back at the hotel, a cleaner catches sight of me eating a potato wedge. She points to her stomach and asks for food. Things can't be going so well if a paid employer is begging a hotel guest for food. And I am not as gung ho as I was as a young man. I feel slightly vulnerable at this truck stop motel. I padlock my backpack to the bed when I go out.

The train schedules of the different trains on the Cape to Cairo route don't necessarily match up, meaning I have a three-day layover at the MA22 Lodge. It's good to have my own space, enjoy hot running water in my bathroom, sleep, chill out and take care of clothes washing. I also wash my sleeping bag which has indescribable smells after the series of grubby trains I have been on.

Finally, after three days of binge-watching a TV series and having lost some social skills following this isolation, I head over to Kapiri Mposhi train station. On the taxi ride over, the driver suddenly stops. He seems frozen.

"What is it? I ask
"Police." Indeed in the distance are police. The taxi driver turns off the road
and we take on some pretty terrible dirt roads in the Toyota Corolla.
"No licence," the youngster tells me with a big smile. I thought he seemed
a bit young to be a taxi driver.
"Ah."

From here to Dar es Salaam I travel aboard a train that is not a colonial
relic. The TAZARA was built by the Chinese in the 1970s, a time when
China was a much more closed and poorer country, but keen to help other
countries in the socialist block. Since then the line has not been run very
efficiently. On board my compartment comprising four beds is full.

An articulate TAZARA employee says to me "TAZARA is not working out."
"But here we are, moving!" I reply.
"Yes, but there are so many hiccups, including late payment for us
employees. Currently, most of us haven't been paid in two months. At
other times it has been many months. But things will change soon. The
Tanzania and Zambia governments are going to make the railway a
concession, and it's probably going to be the Chinese who run it in the
future."
"And how do you feel about that?"
"Good! First and foremost we want to be paid every month."

The staff in the train restaurant are sullen and rude. I notice that they bring
a bowl of water for customers to wash their hands, but not for me. When
my stodgy meal arrives, I say, "Can I also have a bowl to wash my hands,
like everyone else?" He looks down sharply and then returns with a bowl.
Is it because I am scruffily dressed? Would service improve if I was
wearing my three-piece pinstripe suit? I doubt it, and from here on I will eat
food sold at train platforms.

Perhaps the clue to their sullenness was the comment by the TAZARA
employee that they don't get paid regularly.

I get off at Mpika train station to try and get some visuals. When I film
some women selling baskets full of tomatoes to train passengers (shoot
first ask questions later) I am shouted at by a railway employee, not for the
first time. I climb aboard again and walk to the back of the train. Here the
Tanzanian staff shout at me. "What do you want here?" Oh to be back on
those lovely peaceful Zimbabwean trains.

The TAZARA employee I had chatted to gets off here at Mpika, and
another passenger takes his place in our compartment. This young
Zambian unpacks his bag and rubs hand lotion onto his hands. He seems

a little preoccupied. We get talking.

He asks me, "I know someone in Lusaka. He has a girlfriend. But he also secretly has a boyfriend. What should he do?"
"I think he should be honest with himself and with society."
Okay, that's easy to say but homosexuality is a crime in most African countries, so I add "And if society can't handle it, he should go and live in a country where he is free to express himself naturally. We should all be able to be ourselves." Agony Aunt is just one of the many hats I wear, people.

I am assuming my new friend didn't stay too long in Dar es Salaam. Soon after we arrived the Tanzanian government announced a crackdown on all gay people. The Guardian's Peter Burke: "Hundreds of LGBT activists in Tanzania have gone into hiding after a senior official announced a task force aiming to identify and punish gay people in Dar es Salaam. Paul Makonda, the city's administrative head, said he had put together a team of officials and police that would target gay people, who could face lengthy prison sentences... Makonda called for Tanzanians to report gay people and told a news conference he had already received more than 5,700 messages from the public, including more than 100 names."

A medieval witch-hunt then proceeded. The worst part is that these are colonial-era laws being used to target a sector of society that has existed since the beginning of time. In pre-colonial Africa, homosexuality was an intrinsic and accepted part of society. "How far back can homosexuality be traced in Africa? You cannot argue with rock paintings," says author Bernardine Evaristo. Yet homophobia is extreme in most parts of the continent today. According to human rights campaigner Bidi Asimi, "One factor is the increased popularity of fundamental Christianity, by way of American televangelists, since the 1980s. While Africans argued that homosexuality was a Western import, they in turn used a Western religion as the basis for their [anti-gay] argument. Reinforcing this is the fact that populist homophobia has kept many politicians in power. Across Africa, if you hate gay people, you get votes."

We wait at the Zambia-Tanzania border for a couple of hours. Every time I stick my head out the window kids scream at me "Mzungu! Mzungu!" (White person, White person). "Give me! Give me money!" It's starting to rankle a bit, probably also because I am spending so much time confined to a small space with many people.

At 1860 kilometres, this is the longest single train journey on my Cape to Cairo trip encompassing Zambia and Tanzania. I like crossing borders on trains when one doesn't have to move from one's compartment. Immigration officers come on board and work their way through the train.

"Purpose of your visit?"
"Tourism."
"Profession?"
"Computer specialist."

I am enjoying my new career path which raises no eyebrows.

I ask "Can I take a picture of you stamping my passport?" This would be for my documentary.
"No," is the angry reply, as expected.
"What do you want to take a picture for?"
"Oh just to show my friends at home how it is to cross an international border by train."

The immigration officer stares at me suspiciously. However, I am given a two months entry, while my Zambian hand-lotion friend bemoans that he only gets two weeks. "Why do they give preferential treatment to *mzungus*," he asks, but the screaming, "*Mzungu, Mzungu*" of the kids is still ringing in my ears.

At Makambako station in Tanzania a group of Chinese board the train, and I go and introduce myself, ostensibly because I want to interview them for my documentary. Chinese people on a historic Chinese train—it's almost too good to be true. But approaching them to chat is more than for my documentary. In some bizarre way, it seems like familiarity in a foreign country. Who'd think I'd feel a kinship with Chinese people? I'm not much of an African if it's all so exotic and different and it's a relief to spend time with a group of Chinese. I mean they're not even "Westerners" (if that's what I am).

The Chinese on the train are four young women and one young man all with bright intelligent eyes, and all exchange students teaching in Tanzania for a year.

"We thought this would be our entry to living in East Africa in the future, but now we have changed our mind".

I ask them what living in Tanzania has been like.

"Slow! They do everything slowly: walk slowly, eat food slowly… In China, everything is done very quickly. It's not very efficient here."
The second young teacher adds, "It's very difficult to communicate because they stick to their own ideas."
A third young teacher says, "Things go slowly, but peacefully. They don't get angry."

The TAZARA line was built by the Chinese in the 1970s when China was a relatively poor communist country. Today China is a powerful, wealthy, one-party-communist-free-market powerhouse that has been ramping up infrastructure investments in Africa dramatically in recent years.

I ask the students what they think about this involvement in Africa.

"It's a friendship. We build a friendly relationship—cooperation."
This sounds like an official line but another student has a more pragmatic perspective. "I don't think it's about friendship. It's a political strategy. Every developed country does this. I think friendship is among people. We establish friendships, not the government."

What is for sure is that the number of highways, airports and railways built by the Chinese in Africa is massive. But this is also huge debt for African governments to take on. On the other hand, taking on debt is probably the only way to expand infrastructure.

Train station stops are an opportunity for travellers to stock up on fruit and vegetables sold by vendors who run from window to window. The train descends slowly through a series of switchbacks and tunnels from the cool highlands to the lowlands. The scenery is spectacular: mountains and plains fringed by palm plantations. The air is hot and sticky.

Now the rhythmic sounds the train makes have become my music. I am in sync with the iron snake.

After 72 hours, and exactly 24 hours late, we arrive in Dar es Salaam. There are many reasons for undertaking this Cape to Cairo journey. Most of all it's a take-two. Twenty years ago I travelled from Cape Town to Dar es Salaam using only trains and making my first documentary travelling with friend and presenter Andrew Schmidt. But that bag containing the tapes was stolen out of a small hotel south of Dar es Salaam. I'm back for my second effort and taking it all the way up the continent.

I bypass Dar es Salaam and hop onto a couple of buses north to Mombasa, Kenya. Yes, sadly by bus, as there is no train connection on this stretch. Halfway between Dar es Salaam to Mombasa, I spend the night in Tanga where I arrive after three days of train travel directly followed by a six-hour bus ride. I connect by minibus to Mombasa at 5 am the following morning and go directly to the train station. It is starting to feel somewhat like the Amazing Race because my Ethiopian visa's validity began on the day they issued it in South Africa, meaning the clock is ticking to get in and out of Ethiopia before the visa expires.

The Mombasa Train station is brand new, impressive and Chinese-built. I get one shot of the exterior just in time before a security guard arrives to tell me off.

"No cameras."

All passengers' bags are checked by sniffer dogs and security is tight. Walking onto the platform I spot a bust of Zheng He, "Chinese navigator and diplomat... who paid four visits to Mombasa between 1405 and 1433... enhancing mutual understanding between China and Kenya and strengthening Kenya-China friendly exchanges." There's the friendly Chinese in Africa again. Interestingly, someone who came from China and whose mission was to control trade in East Africa is celebrated in a contemporary Chinese-built train station in Kenya. Or as historian Professor Geoff Wade puts it, "The maritime forces sent abroad in the first third of the 15th century were intended to achieve the recognition of Ming dominance of (or perhaps suzerainty over) all the polities of the known maritime world. To achieve this they used force or the threat thereof... They were engaged in that early form of maritime colonialism by which a dominant maritime power took control (either through force or the threat thereof) of the main port polities along the major east-west maritime trade network, as well as the seas between, thereby gaining economic and political benefits." Is it right that a former imperialist should be celebrated here? Is the Mombasa train station bust of Zheng He China positioning itself in Africa in the 21st century?

The Mombasa-Nairobi line is new, fast and air-conditioned. That evening we pull into Nairobi train station in the darkness. There is a sea of taxis and drivers jostling for passengers. I walk purposefully past them to a taxi parked at the back, with its driver looking relaxed and unperturbed. I approach him. I agree on a fee for Tony to take me to the nearby YMCA, and he is my taxi driver for the next 24 hours in Nairobi. The YMCA is very basic and very cheap. And it is a sentimental stop as I stayed here two and half decades earlier, with a group of 11 university students, and we held a spaghetti-eating competition within these very walls.

Where else in the world can you get into a taxi in a capital city, and minutes later enter a national park located on the periphery of the city? That is what I do with Tony at dawn the following day at the Nairobi National Park. I don't have a tripod, so to get close-ups I have to physically get close up! That is all fine and well except if one is in a national park with wild animals. Wanting to get better shots of hippos, I get out of the taxi and walk closer. I should know better, and I am castigated by a passing tour guide in a safari vehicle. He shouts at Tony in Swahili and turning to me says, "I should report you for getting out of a vehicle here. It is illegal." Fortunately, he doesn't, and we continue our taxi safari. I get shots of buffalos, hippos, and buck—from within the taxi.

That same evening I am on a night bus north to the Ethiopian border. There are no trains on this route until Khartoum. In the middle of the night, the bus makes a stop and thinking it is an opportunity to stretch our legs I get out and stand nearby. The next thing the bus disappears. I start running after it. Indeed I am sprinting. But the bus has gone off into the distance. I am standing in the middle of bandit territory, late at night, with my bag on the bus which has disappeared, and with no mobile phone signal. What now? I am thinking to myself that the psychic didn't warn me about this.

I walk back to the drop-off point. There is a lady there who explains to me that the bus will come back, it is just taking a detour. I have asthma, probably from the shock. But my asthma pump is on the bus. Finally, the bus does return and I am back on board reunited with my possessions, and the fidgety passenger next to me.

We arrive at the border town of Moyale at dawn. Walking up the stairs of the new immigration building, I am stopped by a hard-arsed-looking customs official. He instructs me to leave my bag with him. I comply. My money bag with my passport is tucked under my trousers. At the immigration counter, I am asked the usual question.

"What is your job?"
"IT" I reply. That seems to satisfy them.

I walk back across the large new empty immigration hall, and down the stairs outside. The hard-arsed customs guy is sitting next to my bag. I show him my stamped passport, and giving him the satisfaction of one whose uniform has let quite a lot of power go to his head, politely I ask:

"Would you like to check my bag?"
He hesitates for a moment, and then says with some satisfaction, "You can go."

Goodbye friendly Kenya, hello Ethiopia.

I walk into the Ethiopian border town of Moyale and drink a cup of Ethiopia's famous coffee at a local joint. With some local assistance, I find a minibus heading north to Yabello. Here, I will rest my weary head on a fairly disgusting pillow at the Yabello Hoteli. I haven't slept for some time. But first I buy my bus ticket north to Addis Ababa for the following day at 5 am. To be on the safe side, and because of past experience, I arrange for two separate tuk-tuk taxi drivers to fetch me in the morning. If both arrive I'll pay the one-off. Surprise surprise, in the morning neither driver appears. The clock is ticking and there is zero traffic on the road. A crazy man is chased away from the petrol station I am waiting at. Otherwise, all is silent and the bus station is just too far to walk to. Eventually, the first vehicle appears. It is an NGO-looking Landcruiser. I jump into the road waving them down. Thank goodness they stop, and agree to drop me off at the bus station. I am soon travelling north on a large Ethiopian bus.

At a none-too-hygienic toilet stop, a fellow passenger sidles up to me. His questioning about my reason for being in Ethiopia starts to feel more like an interrogation. I guess some things don't change. I lived in Ethiopia in the 1996-1998 period when their communist dictatorship, modelled on the extreme Albanian form of communism, had only recently ended. Albania has subsequently embarked on a journey to democracy. Ethiopia not so much.

A little later on, the bus passes through the town of Shashamene. What would have been my first documentary project (before the East Africa debacle of 1999) but which was stillborn was to have been set here back in 1997. Shashamene is the area where Ethiopian Emperor Heile Selassie gave land to Rastafarians wanting to return to Africa from the diaspora, starting in the 1940s. I met a young Brit with a video camera in Addis Ababa who had the Rastafarian documentary idea and we travelled down to Shashamene. The initial meeting with the Rastafarians whose provenance is the UK and the Caribbean was not friendly. "You can't just arrive here and start filming us! You need to have arranged it." For some reason, the young Brit and I gave up on the video project, yet funnily enough, we hung out with the Rastafarian community anyway for several days. They smoked marijuana consistently, as did the Brit and I—perhaps that explains our loss of motivation in the project we had set out to do.

Their stories were interesting. One of the old-timer Rastafarians had flown from the Caribbean to Senegal decades earlier and then travelled across Africa to Ethiopia—without a passport. "I am back in the motherland. Why would I need a passport?" This meant waiting for days or weeks at border posts in the hope of eventually being let in without any documents. When I told another red-eyed Rastafarian, who was originally British, that I'm South African, he told me about travelling down to Morocco in the 1950s and then getting a lift with a South African couple right the way across North Africa to Egypt.

Back to the present, my bus arrives in Addis Ababa. The city has changed dramatically over the last two decades, with many new modern buildings. I barely recognise it. I have a few days off here, as I have to arrange my Sudan visa. In some cases getting visas in neighbouring countries is the next best option to getting them in one's home country—and sometimes easier and cheaper. That is certainly the case for the Sudanese visa.

Meanwhile, public transport out of Addis Ababa has been prohibited for a few days because of violence and unrest around Ethiopia which I narrowly missed on my bus journey up. I hang out with Maurizio Melloni who I know from my time here in the 1990s.

Ethiopia has a federal system which is supposed to be a way of tying together a multi-ethnic state—by allowing each ethnicity a certain amount of independence. Amazingly the right to secede from the state forms part of that federal system. Like many other newly independent African states, ethnic issues have bedevilled Ethiopia. But unlike other African states, where European colonialism can be apportioned some of this blame, Ethiopia is the only African country, aside from Liberia, not to have been colonised. Ethiopia's multi-ethnic state is a result of its own consolidation processes. Meaning for once, the ethnic strife here cannot be blamed on Europeans. African states are still very new, and their boundaries were artificially created by Europeans bringing various ethnic groups into single countries. Divide-and-rule tactics were frequently employed to control these colonies, resulting in ethnic issues later down the line, most infamously in Rwanda. European statehood has experienced a more organic evolution, and even there the nation-state is a bit precarious. In the 1990s the former Yugoslavia broke up into several distinct countries.

With Maurizio, a local and a former tour guide, I can count on solid advice on Ethiopian travel. Because of the ban on buses in and out of Addis Ababa due to ethnic strife, and as my Ethiopian visa is about to expire, the only option is to fly over to Khartoum. But there are no trains on this route. And that's the purpose of my journey. So I don't feel too bad about this short plane hop.

On arrival in Khartoum, I walk the city all day long. It is dusty and windy. I nearly lose my life crossing Africa Road as a result of looking the wrong way. I am still accustomed to cars driving on the left. A fully loaded minibus barrelling along at high-speed hoots and I jump out of the way just in time.

While in Khartoum I check out the famous whirling dervishes. These Sufis dance round and around in a circle, entering into a state of trance, the idea being to reach religious ecstasy. It is quite a sight.

I buy my tickets for the train north. It will be a 4 am start the following morning. To be on the safe side, I arrange a taxi ride with two separate drivers. Surprise, surprise neither of them is at the hotel at 4 am. I wait a while then start walking the deserted Khartoum night streets, alone with my backpack, and my valuables (Forex anyone?). Eventually, I get to a busier road and find a taxi to take me to the station.

This is another of the new Chinese-built trains. There are more planned for the region that will hopefully link up East Africa with Sudan. That will bring the Cape to Cairo by train route closer to reality. On board, I get talking to Musab and interview him on camera. He tells me he is just back from many years of working in Saudi Arabia. Musab says road transport is not safe in Sudan, so the train is a better option.

An elderly man asks me if I have police authorization to shoot a video. I think for a moment and then say, "Ah Police authorisation, yes, yes, I have that". Of course, I don't. Every tourist in Sudan needs to get a special authorisation just to take photos! It took me ages to track down the correct government building in Khartoum where I filled in a form and paid a fee just to take pictures in the country as a tourist. That permission, which I have, excludes video.

I disembark at Thshendi train station and take a taxi to the Meroe pyramids. These were the burial sites for the Meroe kings and queens. Many were damaged by European treasure hunters but they are being restored. I am the only tourist at these pyramids. A slightly different experience to visiting pyramids in Egypt.

At Atbara bus station I spot a Catholic priest. Funny how I make a beeline for the only Christian I have seen in Sudan, just like I made a beeline for the Chinese tourists on the TAZARA train—seeking some commonality in a foreign land. "It can't be easy being a Catholic in Sudan?" I ask the priest innocently. Three decades of Sharia law will only come to an end a couple of years after my visit to Sudan. The Catholic priest just smiles at my pointed question.

The bus north through the desert travels dangerously fast, just as Musab had warned me. It is a relief to eventually get into Wadi Halfa. Here I meet up with a tour guide who recognises me from the Sudan Embassy in Khartoum. We're talking about the tricky political situation in Ethiopia when he adds, "Don't get into conversations like this in Egypt. There are all sorts of government people listening." This I had already an inkling of.

My Wadi Halfa hotel is a dirty dump. I am next door to the shared ablution facilities and am awoken at dawn by the expectoration and other toilet actions whose sounds are carried effectively by the tiles that line all the walls.

From Wadi Halfa I connect to the overnight ferry to Egypt on Lake Nasser.

In the town of Aswan, I need a hotel, and I have no guidebook. So I wander along the main road until I spot a sign for a hotel. I walk up the stairs to the reception area. A room here is just 10 dollars a night, and this cheap price is the plus side of a place with tourism and competition. The downside is… many tourists! Actually, I am pretty excited to see another tourist. That's because I haven't seen any for quite a long time. So at the reception desk, I turn to this backpacker, a young male European, with a smile and say, "Howsit going?" He stares at me like I am crazy (as if friendliness were a criminal act). I am indeed back on the well-trodden path of backpackers and tourists! I am almost constantly asked by Egyptians, "What country do you come from?" It's like it's a mantra. This is mass tourism, and tourists are commodified here. I miss Sudan.

Many years ago when I crossed the Sahara from Morocco down to Senegal, I recall meeting a Mauritanian who when he discovered I am South African got very excited.

"Oh—are you travelling all the way to South Africa?"
"No. Just to West Africa."

He seemed so disappointed. Like I had let him down. Now I am travelling all the way up Africa and I have been met with complete disinterest by anyone I may have mentioned this fact to. Of course, it is something one does for oneself. It is not always easy alone, and conditions can be basic but I have my eye on the end goal, now just one more train away—Cairo.

I walk along the pre-dawn Aswan streets to catch this last train, police lights flashing en route to the train station. I suppose the police presence is reassuring. As usual, I am on the lookout for someone to interview on this eleventh and final train, and luckily I meet Medhat, a young Egyptian tour guide from Cairo.

I tell Medhat, "My six-week journey is coming to an end, yet I wish it would just go on."
Medhat says, "You should just keep moving. I was diagnosed with depression following the collapse of tourism after the revolution and the advice I was given by a doctor was to just keep moving, keep busy."

I arrive at the train station in Cairo, walk across Tahrir Square and take the elevator up to my hotel. I am elated! Ecstatic! I have done it! Cape to Cairo!

The Egyptian mantra of, "What country do you come from?" reaches new heights at Cairo airport, when the immigration officer, holding my passport in his hand, asks me, "What country do you come from?"
I muster a tiny bit of diplomatic skills and say, "South Africa." I feel a bit of relief to be stamped out of another police state having been filming without permission!

It's a short hop over the Mediterranean to Greece. What awaits? Navigating bureaucracy to get permanent residence, following my heart, and a leap into the unknown.

Epilogue

Journalism is in my blood, and filmmaking is even more so. What a wonderful job where you get to meet people from all walks of life, ask them all kinds of personal questions and get to be creative! In that order.

Now, I live on a little Greek island and sometimes it feels like Aegina is my Saint Helena island. My island of exile: where I live in comfort yet am so far away from the battlefields that I so miss.

About the author

Neil Shaw is a South African documentary filmmaker who has produced content in 34 African countries for the Associated Press, Al Jazeera, the United Nations, South African broadcasters, the South African and UK governments and several NGOs.

www.neilshaw.tv

www.youtube.com/@NeilShawTravels